PROSPERITY FOR ALL

PROSPERITY FOR ALL
HOW TO PREVENT
FINANCIAL CRISES

ROGER E. A. FARMER

OXFORD
UNIVERSITY PRESS

OXFORD
UNIVERSITY PRESS

Oxford University Press is a department of the University of Oxford. It furthers the University's objective of excellence in research, scholarship, and education by publishing worldwide. Oxford is a registered trade mark of Oxford University Press in the UK and certain other countries.

Published in the United States of America by Oxford University Press
198 Madison Avenue, New York, NY 10016, United States of America.

Library of Congress Cataloging-in-Publication Data
Names: Farmer, Roger E. A., author.
Title: Prosperity for all : how to prevent financial crises /
Roger E.A. Farmer.
Description: New York : Oxford University Press, 2016. | Includes
bibliographical references and index.
Identifiers: LCCN 2016008326 (print) | LCCN 2016018865 (ebook) |
ISBN 9780190621438 (hardback) | ISBN 9780190621445 () |
ISBN 9780190621452 () | Subjects: LCSH: Economic policy. | Monetary policy. |
BISAC: BUSINESS & ECONOMICS / Economics / General. |
BUSINESS & ECONOMICS / Economic Conditions. |
BUSINESS & ECONOMICS / Economics / Macroeconomics.
Classification: LCC HD87.5 .F37 2016 (print) | LCC HD87.5 (ebook) |
DDC 330.15/6—dc23
LC record available at https://lccn.loc.gov/2016008326

1 3 5 7 9 8 6 4 2
Printed by Sheridan Books, Inc., United States of America

There is so much to learn, for men,
That I dare not go to bed again.
The swift, the swallow, the hawk, and the hern.
There are millions of things for me to learn.

From "The Child in the Orchard,"
by Edward Thomas (1979, p. 149)

CONTENTS

PREFACE

This book arose from a series of three lectures that I gave in 2013 while I was a visiting Senior Houblon-Norman Fellow at the Bank of England. I have since updated the lectures and expanded them with material developed from my published research, from a series of undergraduate lectures that I gave at the University of California Los Angeles in 2014 and 2015, a number of Op Ed pieces, and from material that has appeared on my blog, *Roger Farmer's Economic Window*.

This volume is written for anyone with an interest in how to prevent financial crises and achieve prosperity for all. I endeavored to make my ideas accessible to anyone with a basic knowledge of economics, and I hope my book appeals to students, practitioners of economics, policymakers, and the general public.

During the process of seeking a publisher for the manuscript, I received feedback from several reviewers. I do not know their identities, but it seems clear from the content of the reviews that some of my reviewers were academic economists with PhDs, some were journalists or bloggers, and some were practitioners of economics in business or government. The feedback I received revealed a great deal about the economics discipline.

The reviews were laudatory and enthusiastic about my original ideas and contributions, and the readability of the manuscript. But, there was a disconnect between academic economists and practitioners of economics. Academic reviewers treated the manuscript in the same way they would treat a research manuscript submitted for publication in an academic journal. They tried to fit the ideas into their own preconceived views of science. They debated assumptions, questioned interpretations, and asked for reconciliation. I have provided technical appendices in Chapters 6, 8, and 9 primarily for these academic economists to show them the engine under the hood. Everything I say in this book is backed up by 35 years of academic research. These appendices are guides for informed readers who want to move beyond the verbal claims of each chapter. Those of you who wish to explore my arguments in more detail may read the academic sources referenced in extensive footnotes.

This book is an unashamed attempt, written in simple language, to persuade both academic and nonacademic readers alike why economics must change and how to change it. It is a book with original ideas designed to challenge you to think. If, after reading it, you think you have understood what I said, you probably have understood it.

One reviewer wrote that reading the manuscript was "like reading a fun and fascinating detective story." I hope you will agree. Economists have become far too concerned with developing rigorous mathematical arguments that read like theorems. Trust me, you do not need a PhD to understand a simple argument made in words. I cannot think of a better way to respond to potential academic critics than to quote from a 1937 *Quarterly Journal of Economics* article in which John Maynard Keynes responded to critics of *The General Theory*:

> There are other criticisims [sic] also which I should be ready to debate. But tho [sic] I might be able to justify my own language, I am anxious not to be led, through doing so in too much detail, to overlook then the substantial points which may, nevertheless, underlie the reactions which my treatment has produced in the minds of my critics.

I am more attached to the comparatively simple fundamental ideas which underlie my theory than to the particular forms in which I have embodied them, and I have
no desire that the latter should be crystalized [sic] at the
present stage of the debate. If the simple basic ideas can
become familiar and acceptable, time and experience and
the collaboration of a number of minds will discover the
best way of expressing them. I would therefore, prefer to
[clarify how I differ from previous theories]. (pp. 211–212)

Like Keynes before me, I believe there is not one equilibrium
unemployment rate. There are many. And the rate that occurs
is chosen by the self-fulfilling beliefs of participants in the
stock market. Unlike Keynes, I do not believe that fiscal policy
is the right solution to a depression. Instead, I argue for the
implementation of a new financial policy of asset market control, operated by a nation's central bank and/or by its national
treasury.

It has been eight years since the onset of the last financial
crisis and, despite calls for new ideas, academic economists,
central bankers, and politicians continue to work with out-
dated models and seat-of-the pants theorizing. Some commen-
tators have challenged this orthodoxy, but the predominant
challenge has come from those who would return to discarded
theories of the 1950s. The ideas contained in this book present
an alternative macroeconomic paradigm.

ACKNOWLEDGMENTS

I have been privileged to work with a series of graduate students and coauthors, all of whom have influenced me as I developed the ideas in this book. I thank Viviane André, Jess Benhabib, Rosalind Bennett, Amy Brown, Andreas Beyer, Athanasios Bolmatis, Anton Cheromuhkin, Sangyup Choi, John Duffy, Leland E. Farmer, Jang-Ting Guo, Jérôme Henry, Andrew Hollenhorst, Thomas Hintermaier, Mingming Jiang, Masanori Kashiwagi, Panagiotis Konstantinou, Vadim Khramov, Amartya Lahiri, Kevin Lansing, Massimiliano Marcellino, Ken Matheny, Giovanni Nicoló, Carine Nourry, Konstantin Platonov, Dmitry Plotnikov, Yuji Sakurai, Alain Venditti, Daniel Waggoner, Ralph Winter, Michael Woodford, Pawel Zabczyk, and Tao Zha. I owe a huge debt to Costas Azariadis, who taught me the meaning of self-fulfilling prophecies.

I thank the Trustees of the Houblon-Norman Foundation for providing me with a Senior Fellowship at the Bank of England in 2013, where many of the ideas I discuss here were brought into focus. I benefited enormously from conversations with then-Governor Sir Mervyn King, Governor Mark Carney, Deputy Governor Sir Charles Bean, Paul Fisher, Spencer Dale, Paul Tucker, Martin Weale, David Miles, and Andrew Haldane. I have drawn liberally from two articles that I wrote for the *Bank of England Quarterly Bulletin* (Farmer, 2013c, 2013d) and from a chapter that was published in the book, *Rethinking Expectations,* published by Princeton University Press (Frydman & Phelps, 2013). I thank Mark Cornelius of the Bank and Peter Dougherty of Princeton University Press for permission to quote liberally from these previously published sources.

I have been privileged to present the ideas in this book at seminars, public lectures, and conferences throughout the world and I am grateful to have received feedback from many colleagues who have discussed my work both formally and informally. Among those who have provided invaluable feedback are Fernando Alvarez, David Andolfatto, Costas Azariadis, William A. Barnett, Raymond Barrell, Alberto Bisin, Olivier Blanchard, Markus K. Brunnermeier, Sir Alan Budd, James Bullard, Vitor Constâncio, Diane Coyle, Paul De Grauwe, Harold Demsetz, Michael De Vroey, Gauti Eggertsson, Larry Elliott, Martin Ellison, Zeno Enders, Charles L. Evans, Emmanuel Farhi, Roman Frydman, Xavier Gabaix, Nicolae Gârleanu, Valentin Haddad, Arnold Harberger, Leo Kaas, Nobuhiro Kiyotaki, David Laidler, Kevin Lansing, Axel Leijonhufvud, Richard Lipsey, Robert E. Lucas Jr., N. Gregory Mankiw, Marcus Miller, Thomas Palley, Michael Parkin, Edmund Phelps, Simon Potter, Sir David Ramsden, Andrew Scott, Karl Shell, Nancy Stokey, Lawrence H. Summers, Aaron Tornell, Harald Uhlig, Mark Weder, Ivan Werning, Stephen Williamson, Martin Wolf, Michael Woodford, and Simon Wren Lewis.

Thanks once more to Giovanni Nicoló and Konstantin Platonov, who prepared the index and checked the mathematical appendices, and to Leland E. Farmer and Paul Fisher for their detailed comments. Most importantly, I thank C. Roxanne Farmer, who edited the entire manuscript and whose insights and encouragement inspired me to translate my ideas into terms that, I hope, are understandable to the general reader. I received comments from several anonymous referees and I thank all of them for their suggestions. Last, a special thanks to David McBride, Scott Parris and Anne Dellinger for their editorial wisdom, encouragement, and support, and to the entire team at Oxford University Press who have worked tirelessly to bring this project to completion.

1

PROSPERITY FOR ALL

What caused the Great Depression? What caused the Great Recession? How can we prevent financial crises? What is wrong with macroeconomics? Why must economics change and how can we change it? This book asks and answers these questions.

My answers are simple. The Great Depression and the Great Recession were both caused by crises of confidence in the financial markets. Each episode was accompanied by a market crash that wiped trillions of dollars from national wealth.[1] As wealth fell, expenditures fell. Firms fired workers and produced fewer goods. As production fell, profits fell, and the pessimistic beliefs of asset holders were validated. Depressions are self-fulfilling prophecies.

My narrative may sound simple and plausible, particularly if you earn your living by trading in the financial markets; but, it is inconsistent with the body of economic theory that we have been teaching at our colleges and universities for the past thirty-five years. In the following chapters, I have two goals. The first goal is to fix macroeconomic theory. I provide a new paradigm that squares the narrative of a financial panic with the microeconomic paradigm of rational choice. The second goal is to use the insights from my paradigm to fix the financial system. We must design a new financial policy that stabilizes financial markets and guarantees prosperity for all.

The Role of the State

The Great Recession that began in 2007 is still affecting all of us in ways that were unimaginable to mainstream economists in the decades following World War II (WWII). Unemployment peaked in the United States at 10% and is only now beginning to fall to prerecession levels. Per-capita growth in the United Kingdom and in the United States is lackluster by postwar standards, and Europe and Japan are mired in deep troughs with no end in sight. What can we do about it? What *should* we do about it?

A free market economy is the best way that human beings have yet devised to organize economic activity. But, every market system works within a set of laws and regulations. The question we must ask ourselves is not: Do we wish to live in a free market or a socialist economy? It is: What set of regulations can we put in place to ensure markets provide the maximum prosperity for all?

If a politician or commentator argues that the state should intervene in a contract between two or more people, the burden is on him or her to provide a clear explanation for the failure of free markets to deliver an optimal outcome. Any argument for the control or regulation of markets must be clearly defended. I have such a defense. There is a simple answer to the question: Why do markets fail? In the following pages I explain that answer and I offer a set of policies designed to ameliorate and, I hope, to prevent the worst effects of financial crises.

A Normative Question and a Positive Question

Modern economic systems consist of billions of human beings interacting with each other in social networks. The economic component of social interaction involves decisions that allocate raw materials, labor, and capital to the production of commodities and the allocation of finished goods to people throughout the world. In preindustrial societies, most of the commodities produced were agricultural goods necessary to sustain life. With the advent of industrialization in the eighteenth century, a larger share of output was devoted to manufactured goods and, in modern, advanced nations, the largest share of production is in the service sector. In the United States today, barely 1% of American workers are employed in agriculture, 20% are employed in manufacturing, and the remaining 79% are employed in services.[2]

There are many possible ways of organizing economic interactions among people. For example, we might choose a committee of experts and assign them the task of deciding on the allocation of resources between the production of consumption goods and the production of investment goods. This is the method chosen in the Soviet Union and in Communist China in the mid twentieth century. Alternatively, we might design a set of laws and allow individuals to interact freely in markets subject only to the constraint that they do not break those laws. This is the method chosen by most western democracies. Economics compares alternative methods for allocating resources and asks if one economic system is better than another.

To compare alternative economic systems, economists imagine the existence of an omniscient social planner who has perfect knowledge of the preferences of every person in society. Of course, no such being exists. But the fiction is a useful one that allows us to break the issue of comparative economic systems into a normative question and a positive question. The normative question asks: What objective should we assign to the social planner? The positive question asks: Does a given economic system implement the solution to the social planner's problem efficiently?

Different people will give different answers to the normative question. For example, we might assume, as did nineteenth-century British utilitarian Jeremy Bentham, that the social planner should attempt to achieve the greatest happiness for the greatest number of people.[3] Given that we live in a society with large differences in inherited wealth, to achieve a utilitarian objective, the social planner would need to redistribute wealth from rich to poor.

Alternatively, we might argue that the existing distribution of wealth, however unequal, is nevertheless just. This case is made by conservatives who claim that, from whatever the social starting point, some people will accumulate wealth through the fruits of their labor and that the act of personal accumulation should be encouraged for the good of all. According to that perspective: A rising tide lifts all boats.

In this book, I do not ask the normative question: Is the distribution of resources just? I have a far narrower goal. I address the positive question: How can we design institutions that allocate resources efficiently?

In an agricultural society, the social planner might direct half the working population to the activity of growing corn and she might direct the other half of the working population to remain unemployed. If the unemployed people would prefer to be working, the social planner's allocation would be inefficient. Regardless if the corn is distributed equally to all the people, or distributed unequally based on age, status, or work history, society would be better off if everybody who wished to work was provided a job.

My claim, in this book, is that the unemployment that occurs during financial crises is inefficient. Regardless of how we distribute resources, the youth unemployment rate of 50% that occurred in Greece in 2014 is not an efficient way to run a society. However we choose to address the distribution question, a social planner who tolerates unemployment of 50% is falling asleep on the job. Given a chosen political objective for the social planner—utilitarian or status quo—this book addresses a more limited question: How can we design institutions that provide jobs for everyone who wants one?[4]

The Fatal Conceit

Some economists claim that the notion of institutional design is ill conceived. In an important critique of socialist planning,

Friedrich Hayek argued that economic systems are evolution-ary.[5] He titled his book *The Fatal Conceit* to reflect what he saw as the mistaken idea that human beings can design political and economic institutions that improve on market outcomes. For Hayek, the market is an organic living, breathing entity that evolves in ways that are always, eventually, beneficial to human welfare. There is much to admire in that idea.

For Hayek, private individuals, acting in their own interests, are striving constantly to pursue new ideas, and the engine of capitalism is fueled by individual liberty. Not every enterprise succeeds, but those that do succeed improve the lives of their creators and often the lives of every other human being on the planet. Henry Ford brought us the automobile, Andrew Carnegie developed the steel industry, and Steve Jobs brought hand-held supercomputers to living rooms around the world. In the process, they became billionaires and the rest of us grew rich along with them.

Along with every Henry Ford, Andrew Carnegie, and Steve Jobs, there were hundreds of thousands of failed busi-nesses that drifted into obscurity. Who, today, can remember the Edsel or the eight-track tape player? Entrepreneurs try out ideas. The good ones succeed; the bad ones fail. Importantly, society evolves in ways in which none of us could have con-ceived when we engaged in actions we believed would be in our own self-interest. That, in Hayek's view, is the magic of liberty.

Hayek is right. The market is an evolving social organ-ism in which some business ventures succeed and others fail. But Hayek does not go far enough. The marketplace for ideas is not restricted to business ventures. Political in-stitutions, like business ventures, are organic entities that arise as the outcome of human ingenuity. Successful po-litical ventures survive in the political marketplace just as successful business ventures survive in the economic mar-ketplace. Unsuccessful political institutions are relegated to the dustbin of history.

Two Examples of Successful Institutional Designs

Business cycles were a great deal more stable in the period after WWII than they were during the nineteenth century. And the decades from 1990 through 2007 were a period of tranquility and growth that economists refer to as the *Great Moderation*. I believe the stability of post-WWII business cycles and the reduction in the volatility of business cycles during the Great Moderation were not lucky accidents. They are two examples of successful institutional designs.

Following the Employment Act of 1946, policymakers attempted to stabilize business cycles by introducing new monetary and fiscal policy rules suggested by John Maynard Keynes that were based on the ideas he developed in *The General Theory*.[6] As a consequence, post-WWII business cycles were more stable than their nineteenth-century counterparts. This is my first example of a successful institutional design.[7]

In 1990, the Reserve Bank of New Zealand introduced a new policy called *inflation targeting*, in which it raised or lowered the interest rate on overnight loans with the goal of maintaining a stable inflation rate. That policy was emulated soon after by central banks throughout the world, and it was accompanied by a remarkable reduction in inflation and output volatility, referred to as the Great Moderation.[8] This is my second example of a successful institutional design.

The view that we can design institutions successfully is not without its critics. Former American congressman Ron Paul has argued that the Great Recession was caused by the failed policies of the Federal Reserve System during the 1990s. He advocates a return to the gold standard, a nineteenth- and early-twentieth-century monetary system in which the dollar was pegged to gold at a fixed exchange rate.[9] I disagree with Paul's critique of Federal Reserve policy. In my view, inflation targeting was a successful innovation that worked well while interest rates were positive, but failed when the money interest rate fell to zero and could be lowered no further.[10]

Congressman Paul's defense of the gold standard is a fringe view even among conservatives. For example, influential free market economist Milton Friedman was a staunch defender of the Federal Reserve System and an opponent of a return to the gold standard. Friedman's script for preventing the Great Depression was followed closely by Ben Bernanke, when the Fed intervened in the economy on a large scale in 2009 with a policy known as *quantitative easing*. In a speech honoring Friedman on his ninetieth birthday, Bernanke said: "I would like to say to Milton and Anna [Schwartz]: Regarding the Great Depression. You're right, we did it. We're very sorry. But thanks to you, we won't do it again."[11]

In September 2008, the US financial system imploded and Fed policymakers were faced with a situation they had not seen since the Great Depression. The Bernanke Fed responded by engaging in the policies that Milton Friedman had developed as a consequence of his exhaustive study of the monetary history of the United States.[12] In my view, the Fed intervention prevented a second Great Depression.

There is a lesson to be learned from this episode. Rather than revert to the failed policies of the nineteenth century, as Ron Paul would have us do, we should modify our institutions to reflect what we have learned. Institutional design is an ongoing organic process that must adapt to social and political forces in the same way that profit-making entities adapt to market forces.

Which Free Market?

When Hayek criticized socialism, he was informed by experience.[13] Beginning in the 1920s, Soviet leaders pursued central planning as an alternative to the free market system as a way of allocating resources, and China followed suit when the communists came to power in 1947. Hayek's critique proved prescient as the failed experiments of communism were swept away with the opening of China to trade in 1972 and the fall of the Berlin Wall in 1989.

Hayek believed that central planning was inferior to free markets and that market capitalism is the best possible form of social and economic organization.[14] He was right to infer that some form of market organization is better than central planning at allocating resources and creating wealth. But, that observation does not help us to decide *which* form of market organization is to be preferred.

There is no such thing as *the* free market. All market systems operate within systems of rules that define which property rights will be enforced and which will not. Those rules are themselves determined by the interaction of human beings in a political process that is still evolving. We cannot just decide that goods will be allocated in a free market. We must decide *which* free market. That is what I mean by institutional design.

Why Markets Fail

It is a premise of economic theory that free exchange in markets achieves efficient outcomes. That premise has been elevated to the status of a theorem. That theorem, the *first welfare theorem of economics,* states that: "every competitive equilibrium is Pareto optimal." There are two technical terms used in the definition of the first welfare theorem. The first is the term *competitive equilibrium*; the second is the term *Pareto optimal.*

The concept of a "competitive equilibrium" is a qualification of the terms under which goods can be produced and people can trade with each other. It includes the assumptions that technology can be replicated at any scale, there are no monopolies, there are no costs to changing prices, labor unions do not distort wages, and everyone has access to the same information. Although all these assumptions can be, and have been, disputed. I shall not dispute them here.

The second definition in the statement of the first welfare theorem is the term *Pareto optimal*. A way of organizing the distribution of goods in a society is Pareto optimal if there is no other way of distributing goods that will make at least one person better off without making someone else worse off.

Pareto optimality is a very weak concept that includes many forms of social organization that most of us would find abhorrent. For example, if a selfish dictator owns all the resources in a society and everyone else starves, that form of social organization is Pareto optimal. Reallocating resources to starving children would make the selfish dictator worse off. Pareto optimality says nothing about morality.

If Pareto optimality is such a weak concept, why would we be interested in using it as a benchmark? Because if a form of social organization is not Pareto optimal, then everyone in society—from the very richest to the very poorest person—can agree that we must change the rules of the game. We should all be able to agree on a policy that makes all of us better off.

I make here a simple but strong claim. Free trade in competitive markets does not, in general, lead to a Pareto optimal outcome. I will show that there are two reasons why markets fail. The first is a systemic failure of financial markets. The second is a systemic failure of labor markets. In the following sections I explain why both financial markets and labor markets fail, and I present a policy that can improve the standard of living for all of us. Laissez-faire capitalism is a good deal better than the central planning implemented in Maoist China or Soviet Russia. However, unregulated free markets can sometimes go very badly wrong. There is no excuse for a society that condemns 50% of its young people to a life of unemployment.[15] We can and must seek prosperity for all.

Why the Financial Markets Fail

The financial markets provide a mechanism for all of us to take bets on economic and social outcomes that may or may not unfold in the future. If an oil company thinks there will be a new discovery of oil, it can hedge its position by selling its own current holdings in the futures market. If an exporter of cars sells primarily to an overseas market, that company can insure itself against foreign exchange fluctuations by buying or selling foreign exchange futures. And if any of us wishes to save for our old age, we may take more or less risky positions by purchasing assets that range from low yielding but safe treasury securities to high yielding but risky shares in the stock market. Surely, the opportunity to trade freely in the financial markets is a good thing!

Up to a point, that is true. But, it is subject to an important and damning qualification. Participation in the financial markets is restricted to those who are currently alive. When some people are unable to trade goods, for any reason, we say there is incomplete participation. The first reason why market economies do not deliver Pareto optimal outcomes is *incomplete participation in the financial markets*. We cannot trade in financial markets that open before we are born.

My case against Pareto-efficient financial markets is not purely theoretical. It is also empirical. Stock market prices are far too volatile for their movements to be explained purely by market fundamentals. To measure market volatility, financial analysts use a measure of company value called the *cyclically adjusted price earnings ratio,* or the CAPE. Simple economic theories predict this measure should be constant. In the US data it has been as low as 5 in 1919 and as high as 44 in 1998.[16] Because the wild swings in market capitalization that occur in the real world cannot be explained easily by conventional macroeconomic theory, I infer that those swings are caused by something other than fundamentals.

If market price swings are not caused by fundamentals, then what does cause them? I believe large swings in the CAPE are caused by self-fulfilling bouts of optimism and pessimism on the part of market participants. These inefficient fluctuations in asset prices are not eliminated by trade because those who are most affected by them, our unborn children and grandchildren, are unable to buy and sell assets in the financial markets.

Why the Labor Market Fails

The consensus position among monetary economists today is that unemployment is caused by a friction that prevents wages or prices from moving quickly to equate the quantity of labor demanded with the quantity of labor supplied. I disagree. The concept of "sticky" wages or prices is not a useful one. The problem with the labor market is more fundamental. Unemployment is not caused by the failure of wages or prices to adjust. It is caused by the fact that job search is an activity that has no market price.

Suppose a neurosurgeon learns the Rolling Stones will be playing a concert next month in her town, but the only way to purchase a ticket is by standing in line for 24 hours outside the local ticket office. Although she likes the Rolling Stones, the neurosurgeon chooses not to queue because her time is too valuable. Instead, she pays her teenage son to buy her a ticket by paying him to stand in line in her place. In this example, the activity of queuing has a price, and adjustments in that price ensure the doctor's time is allocated efficiently, saving a patient's life, as opposed to queuing for a Rolling Stones ticket.

Searching for a job is a lot like standing in line for a Rolling Stones ticket. But, unlike my concert example, you cannot pay someone else to go to a job interview on your behalf. There is no price for the activity of job search and, as a consequence, market participants do not receive the signals they need to allocate their time efficiently between job search and work. When there are not enough prices, I say there are *incomplete labor markets*.[17]

Wall Street and Main Street Are Connected

Even if asset markets are inefficient, there is no a priori reason why movements in stock market prices should cause fluctuations in the unemployment rate. One might imagine a situation in which asset price fluctuations are associated with variations in the distribution of income between labor and capital, but unemployment remains constant at the socially efficient rate. This is not what we see in practice.

There is a huge amount of day-to-day volatility in asset markets. A large component of asset price volatility is transitory. These transitory movements do not affect demand and they do not have a recognizable effect on wages, prices, or employment. But, persistent movements in stock prices *do* cause changes in the consumption behavior of households, and those changes are transmitted into changes in economic activity. I have shown in my published work that a persistent fall in the value of the stock market is followed by a substantial increase in the unemployment rate one quarter later. Furthermore, the connection between changes in the stock market and subsequent changes in the unemployment rate has remained stable for seventy years.[18]

The fact that asset price movements are followed by changes in real economic activity does not prove the connection is causal. A classical economist, looking at the same data, might argue that the value of the stock market fell, following the 2008 Lehman Brothers bankruptcy, because rational forward-looking market participants anticipated a very bad event that was about to occur. As I write this book, I do not see any obvious fundamental explanation that can account for an increase in the unemployment rate that has persisted for eight years. I do not believe the unemployed were enjoying additional vacation time, and I conclude there are persistent labor market inefficiencies.

Classical and New Keynesian Schools of Thought

There are two leading explanations for the very slow recovery in the unemployment rate, and the continuing low growth of labor productivity, in the aftermath of the Great Recession.[19] One group of classical economists clings to pre-Keynesian ideas that blame the recession on bad economic policy. The second group of New Keynesians seeks to resuscitate failed interpretations of Keynes on which the profession gave up, rightly in my view, during the 1980s. Both groups are wrong.

The classical economists argue for a policy of austerity and claim we cannot produce more than the economy delivers. Instead, they claim that by lowering taxes and loosening regulations, politicians may unleash the tiger of private enterprise and initiate a surge of growth to propel the economy into a brave new future. Paul Krugman refers to these economists as "austerians."[20]

The austerians have not had it all their own way. Leading financial journalists and their cousins in the blogging community have called for a return to the "Keynesian" ideas that were developed by Sir John Hicks in the United Kingdom, and Alvin Hansen and Paul Samuelson in the United States.[21] Hicks' and Hansen's mathematical interpretation of Keynes' *The General Theory* goes by the name of the *IS-LM model*, and Samuelson's marriage of the IS-LM model with classical theory is called the *neoclassical synthesis*.[22]

The MIT Gang

In a series of opinion pieces, Paul Krugman has pointed to the hegemony of Massachusetts Institute of Technology (MIT) economics—an approach that he identifies with the neoclassical synthesis developed by Samuelson and propagated by leading MIT economists including Samuelson, Robert Solow, and Stanley Fischer. Krugman refers to these people as *the MIT gang*. Other prominent members include former deputy governor of the Bank of England Sir Charles Bean, Nobel Laureate and former World Bank chief economist Joseph Stiglitz, former Fed chair Ben Bernanke, former World Bank chief economist Kenneth Rogoff, and former International

Monetary Fund (IMF) chief economist Olivier Blanchard. This is an impressive list.

The MIT gang was taught to understand macroeconomics with the IS-LM model. Although that was a useful way of summarizing some empirical regularities that characterize recessions, it depends on a set of assumptions that were challenged and overturned during the 1950s and the 1960s. The most important of these assumptions is that consumption depends on income. Research by Milton Friedman at the University of Chicago, and by Albert Ando and Franco Modigliani at MIT, demonstrated conclusively that consumption depends, not on income, but on wealth.[23]

Wealth and Income

The dependence of consumption on wealth, rather than income, is important. Every day, people choose how much of their income to spend on goods and services, and how much to put aside for a rainy day by saving. Saving increases their wealth. Spending generates jobs.

Two thirds of US gross domestic product (GDP) consists of expenditures on consumption goods. New Keynesians argue that consumption expenditure depends on income and that when people spend more for any reason, the increased spending causes GDP to go up by more than the initial increase in spending. That idea, called *the multiplier*, was first developed by Keynes' contemporary Richard Kahn.[24]

Using the concept of the multiplier, New Keynesian economists have advocated that, when unemployment is too high, government should increase employment by borrowing money from the public and using the proceeds to buy goods and services. According to these economists, an increase in government purchases, when the economy is in a recession, will pay for itself. There will be a multiplier effect that raises employment and, as more people are employed, tax revenues will increase.

The New Keynesians are wrong because they are working with an incorrect theory. Consumption does not depend on income. It depends on wealth. Wealth is not just important in theory; it is also important in practice. I have shown in my research that, in the US data, a ten-percentage-point increase in the real value of the stock market leads to a three-percentage-point reduction in the unemployment rate one quarter later. Researchers at the Bank of England and at Hamburg University have replicated my findings from US data and found that similar relationships hold in both the United Kingdom and in Germany.[25]

Wealth consists of the present value of the profits we expect to earn from owning shares, the present value of the rents we expect to earn from owning property, and the present value of the wages we expect to earn from future employment. These are all examples of assets.

An asset is a claim to a stream of future payments. The *present value* of that stream is the amount that someone else would be willing to pay for it. And that, in turn, depends on expectations. Because the stream of payments occurs at different points in the future, the present value of an asset depends on the entire path of expected future interest rates over its lifetime.

In my opinion, when market participants become confident, they are willing to pay more for assets. An increase in the value of paper wealth has real consequences. The values of people's retirement portfolios rise and they feel better able to take a foreign cruise, invest in a college education for their grandchildren, or simply spend more money on all forms of consumer goods, both basics and luxuries. As demand picks up, firms hire more people to produce the goods demanded. Firms become more profitable, unemployment falls, and the spontaneous increase in optimism becomes self-fulfilling. According to my explanation of the facts, beliefs are themselves fundamentals that should be accorded the same methodological status as preferences or technology. When we *feel* rich, we *are* rich.

The Role of the Central Bank

Most economists believe that government has a role in the economy, but they disagree as to what that role should be. Almost everyone would concur with the proposition that central banks should provide a stable currency, and, since 1990, an orthodoxy has developed that the right way to do that is through raising or lowering the interest rate in response to changes in realized or expected inflation. That policy is called *inflation targeting*.

But, although policymakers think that central banks can and should control the inflation rate, there is an almost universal consensus that, in the long run, policymakers can do nothing about the level of economic activity. Some economists even claim the government should do nothing to increase employment in the short run. Milton Friedman was a strong advocate of that position.[26]

The New Keynesians disagree. They believe the economy can become dislodged temporarily from its long-run equilibrium as a consequence of frictions that prevent wages and/or prices from adjusting to economic circumstances. When that happens, New Keynesians say there may be a role for government to intervene to help restore full employment.

I agree with the New Keynesians that the unemployment rate is often not equal to its "natural" rate. I disagree with the position, held by classical and New Keynesian economists alike, that government can do nothing about the long-run level of economic activity. Government has a responsibility not just to maintain a low and stable inflation rate and to stabilize output fluctuations in the short run, but also to maintain full employment *in the long run*. That requires more than the current policy of interest rate control. It also requires that we adopt a new policy of active asset market stabilization.

The Role of the Treasury

In our current situation, when the money interest rate is close to zero, many economists have advocated a large public investment program to restore full employment. In my view, a policy of building new infrastructure will only be successful in increasing employment if it is financed by printing money or by borrowing from the public by issuing short-term as opposed to long-term bonds.

According to the consensus view, public expenditure will have the same stimulus effect on the economy regardless if it is paid for by issuing short-term treasury bills or thirty-year treasury bonds. I disagree. It matters a great deal how a given expenditure is paid for. Public expenditure financed by creating money or short-term debt will increase aggregate demand. Public expenditure financed by issuing long-dated treasury bonds will compete for funds with private investors and cause a reduction in private investment expenditure.

When one recognizes that the way that expenditure is financed matters, it is a short step to recognize that it is all that matters. An increase in government-issued long-dated bonds will cause private expenditure to fall. A reduction in government-issued long-dated bonds will cause private expenditure to rise. If our goal is to increase expenditure, that goal can be achieved by replacing long-dated bonds in the hands of the public with short-dated treasury bills or, better still, with cash.

Let me be clear. In the middle of a depression, when the interest rate is zero, we should try anything and everything to restore aggregate demand. My own preferred policy would be to send a check for $1,000 to every domestic resident, paid for by printing money. That distribution mechanism puts cash in the hands of those people who know best how to spend it: you and me. But, taking a corrective fiscal action after a depression has occurred is like closing the barn door after the horse has bolted. It would be much better to design a policy that prevents a depression from starting in the first place through active treasury trades in the asset markets.

A New Policy to Prevent Financial Crises

This book does not just present a new economic paradigm to explain the facts. I also have a suggestion for a new economic policy, designed to prevent the worst effects of financial crises. The Treasury and/or the central bank should intervene in the asset markets. By buying the market in a recession and selling it in a boom, the Treasury would be mimicking the trades that each of us would make for ourselves if we could participate in the financial markets that open before we are born.

Some have argued that the family, not the government, should solve this problem.[27] Although the family does connect each of us with our children through the bequests that we leave for them, not all parents have the best interests of their children at heart. And even if it were true that the state has no role in child welfare, the family still cannot solve the problem of incomplete participation in financial markets.

If a parent were to act as a substitute for the participation of her child, she would need to purchase an asset with positive payoff in states of the world where her child is born during a recession. To pay for that asset, the parent would sell the market short in states of the world where her child is born during a boom. That pair of trades would leave the child with a positive bequest in the recession state at the cost of leaving her with a debt in the boom. But, because western legal codes prohibit debt bondage, those trades cannot take place.

If parents were allowed to leave negative bequests in some states of the world, the fact that parents care for their children would cause them to trade in a way that would eliminate inefficient asset price fluctuations. Although these trades would not occur at equilibrium prices, their conceptual possibility is required to ensure that the optimal equilibrium is the only one we see in practice.

How to Implement a New Financial Policy

I have argued that government has an obligation to smooth out swings in the financial markets. But how should it do that? The central bank, acting as an agent for the Treasury, should intervene each month in the financial markets by buying or selling shares in an exchange-traded fund (ETF) in the stock market in response to movements in the unemployment rate.[28] If unemployment was judged to be too high, the central bank would buy additional shares in the ETF, and if unemployment was judged to be too low, it would sell them. Just as monetary policy targets the inflation rate, so financial policy should target the unemployment rate.

A conventional view of asset price stabilization would argue that the central bank should include asset prices as one component of the price index that it targets. For example, one might construct an index in which the consumer price index has a weight of 80% and the S&P 500 has a weight of 20%.[29] That is not my argument. The central bank should use conventional interest rate control to target inflation and pursue a separate policy of actively buying and selling risky or long-dated assets to stabilize the unemployment rate.

Monetary policy and financial policy can act independently because they pull different levers. A decision to raise the short-term interest rate would be accomplished by instructions to the trading desk of the central bank to reduce the size of its portfolio. A decision to raise the price of the ETF would be accomplished by instructions to the trading desk to change the risk composition of the central bank's portfolio by buying shares in the ETF in exchange for short-term bonds.

My proposal to stabilize asset markets is an extension of policies followed by central banks throughout the world in the wake of the 2008 crisis, and is similar to proposals for countercyclical capital buffers that have been explored by the Bank of International Settlements (BIS) in Switzerland.[30] It differs from those of the BIS because I believe the transmission mechanism of financial cycles operates primarily through wealth effects. The BIS, in contrast, takes the view that there are frictions in the credit markets. Both positions see active macroprudential policy to be a complement, not a substitute, for the conventional view of asset price stabilization as a component of monetary policy.

A Road Map to the Book

What will you discover as you turn the pages of this book? In Chapter 2, I provide a brief summary of contemporary macroeconomic ideas and lay out the backgrounds of the defendants in my trial of ideas: classical and New Keynesian schools of thought.[31]

In Chapter 3, I present the history of the natural rate hypothesis—a central component of New Keynesian economics. I explain why it was developed and why it is wrong. Chapter 4 proceeds with the case against both classical and New Keynesian economics. I argue that we must bring back unemployment to our models, and I show how New Keynesian economists betrayed the ghost of Keynes by accepting the argument, put forward by classical economists, that all unemployment is voluntary.

Chapter 5 provides five reasons to be skeptical of the New Keynesian agenda by drawing ideas from philosopher Imre Lakatos. I argue that New Keynesian economics is a degenerative research program that survives by making ever-more-implausible modifications to its core model.

Chapters 6 and 7 change tack. There, I present constructive alternatives to classical and New Keynesian thought. Chapter 6 presents a search theory of unemployment that marries Keynesian ideas with classical economics in a new way. In my proposed alternative approach, the Keynesian search model, I reintroduce two key insights from Keynes that have been ignored by New Keynesian economists. There are many steady-state equilibrium unemployment rates, and the unemployment rate that prevails is determined by the animal spirits of market participants.

Chapter 7 moves from the labor market to the asset markets. I introduce an important idea, the efficient markets hypothesis, and I break it into two parts. Financial markets are, I argue, informationally efficient; they are not Pareto efficient. I explain *why* financial markets are not Pareto efficient and I provide empirical evidence to substantiate my claim.

Chapters 8 and 9 explain, in simple terms, the implications of my ideas for simple theories of inflation, unemployment, and the interest rate. Chapter 8 explains the three-equation New Keynesian model that guides monetary policymakers today and it presents the case that this model cannot explain why unemployment is persistent. Chapter 9 provides a three-equation alternative to the New Keynesian model that I call the *Farmer Monetary Model*.

Chapter 10 delivers my case against traditional fiscal policy. When I started this project more than eight years ago, I thought I would be bolstering the case for fiscal intervention. As I developed the theory and examined the evidence, I realized I was wrong. Chapter 10 explains the evolution of my ideas.

Finally, in Chapter 11, I provide my solution for the prevention of future financial crises. Sovereign states should create sovereign wealth funds, backed by the present value of future tax revenues, and they should use those funds to stabilize financial markets.

I have tried to keep the argument accessible to a reader with a basic knowledge of economics. If you read the financial press, there should be nothing here to surprise you. Chapters 6, 9, and 10 contain technical appendices. I have provided them primarily for academic economists to show them how the mathematics that underlies my model differs from the New Keynesian alternative. Everything I say in this book is backed up by thirty-five years of academic research. These appendices are guides for the informed reader who wants to move beyond the verbal claims of each chapter.

I began this section with the metaphor of a trial of classical and New Keynesian schools of thought. The charge is that both schools have perverted the course of economic progress by betraying the important advances achieved with the publication of Keynes' *General Theory*. As you follow through the book, I present the case for the prosecution. It is your job to act as jury, judge, and—if you accept my argument—executioner.

2

KEYNES BETRAYED

Macroeconomics is a child of the Great Depression. Before the publication of Keynes' book, *The General Theory of Employment, Interest and Money*, macroeconomics consisted primarily of monetary theory. Economists were preoccupied with price stability, as we are today, but the idea that government should control aggregate economic activity through active fiscal and monetary policy was absent. At the risk of oversimplifying a complex pattern of ideas, I refer to *the* view of macroeconomics that preceded the publication of the General Theory as *classical economics*.

Classicals, Keynesians, and Bastard Keynesians

Classical economics saw the economy as self-stabilizing. Writing in 1933, Ragnar Frisch revived a metaphor, first used by Swedish economist Knut Wicksell.[1] The economy is like a rocking horse, hit repeatedly by a child with a club. The child represents random shocks to the economy caused by an array of random events. Frisch called this the "impulse." The rocking horse represents the behavior of millions of people, interacting in markets. He called this the "propagation mechanism."

If struck by a club, the rocking horse swings back and forth before it comes to rest. If struck repeatedly and randomly by a club, the horse swings back and forth in an erratic manner with a path that depends on the entire history of blows and on the internal dynamics of the rocker. Almost all economists who model the macroeconomy today accept Frisch's vision of economic dynamics. Importantly, the propagation mechanism in Frisch's metaphor is self-stabilizing.

In my book *How the Economy Works*, I introduced an alternative metaphor designed to capture the essence of Keynesian economics.[2] The economy is like a boat on the ocean with a broken rudder. As the club hits the rocking horse, so the wind blows the boat. In the windy boat metaphor, there is no self-correcting market mechanism to return the boat to a safe harbor. We must rely, instead, on political interventions to maintain full employment. That is the essential insight of Keynes' General Theory.

After WWII, academic economics sought to reconcile Keynes' economics with the classical ideas embodied in the microeconomics of the day. During the mid nineteenth century, French economist Léon Walras had developed the microeconomic theory of general equilibrium. During the 1920s, Sir John Hicks was a key player in the development of that theory. In an important book, *Value and Capital*, Hicks introduced the idea of a temporary equilibrium.[3] He invited us to simplify our view of markets by envisioning a sequence of periods. For Hicks, a period was a week, and each week the people in the economy would come together to trade goods.

In *Value and Capital*, an auctioneer mediates the market that occurs each week. His job is to ensure no trades take place until all demands and supplies have been equated by market prices. In between weekly market meetings, people carry assets that represent claims to future goods. These assets include money and bonds, and, in modern versions of temporary equilibrium theory, they also include stocks, insurance contracts, and options.

After reading the first draft of Keynes' *General Theory*, Hicks became disillusioned with his own theory of temporary equilibrium, which was unable to provide an explanation for the mass unemployment he observed in the United Kingdom in the 1920s and in the United States during the Great Depression. Hicks embraced the Keynesian idea that mass unemployment is caused by insufficient aggregate demand, and he formalized that idea in the IS-LM model.[4]

The program that Hicks initiated was to understand the connection between Keynesian economics and general equilibrium theory. But, it was not a complete theory of the macroeconomy because the IS-LM model does not explain how the price level is set. The IS-LM model determines the unemployment rate, the interest rate, and the real value of GDP, but it has nothing to say about the general level of prices or the rate of inflation of prices from one week to the next.

To complete the reconciliation of Keynesian economics with general equilibrium theory, Paul Samuelson introduced the neoclassical synthesis in 1955.[5] According to this theory, if unemployment is too high, the money wage will fall as workers compete with each other for existing jobs. Falling wages will be passed through to falling prices as firms compete with each other to sell the goods they produce. In this view of the world, high unemployment is a temporary phenomenon caused by the slow adjustment of money wages and money prices. In Samuelson's vision, the economy is Keynesian in the short run, when some wages and prices are sticky. It is classical in the long run when all wages and prices have had time to adjust.

Although Samuelson's neoclassical synthesis was tidy, it did not have much to do with the vision of the General Theory. Keynes envisaged a world of multiple equilibrium unemployment rates where the prevailing rate is selected by the propensity of entrepreneurs to take risks. He called this propensity *animal spirits*.

In Keynes' vision, there is no tendency for the economy to self-correct. Left to itself, a market economy may never recover from a depression and the unemployment rate may remain too high forever. In contrast, in Samuelson's neoclassical synthesis, unemployment causes money wages and prices to fall. As the money wage and the money price fall, aggregate demand rises and full employment is restored, even if government takes no corrective action. By slipping wage and price adjustment into his theory, Samuelson reintroduced classical ideas by the back door—a sleight of hand that did not go unnoticed by Keynes' contemporaries in Cambridge, England. Famously, Joan Robinson referred to Samuelson's approach as "bastard Keynesianism."[6]

The New Keynesian agenda is the child of the neoclassical synthesis and, like the IS-LM model before it, New Keynesian economics inherits the mistakes of the bastard Keynesians. It misses two key Keynesian concepts: (1) there are multiple equilibrium unemployment rates and (2) beliefs are fundamental. My work brings these concepts back to center stage and integrates the Keynes of the General Theory with the microeconomics of general equilibrium theory in a new way.

Macroeconomics at Penn during the 1980s

Not everything I say in this book is new, and the insights I present are drawn from several different traditions. The school that most influenced my ideas was developing when I was an assistant professor at the University of Pennsylvania during the 1980s.[7] At that time, Costas Azariadis wrote an important paper with the intriguing title of "Self-Fulfilling Prophecies" and David Cass and Karl Shell introduced the term *sunspots* into economics in a new way.[8] All three authors were writing about the same idea: business cycles might be driven by arbitrary swings in the beliefs of market participants that have nothing to do with the so-called fundamentals of the economy.

Sunspots had been used previously by Stanley Jevons, who thought the sunspot cycle influenced business cycles through the effects of solar flares on agriculture.[9] The modern use of *sunspots* is different. Cass and Shell used it as a spoof to mean the effect of nonfundamental shocks to business and consumer confidence that influence the economy only because people believe they will.

The idea that confidence matters was not new; it appears in Keynes's General Theory where Keynes used the term *animal spirits* to mean the same thing. What was new in the work of Azariadis, and Cass and Shell, was that beliefs matter even in economic models that follow all the dictates of standard microeconomic theory. People are rational, prices are fully flexible, and people know with certainty the probabilities that future prices will be realized.

Shell presented the first work on "sunspots" in Paris in 1977 in a seminar run by legendary French economist Edmond Malinvaud.[10] The idea that confidence can be an independent driver of business cycles in models of this kind was so revolutionary that it was met with disbelief from Malinvaud.[11]

In 1977, Karl Shell and Costas Azariadis were living in West Philadelphia and they would often walk home together from the office. It was on these evening strolls that Karl discussed the sunspot idea with Costas. He, too, was initially skeptical.[12] Azariadis believed the result that "sunspots matter" must be a special case that would not persist in more robust examples of economic models. After investigating dynamic models more carefully, he established that self-fulfilling prophecies are pervasive in models of overlapping generations in which people are born and people die, and he went on to publish a path-breaking paper on the topic.[13]

Initially, the sunspot agenda was dismissed because the models used to convey the idea were technically demanding and did not have much empirical content. That soon changed. Writing with Michael Woodford, who was then an MIT graduate student visiting Penn, Woodford and I showed how to construct a monetary model in which beliefs drive business cycles independently in a version of the model that had been used by Robert Lucas to introduce modern theories of expectations to the profession.[14]

Soon after the publication of the papers by Azariadis and by Cass and Shell, the idea that self-fulfilling prophecies can drive business cycles became mainstream. In coauthored papers with Jess Benhabib of New York University and Jang-Ting Guo of the University of California Riverside, we applied the idea to the model that was, by then, sweeping the profession: the real business cycle (RBC) model of Finn Kydland and Edward C. Prescott.[15] I went on to write a textbook on the topic, *The Macroeconomics of Self-Fulfilling Prophecies*, which remains to this day a standard reference book and is used in graduate programs around the world.[16]

It was clear to many of us, even back then, that self-fulfilling beliefs could explain business cycle fluctuations at least as well as the real-business-cycle paradigm that came to dominate graduate programs for the next thirty-five years. But, the sunspot agenda did not have a single strong leader and the figures who wrote the first two papers in the area, Azariadis, and Cass and Shell, were dismissive of the practical and empirical relevance of their ideas.[17]

Two Generations of Models in Which Confidence Matters

In a survey paper published in 2014, I distinguished between first- and second-generation endogenous business cycle models.[18] I used the term *endogenous business cycle models* to mean models in which confidence influences outcomes independently, as opposed to "RBC models," in which all economic fluctuations are caused by shifts in technology.[19]

In first-generation endogenous business cycle models, the economy retains the self-correcting mechanisms that Frisch described in his rocking-horse metaphor. Confidence shocks do rock the horse, but in this respect they are no different from productivity shocks, strikes, hurricanes, and monetary disturbances. Classical economists like Arthur Pigou, who wrote about business cycles in his 1927 book, *Industrial Fluctuations*, would not have been surprised by the notion that confidence matters for economic activity. All the work cited in the previous section, including that described in *The Macroeconomics of Self-fulfilling Prophecies*, falls into this category. These models lead to Pareto-inefficient fluctuations, but the social cost of business cycles is small.

In a more recent book, *Expectations, Employment and Prices,* published in 2010, I described a second generation of endogenous business cycle models. In these models, confidence does not just rock the horse; it knocks it over.[20] The difference is between models in which the economy can be pushed away temporarily from its steady state and models in which it can be pushed into an entirely different steady state. In the first case, the economy is self-stabilizing and, most of the time, the allocation of resources is "almost" Pareto efficient. In the second case, the stabilization mechanism is broken and the allocation of resources is very far from being Pareto efficient most of the time. In my opinion, the idea that economic equilibrium can be Pareto inefficient, most of the time, is *the* most important idea to emerge from Keynes' General Theory.

My Connection with Keynes

In the following pages, I am sometimes highly critical of mainstream economic ideas. I am not alone in my criticisms. A significant number of Post-Keynesian economists—for example, Joan Robinson, Paul Davidson, and Hyman Minsky— have also critiqued the foundations of New Keynesian economics. In common with the Post-Keynesians, I believe that expectations are an important independent driver of business cycles and that market economies can sometimes get stuck in equilibria with high, persistent, involuntary unemployment. Unlike the Post-Keynesians, however, my methods are unashamedly neoclassical. I favor the use of formal models and I am perfectly happy to assume that wages and prices are flexible. The Post-Keynesians emphasize the fact that we cannot rationally calculate the probabilities of future events because the world is changing in a way that is unknown and unknowable. Although that idea is important and powerful, it does not play a central role in the theory

I present in this book. The actors who populate my models are fully aware of the probability of any future event.

In the remaining chapters, I reintroduce two central themes of Keynes' General Theory and recombine them with classical economics in a new way. I combine the idea that business cycles are driven by animal spirits, with the idea that the unemployment rate may be permanently above its so-called natural rate. The ideas that I develop represent a new macroeconomic paradigm that offers an alternative explanation of the history of unemployment, interest rates, and inflation from the New Keynesian narrative that currently dominates thinking at central banks around the world. My work implies that central banks and national treasuries should adopt a new financial policy in which they intervene actively to stabilize financial markets. By adopting this policy, it is my hope that we may provide an environment in which market capitalism may thrive, without killing the goose that lays the golden egg.

3

THE DEMISE OF THE NATURAL RATE HYPOTHESIS

The history of economic thought in the twentieth century is the history of a struggle between classical and Keynesian ideas. Two events have transformed this history since 1900. The first was the Great Depression of the 1930s, a prolonged period of high unemployment and low growth. The second was the Great Stagflation of the 1970s, a period of simultaneous high inflation and high unemployment. I believe the Great Recession is a third transformative event. Just as the Great Depression and the Great Stagflation changed economics forever, so will the Great Recession.

The 1920s was the era of the economics of Adam Smith.[1] Markets work well and the business cycle is self-stabilizing. The economists of the 1920s accepted a concept, Say's Law, attributed to eighteenth-century French economist Jean-Baptiste Say.[2] Say's Law asserts that "supply creates its own demand" and it is widely interpreted to mean there can be no such thing as involuntary unemployment. The Great Depression ended the widespread acceptance of Say's Law and it set the stage for the transformation of economic thought that followed the publication of Keynes' masterpiece, *The General Theory of Employment, Interest and Money*.

The 1950s was the era of the economics of John Maynard Keynes. Markets mess up sometimes and government must get in there and fix them. The economists of the 1950s accepted a concept attributed to Keynes, who asserted that sometimes people could be involuntarily unemployed. The Great Stagflation ended the widespread acceptance of Keynes' concept of involuntary unemployment and it set the stage for a second transformation of economic thought.

The 1980s initiated a rebirth of the same classical ideas that had characterized 1920s economics. But, instead of the verbal theories of the 1920s, the rebirth of classical economics was expressed in the language of mathematics. Because the mathematics was hard, the ideas were simplified and, initially, the new classical resurgence paled in comparison with the rich verbal theories of business cycles expressed by Cambridge economist Arthur Pigou.[3] As my colleague Axel Leijonhufvud once remarked, "Modern macroeconomics is a lot like modern Hollywood movies; the pyrotechnics are spectacular but the plots are sadly lacking."

The Great Depression and the Great Stagnation each saw the death of a great idea. After the Great Depression, it was the demise of Say's Law. After the Great Stagflation, it was the demise of the concept of involuntary unemployment. In this chapter, I make the case that the Great Recession will lead to the death of a third great idea. The next great idea that is about to fall is called *the natural rate hypothesis* (NRH).

What Is the Natural Rate Hypothesis?

The NRH is the idea that unemployment has an inherent tendency to return to some special "natural rate" that is a property of the available technology for finding jobs. It is a fact of nature, a bit like the gravitational constant in celestial mechanics. The theory of the NRH has been taught to every economist in every top economics department for the past thirty years. As part of the package, economists learn the natural rate cannot be influenced by fiscal or monetary policy.

Even today, the NRH is a central component of New Keynesian economics and, with very few exceptions, central bankers, politicians, and economic talking heads use the theory of the natural rate of unemployment to explain their views on the appropriate stance of monetary policy. I believe the NRH is false, and this fact has important consequences. If central bankers are working with a false theory, they are likely to make bad decisions that affect all our lives.

What Is the Phillips Curve?

The genesis of the NRH is connected intricately with the history of the Phillips Curve, an important empirical and theoretical relationship that is supposed to connect the inflation rate with the unemployment rate. The Phillips Curve began life as a scatter plot of inflation against unemployment. It was first constructed by the New Zealand economist A. W. Phillips, or Bill Phillips to his friends.[4] Phillips plotted UK wage inflation on the vertical axis of a graph and the unemployment rate on the horizontal axis. He found the points fell around a downward-sloping curve that has ever since been associated with his name.

Figure 3.1 is a stylized representation of the Phillips Curve that appeared in Phillips' original article. The vertical axis of this graph measures the rate of change of money wages; the horizontal axis measures the unemployment rate. The downward-sloping curve is the relationship between these two variables that Phillips estimated using UK data.

How Did Theorists Explain the Phillips Curve?

Phillips fit a curve to UK data from 1861 through 1913 and he showed that data from later time periods could be explained by the same equation as data from the nineteenth century. His contemporaries saw the conformity of data from the 1950s, with a curve estimated from nineteenth-century and early-twentieth-century data, as evidence that the Phillips Curve is a stable

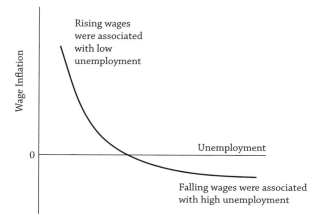

Figure 3.1 The Phillips Curve in the United Kingdom from 1861 to 1957.

structural equation. Its shape and position were thought to be constants that bear the same relationship to theoretical economics that the gravitational constant bears to theoretical physics.

The Phillips Curve was published at the same time that Keynesian economists were struggling to understand how to connect Keynesian economics, in which there is involuntary unemployment, to classical economics, where there is not. The solution to that puzzle was Paul Samuelson's neoclassical synthesis.[5] Samuelson embraced the Phillips Curve as a missing link that connected the short run, during which involuntary unemployment arises because wages and prices are sticky, with the long run, when there is no involuntary unemployment because all wages and prices are perfectly flexible.

Samuelson thought of unemployment as a measure of the gap between the quantity of labor supplied and the quantity of labor demanded. In his view, the labor market is typically in a state of disequilibrium. An excess supply of labor causes wages to fall and an excess demand for labor causes wages to rise. The higher the excess demand for labor, the faster wages will rise. The higher the excess supply of labor, the faster wages will fall. The Phillips Curve, according to Samuelson, was a "wage adjustment equation" that represented an empirical confirmation of his theory.

The idea that wage inflation is a wage adjustment equation became part of the hard core of macroeconomic theory and, to this day, a version of the Phillips Curve informs the judgments of policymakers in treasuries and central banks throughout the world.[6] To borrow a phrase from Keynes' *The General Theory*, the Phillips Curve conquered the profession as "surely as the Spanish Inquisition conquered Spain."[7]

Why Do New Keynesian Economists Cling to the Phillips Curve?

Phillips' evidence from the late nineteenth and early twentieth century was consistent with Samuelson's theory. The facts soon changed and, in all economic data since 1960, simple scatter plots of wage inflation against the unemployment rate do not show the same fixed relationship with each other that characterized the earlier data. The Phillips Curve, as it was originally defined, no longer exists. Why, then, do New Keynesian economists still cling to a false idea?

An analogy with the science of astronomy may help explain why the Phillips Curve remains a central part of macroeconomic models. Before Einstein transformed the science of mechanics with the theory of relativity, theoretical physicists invented a planet called Vulcan, to explain the anomalous orbit of Mercury. Thomas Levenson tells the story: "For more than fifty years the world's top scientists searched for the 'missing' planet Vulcan, whose existence was mandated by Isaac Newton's theories of gravity ... [and] some of the era's most skilled astronomers ... claimed to have found it. There was just one problem: It was never there."[8]

The Phillips Curve is like the planet Vulcan. It has not been there in the data since the 1950s. It is important, not because it is true, but because the New Keynesians need it to be true. Just as the planet Vulcan was relied on by theoretical physicists to explain an anomaly in Newtonian mechanics, so the existence of the Phillips Curve is relied on by theoretical New Keynesian economists to explain an anomaly in classical economics. Changes in the supply of money that ought to have no effect on the real economy do, in fact, appear to matter.

The Failure of the Phillips Curve as a Policy Tradeoff

Writing in 1960, Paul Samuelson and Robert Solow were not yet aware that the evidence for their theory was fast evaporating. They published a paper in which they argued that the Phillips Curve represents an exploitable policy tradeoff.

Using empirical estimates of a Phillips Curve in US data, Samuelson and Solow claimed that, if policymakers wished to maintain unemployment at 3%, they would need to accept an inflation rate of 5%. If they wished to bring inflation down to 3%, they would need to accept an unemployment rate of 5%.[9] These were not the only alternatives. According to Samuelson and Solow, a policymaker could choose any unemployment rate. But, social engineering of the unemployment rate would come with a cost. The lower the desired unemployment rate, the higher the rate of inflation.

Samuelson and Solow's argument sounded plausible, but it relied on the assumption that the Phillips Curve is a stable, structural relationship between inflation and unemployment. For their argument to make sense, the Phillips Curve must remain stable when the government tries to change the unemployment rate through alterations in monetary or fiscal policy. The evidence demonstrates that that is *not* the case.

Beginning in the mid 1960s, the United States printed money to help pay for the Vietnam War. The economy experienced a period of rapid growth and a buildup of inflation, but the unemployment rate did not behave in the way that Samuelson's theory predicted. The inflation rate, as measured by the annualized percentage change in the consumer price index, went from a low of −0.7% in March 1955 to a high of +13.7% in March 1980. If the historical Phillips Curve had held up in US data, the unemployment rate should have been less than 1%. Instead, by 1980 it was 6.3% and rising. This period of high inflation and simultaneous high unemployment is called the *Great Stagflation*.

Why Did the Phillips Curve Shift?

Why was the Phillips Curve stable for such a long time and why did it shift during the 1960s? The answer is that the connection between unemployment and inflation that we see in the data depends on the institutions that govern the supply of money. We call these institutions *monetary regimes*.

From 1861 through 1957, the period when Phillips carried out his empirical work in the United Kingdom, the monetary regime was the *gold exchange standard*. Under the gold exchange standard, a reserve currency, initially the British pound, but later the US dollar, was convertible into gold at a fixed rate. All other countries fixed their exchange rates to the reserve currency, which became an internationally acceptable method for discharging debts.

In the period after WWII, the gold exchange standard led to the buildup of unsustainable imbalances in the foreign currency reserves held by individual countries. Some countries exported more goods and services than they imported; these countries accumulated reserves of foreign exchange. Other countries imported more goods and services than they exported; these countries eventually ran out of foreign exchange reserves and were forced to devalue their currencies against the dollar. In 1971, the system became unsustainable and Richard Nixon suspended the convertibility of the dollar into gold, thereby ending the gold exchange standard and ushering in a new monetary regime.

After 1971, the monetary regime used was the *floating exchange rate system*. Under the floating exchange rate system, domestic money creation is no longer constrained by random discoveries of gold. Instead, national governments are free to create money subject only to the constraint that their citizens continue to recognize its value by using it as a means of payment.

Inflation, as Milton Friedman once said, is "always and everywhere a monetary phenomenon."[10] Inflation cannot persist for long in the absence of money creation, and the ability of a country to print money is connected to the monetary regime. Under a gold exchange standard, inflation is constrained by the rate at which gold can be mined. Under a floating exchange rate system, it is constrained only by the policies of a nation's central bank. The Phillips Curve disappeared during the 1960s because the gold exchange standard gradually collapsed as countries changed the pegs that pinned their currencies to gold. When the gold exchange standard was abandoned in 1971, the genie was finally out of the bottle and expectations in the modern monetary system were and are anchored only by the credibility of each nation's central bank.

The Birth of the Natural Rate Hypothesis

The Great Stagflation was a blow to the Samuelson–Solow view of the Phillips Curve as a policy tradeoff. But, it was not a surprise to everyone. In two separate articles, Milton Friedman and Edmund Phelps both predicted there is no long-run tradeoff between inflation and unemployment.[11] In his 1968 presidential address to the American Economics Association, Friedman argued there is a unique steady-state equilibrium unemployment rate, and he coined the term the *natural rate of unemployment* to refer to this idea.[12]

According to Friedman, Solow and Samuelson were plotting the wrong variable on the axis of the Phillips Curve. It is not the money wage that adjusts in response to an excess demand for labor; it is the money wage adjusted for cost-of-living increases. Economists call this the *real wage*. If unemployment is above its natural rate, Friedman argued that *real wages* will fall, firms will employ more workers, and the unemployment rate will drop. If unemployment is below its natural rate, *real wages* will rise, firms will fire some workers, and the unemployment rate will increase. With the publication of Friedman's presidential address, the NRH entered the lexicon of modern macroeconomics.

The Phelps–Friedman idea was revolutionary. Phelps and Friedman argued that there is a different Phillips Curve for every level of expected price inflation and that unemployment can only differ from its natural rate if people have incorrect expectations. According to this theory, there is no long-run trade-off between inflation and unemployment, and the long-run Phillips Curve is vertical at the natural rate of unemployment.

Figure 3.2 illustrates this idea. In the figure, two different Phillips Curves are plotted: one for a high level of expected price inflation and one for a low level of expected price inflation. The vertical dashed line is what Friedman called the *natural rate of unemployment.* It is the unemployment rate that prevails when the quantity of labor demanded is equal to the quantity of labor supplied.

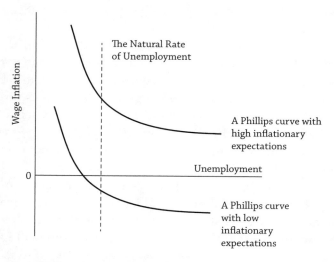

Figure 3.2 Expectations and the Phillips Curve.

Expectations and the Phillips Curve

If there is no tradeoff between inflation and unemployment, why did the Phillips Curve exist in a century of data? Milton Friedman and Edmund Phelps explained that conundrum by developing models in which there is inertia in the way that wages are set. In one simple version of their idea, wage contracts last for several years and, each year, some fraction of workers and firms renegotiate future wages. The wage that is written into contracts between firms and workers depends, in part, on the prices of commodities that people expect to hold over the life of the contract.[13]

Suppose that people expect that, on average, next year's prices will be 3% higher than this year's prices. In this example, an expected inflation rate of 3% will be written into wage contracts. If the realized inflation rate between this year and next is also 3%, price expectations will turn out to be correct. Because wage contracts are chosen to equate the quantity of labor demanded with the quantity of labor supplied, when expectations are correct, the unemployment rate will be equal to the natural rate of unemployment.

What if an unanticipated event occurs between this year and next? For example, suppose the government prints more money than people had anticipated.

If an unanticipated event causes realized inflation to be higher than anticipated, prices will increase more than workers and firms had expected when they entered into labor contracts. Because their wage bill is fixed by contract, firms will earn higher profits than they expected and they will hire additional workers. In this scenario, firms will employ more workers than they otherwise would and the unemployment rate will be below its natural rate.

If an unanticipated event causes realized inflation to be lower than anticipated, prices will increase less than workers and firms had expected when they entered into labor contracts. Because their wage bill is fixed by contract, firms will earn lower profits than they expected and they will lay off workers and may even be forced into bankruptcy. In this scenario, firms will employ fewer workers than they otherwise would and the unemployment rate will be above its natural rate.

This explanation does not depend on the assumption that the expected inflation rate is 3%. It holds for any inflation rate. The important point is that random events may cause realized inflation to differ from expected inflation and that unemployment will be below its natural rate when inflation is higher than expected and it will be above its natural rate when inflation is lower than expected. When the inflation rate is equal to the expected inflation rate, the unemployment rate will be exactly equal to the natural rate of unemployment.

If this theory of the Phillips Curve is correct, a policymaker may be able, temporarily, to bring the unemployment rate below its natural rate by printing money and stimulating aggregate demand. But, the mechanism that causes the reduction in unemployment works essentially by fooling workers and firms into writing wage contracts that do not reflect inflation correctly.

Unemployment can only be different from its natural rate if inflation is different from the inflation rate that people expected when they entered into these contracts. When inflation becomes fully anticipated, the unemployment rate will return to its natural rate. Importantly, the natural rate of unemployment is consistent with *any* inflation rate in the long run.

The Advent of Rational Expectations

Friedman assumed that expectations are determined by extrapolating from the past to the future. He called this theory *adaptive expectations*.[14] This theory is plausible and appeals to common sense. It also explains the data successfully. But, the theory of adaptive expectations assumed that people forecast the future with a mechanical rule. And that assumption has an important drawback. If people use a mechanical rule to forecast the future, their behavior can be manipulated by the government in an implausible way.

If expectations were adaptive, a government that wished to exploit the Phillips Curve could keep increasing the money supply at ever-faster rates. A policy of that kind would fool the public into writing contracts in which employment was consistently below its natural rate. That policy is unlikely to be effective for long because it would only succeed if the government were able to fool the public consistently. Conceptualizing what would happen in this situation draws attention to the deficiency of Friedman's assumption of adaptive expectations. People are not automata. As Abraham Lincoln famously said: "You can't fool all of the people all of the time."

In 1972, Robert Lucas published an influential paper that shaped the course of macroeconomics for the next 40 years.[15] According to Lucas, the public does not use the same forecast rule in every situation. Instead, the public's forecast rule adapts so that expectations of inflation are always right on average. Using a concept first proposed by John Muth, Lucas argued that *expectations are rational.*[16] The *rational expectations hypothesis* states that, although no one can predict the future perfectly, predictions of future prices and inflation should be correct on average.

The rational expectations hypothesis is a sensible idea. It does, however, have its limitations. It makes most sense as a consistency requirement for an economic model. We should not build economic models in which, if the environment is stationary, expectations are consistently wrong on average. If something important changes, however, it may take time for the public to change the way it forecasts. And if changes to the environment are infrequent, expectations may be rational most of the time, but subject to systematic bias in the period after a change.

The Natural Rate Hypothesis Is Religion, Not Science

A central theme in my recent body of work is that the NRH is false. I was led to this conclusion initially in joint work with

Andreas Beyer of the European Central Bank. That work is published in our 2007 paper "Natural Rate Doubts."[17]

Because economists cannot conduct experiments, any test of a hypothesis must make assumptions about what does and what does not change. In this section I explain an empirical test, drawn from my published work, which uses data from the US economy to test the NRH.[18] To conduct the test, I maintain the assumption that the rational expectations hypothesis is true and I use decade-long averages of data on inflation and unemployment. I maintain the rational expectations assumption because I find it difficult to believe expectations will remain biased systematically for periods of ten years at a time.

By averaging out months when the unemployment rate is high with months when the unemployment rate is low, I generate a statistic that should be close to the natural rate of unemployment in every decade. Rational expectations implies that decade-long averages of the monthly inflation rate should contain as many months when inflation was greater than expected as months when inflation was lower than expected. If the NRH and the rational expectations hypothesis are both true simultaneously, a plot of decade averages of inflation against unemployment should reveal a vertical line at the natural rate of unemployment. In Figure 3.3, I show this prediction fails dramatically.

Each point in Figure 3.3 represents a decade average of monthly unemployment (plotted on the horizontal axis) against a decade average of monthly inflation, measured by the annualized percentage change of the consumer price index (CPI; plotted on the vertical axis). There is no tendency for these points to lie around a vertical line. If we exclude the most recent five years, this figure is upward sloping. If we include these years, it is closer to being horizontal than vertical.[19] Each observation on this graph is an average taken over 120 months. Because it is unlikely that expectations are biased systematically when averaged over periods of this length, I conclude the NRH is false.

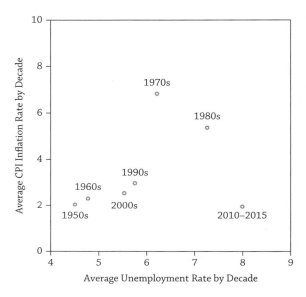

Figure 3.3 Average Inflation and Unemployment by Decade for the United States.
Source: Bureau of Labor Statistics and author's calculations.

Defenders of the NRH might choose to respond to my empirical findings by arguing that the natural rate of unemployment is time varying. But, I am unaware of any theory that provides us in advance with an explanation of how the natural rate of unemployment varies over time. In the absence of such a theory, the NRH has no predictive content. A theory like this—which cannot be falsified by any set of observations—is religion, not science.

Conclusion

I have packed a lot into this chapter. Let me review the main ideas. The Phillips Curve is a downward-sloping relationship between wage inflation and the unemployment rate that characterized UK data for more than a century. It was seized on by Samuelson as a building block in his interpretation of

Keynesian theory. For Samuelson, the Phillips Curve connects the short run, when prices are sticky, with the long run, when prices are flexible. The disappearance of the stable Phillips Curve blows a hole in Samuelson's theory.

When the world left the gold exchange standard in 1971, the Phillips Curve began to shift and there was no longer a stable relationship between inflation and unemployment. Phelps and Friedman argued we should never have expected there to be a stable Phillips Curve in the first place; instead, there is a different Phillips Curve for every level of expected inflation. We only saw one Phillips Curve before 1970 because expectations were anchored by the gold exchange standard and the inflation rate was constrained by the discovery of gold deposits.

Milton Friedman coined the term *natural rate of unemployment* to mean the unemployment rate the economy would converge back to after prices and expectations had been given time to adjust. Soon after Friedman developed the NRH, economists accepted a new theory of expectations called *rational expectations*. If the NRH is true and if people have rational expectations, we should expect to see a vertical Phillips Curve that holds between decade averages of unemployment and inflation. The fact that we do not see a vertical Phillips Curve when we average data over decades demonstrates the NRH is false.

However, although the NRH is false, it has been responsible for a great deal of damage. The NRH was widely accepted not only by economists like Milton Friedman, who were skeptical of the role of government in maintaining full employment, but also, when they had absorbed evidence from the 1970s, it was accepted by economists like Paul Samuelson and Robert Solow, who are Keynesians. The NRH is at the core of contemporary New Keynesian theories used by academic economists and policymakers today to understand the Great Recession. We should all be concerned by the continued use of the NRH. The fact that the NRH is false has important consequences for economic policy and its impact on our lives.

Because our central bankers are working with a false theory, it will be difficult or impossible for them to prevent the next Great Depression. Having a great policymaker, armed with New Keynesian theory, is like having a great soccer goalkeeper in a basketball game. Some say that Michael Jordan is the best basketball player who ever lived. And many soccer fans claim that the best goalkeeper in the 2014 World Cup was Germany's Manuel Neuer. Neuer is a great player, but only when he's playing soccer. Having Manuel Neuer on your team is not much help when you're playing basketball against Michael Jordan.

4

LET'S STOP PRETENDING UNEMPLOYMENT IS VOLUNTARY

Unless you have a PhD in economics, you probably think it uncontroversial to argue that we should be concerned about the unemployment rate. Those of you who have lost a job, or who have struggled to find a job on leaving school, college, or a university, are well aware that unemployment is a painful and dehumanizing experience. You may be surprised to learn that, for the past thirty-five years, the models used by academic economists and central bankers to understand how the economy works have not included unemployment as a separate category.[1] In almost every macroeconomic seminar I attended, from 1980 through 2007, it was accepted that all unemployment is voluntary.

In 1960, almost all macroeconomists talked about *involuntary unemployment* and they assumed, following Keynes, the quantity of labor demanded is not equal to the quantity of labor supplied.[2] That view of economics was turned on its head, almost single-handedly, by Robert Lucas.[3] Lucas persuaded macroeconomists that it makes no sense to talk about disequilibrium in any market and he initiated a revolution in macroeconomics that reformulated the discipline using pre-Keynesian classical assumptions.

The idea that all unemployment is voluntary is called the *equilibrium approach to labor markets*. Lucas wrote his first article on this idea in 1969 in a coauthored paper with Leonard

Rapping. His ideas received a big boost during the 1980s when Finn Kydland, Edward C. Prescott, Charles Long, and Charles Plosser persuaded macroeconomists to use a mathematical approach, called the *Ramsey growth model*, as a new paradigm for business cycle theory.[4] The theory of real business cycles, or RBCs, was born. According to this theory, we should think about consumption, investment, and employment "as if" they were the optimal choices of a single representative agent with superhuman perception of the probabilities of future events.

Real Business Cycles

The theory of RBCs began with simple equilibrium models in which random shocks to the level of technological innovation are the sources of swings in growth and employment. It soon developed into a much more ambitious program. In RBC theory there is no unemployment because RBC theorists assume there is continuous market clearing. They argue that unemployment is not a useful concept and that, instead, we should represent labor market activity by the number of hours spent in paid employment by a representative household. If there is no unemployment, how can there be a natural rate of unemployment? There too, RBC theory has a response. According to RBC economists, there is a natural rate of *employment* that represents the hours of paid employment of a representative worker when productivity is at its average level over the business cycle.

Starting in the 1980s, the tools of rational expectations and continuous market clearing swept the profession. Classical ideas spread outward from the Universities of Chicago and Minnesota, and soon prominent graduate economics programs throughout the world were training their students to study the macroeconomy using classical tools. This new approach was called *dynamic stochastic general equilibrium* (DSGE) theory.

All Models Are Wrong

I have lost count of the number of times I have heard students and faculty repeat the mantra in seminars that "all models are wrong." This aphorism, attributed to statistician George Box, is the battle cry of the Minnesota calibrator, a breed of macro-economist inspired by the new RBC program and promoted by then-Minnesota economist Edward C. Prescott, one of the most influential economists of the past century.

Of course all models are wrong. That is trivially true; it is the definition of a model. But, the cry has been used for three decades to poke fun at attempts to use serious mathematical and statistical methods to analyze data. Data that are observed on a single variable at different points in time is called a *time series*, and the branch of economics that uses mathematical and statistical methods to analyze time series is called *time series econometrics*. Time series econometrics was inconvenient to the nascent RBC program Prescott pioneered because the models he favored were, and still are, overwhelmingly rejected by the facts. That is inconvenient.

Prescott's response was pure genius. If the model and the data are in conflict, the data must be wrong. He advocated a new approach that uses data selectively to judge a theory and he called this new approach "calibration." Time series econometrics, according to Prescott, was crushing the acorn before it had time to grow into a tree. His response was not only to reformulate the theory, but also to reformulate the way in which that theory was to be judged. In a puff of calibrator's smoke, the history of time series econometrics was relegated to the dustbin of history to take its place alongside alchemy, the ether, and the dodo bird.

Real Business Cycles and the High School Olympics

How did Prescott achieve this remarkable feat of prestidigitation? First, he argued we should focus on a small subset of the properties of the data. Since Ragnar Frisch developed the rocking-horse model we met in Chapter 2, economists have recognized that economic time series can be modeled by simple equations in which this year's GDP is equal to a multiple of last year's GDP plus a random shock. These time series move together in different ways at different frequencies. For example, consumption, investment, and GDP are all growing over time. The low-frequency movement in these series is called the *trend*. Prescott argued that the trends in time series are a nuisance if we are interested in understanding business cycles and he proposed to remove them with a filter. Roughly speaking, he plotted a smooth curve through each individual series and subtracted the wiggles from the trend. Importantly, Prescott's approach removes a different trend from each series and the trends are discarded when evaluating the success of the theory.

After removing trends, Prescott was left with the wiggles. He proposed that we should evaluate our economic theories of business cycles by how well they explain co-movements among the wiggles. When his theory failed to clear the eight-foot hurdle of the Olympic high jump, he lowered the bar to five feet and persuaded us all that leaping over this high school bar was a success. Keynesians protested. But they did not protest loudly enough and, ultimately, it became common—even among serious econometricians—to filter their data in the way Prescott proposed. The filtering algorithm proposed by Prescott became known among economists as the *Hodrick–Prescott filter*.[5]

The New Keynesian Surrender

Prescott's argument was that business cycles are all about the co-movements that occur among employment, GDP, consumption, and investment at frequencies of four to eight years. These movements describe deviations of a market economy from its natural rate of unemployment that, according to Prescott, are caused by the substitution of labor effort of households between times of plenty and times of famine. A recession, according to this theory, is what former-MIT economist Franco Modigliani famously referred to as a "sudden attack of contagious laziness."[6]

The Keynesians disagreed. They argued that whatever causes a recession, low employment persists because of "frictions" that prevent wages and prices from adjusting to their correct levels. The Keynesian view was guided by Samuelson's neoclassical synthesis, which accepted the idea that business cycles are fluctuations around a unique classical steady state. Initially, Keynesian economists rejected market-clearing models of the labor market. But Minnesota launched wave upon wave of newly minted calibrators onto the PhD job market and it was not long before the tidal wave of new classical ideas burst through the floodgates of Keynesian resistance. With the publication of an influential volume of readings in 1991, edited by N. Gregory Mankiw and David Romer, New Keynesian economics was born.[7]

New Keynesian researchers discarded the Keynesian concept that unemployment can be involuntary and replaced it with the Minnesota doctrine in which the quantity of labor demanded is always equal to the quantity of labor supplied. Using the Minnesota model as a starting point, they added small costs of changing prices to capture the empirical fact that changes to the money supply are not transmitted instantly to wages and prices. In this respect, they were following in the MIT tradition of the neoclassical synthesis pioneered by Samuelson twenty-five years earlier.

Gradually, New Keynesian economists incorporated more frictions and additional shocks into their models, including shocks to confidence, monetary disturbances, and news shocks. By the onset of the Great Recession, New Keynesian macroeconomists had developed mathematical equations that captured the ideas of 1920s business cycle theories described by classical economist Arthur Pigou in 1927.[8]

By accepting the neoclassical synthesis, classical and New Keynesian economists both accepted that the economy is a self-stabilizing system that, left to itself, would gravitate back to the unique natural rate of unemployment. The New Keynesians agreed to play by Prescott's rules. Not only did they dispense with the important Keynesian idea of involuntary unemployment, they also gave up on the use of strict econometric methods to distinguish between models. Like the RBC economists, the New Keynesians filtered their data and set the bar at the high school level.

In my view, Keynesian economics is not about the wiggles. As I discuss in my book *Expectations, Employment and Prices,* it is about permanent long-run shifts in the equilibrium unemployment rate caused by changes in the animal spirits of participants in the financial markets.[9] By filtering the data, we remove the possibility of evaluating a model that predicts that shifts in aggregate demand cause permanent shifts in unemployment. We have given up the game before it starts by allowing the other team to move the goal posts.

Labor Markets Don't Clear; Let's Stop Pretending They Do

Ever since Robert Lucas introduced the idea of continuous labor market clearing, the idea that it may be useful to talk of something called "involuntary unemployment" has been scoffed at by serious economists. It's time to fight back. The concept of "involuntary unemployment" does not describe a loose notion that characterizes the sloppy work of heterodox economists from the Dark Side. It is a useful category that describes a group of workers who have difficulty finding jobs at existing market prices.

The idea that the labor market is well described by a model in which a market wage adjusts to equate the quantity of labor demanded with the quantity of labor supplied bears little resemblance to anything we see in the real world. What makes me so confident of that claim?[10]

Employment varies over time for three reasons. First, people work longer or shorter hours. Second, people enter and leave

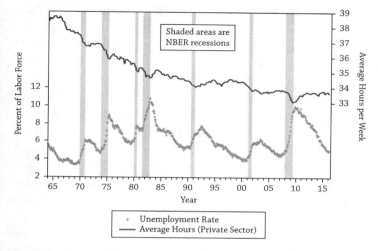

Figure 4.1 Hours and Employment in the United States. NBER, National Bureau of Economic Research.

Source: Bureau of Labor Statistics and NBER.

the labor force, and third, some people lose jobs and others find jobs. Figure 4.1 plots data from 1964 through 2015 on average weekly hours of production of nonsupervisory workers in the private sector (measured on the right axis) and the unemployment rate (measured on the left axis). The solid line is average weekly hours. The line marked by crosses is the unemployment rate. The gray shaded areas are National Bureau of Economic Research recessions.

The facts are clear. Although hours do fall during recessions, the movements in hours are swamped by movements in the unemployment rate. Consider, for example, the 2008 recession. Average weekly hours fell from 34 hours per week to 33 hours per week. The unemployment rate, in contrast, increased from 4% to 10%.

The main story in the data on average weekly hours is that they declined from 39 hours per week in 1964 to 34 hours per week in 2015. As American workers got richer, they chose collectively to take a larger share of their wages in the form of leisure. These movements are important if our goal is to understand long-term trends. They do not, however, tell us much about recessions.

What about the labor force participation rate? Recently, there has been a great deal of angst among policymakers who are asking if the fall in the participation rate that occurred during the Great Recession was cyclical or structural. Figure 4.2 sheds some light on this question.

This figure shows data from 1964 through 2015 on the labor force participation rate (measured on the right axis) and the unemployment rate (measured on the left axis). The solid line is the labor force participation rate. The line marked by crosses is the unemployment rate. The gray shaded areas are National Bureau of Economic Research recessions. Figure 4.2 demonstrates there is no clear tendency for the participation rate to drop in recessions. For example, participation was higher at the end of the 1982 recession than at the beginning, and during

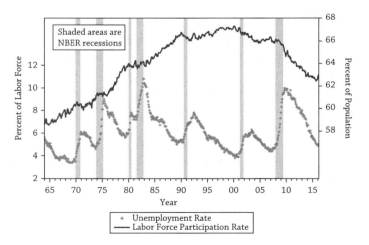

Figure 4.2 Participation and Unemployment in the United States. NBER, National Bureau of Economic Research.

Source: Bureau of Labor Statistics and NBER.

a number of other postwar recessions it has remained flat. The chart demonstrates that changes in the labor force participation rate, like changes in average weekly hours, do not contribute much to the decrease in employment that occurs during recessions.

If the participation rate is not a cyclical phenomenon, why does it vary over time? When we break down the participation rate into female and male participation, a more detailed story emerges. Figure 4.3 shows that breakdown. The solid line represents female labor force participation as a percentage of the female population. The dashed line is male labor force participation as a percentage of the male population. In 1964, only 38% of women were part of the labor force. During the 1960s, more women moved from the home to the workplace and, by 2000, the female labor force participation rate had increased to 60%. The increase in the female labor force participation rate

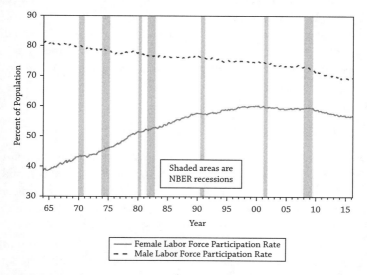

Figure 4.3 Male and Female Labor Force Participation in the United States. NBER, National Bureau of Economic Research.

Source: Bureau of Labor Statistics and NBER.

explains the upward-sloping part of the total participation rate, both male and female, graphed in Figure 4.2.

To explain the decline in the labor force participation rate after 2000, we need to look at demographics. Male labor force participation in 1964 was at 80%. That figure declined gradually during the next forty years and, by 2015, it had decreased to 69%. After 2000, female labor participation also began to decline and it now stands at 57%. The decline in the male labor force participation rate throughout the entire period, and the decline in the female participation rate after 2000, is explained by a change in the age distribution of the population. During the twentieth century, improvements in health care and the increased availability of contraception led to a decline in birth rates. A reduced birth rate has led to an aging population, and as the population aged, there were fewer people of either sex of working age.[11]

The data are clear. The movements in the labor force participation rate during recessions are tiny, and they are swamped by secular trends explained by sociology and demographics. The decline in the labor force participation rate that occurred after the 2008 recession is part of a long-term trend and, in my view, there is not much that fiscal or monetary policy can do, or should do, to counteract it.

Conclusion

For the past thirty-five years, classical and New Keynesian economists have adopted the assumption of continuous market clearing. In the models constructed by both groups, a recession is a period when households decide to take a vacation because the current value of their time is low relative to more prosperous times. In the period from 1980 up through 2007, with very few exceptions, economists at central banks and universities all adopted the assumption of continuous market clearing. Even today, eight years after the end of the Great Recession, many of them still do.

The assumption of continuous market clearing is not, in my view, a plausible explanation of the data described in Figures 4.1 and 4.2. There are three reasons why employment fluctuates over time. People vary the average number of hours worked per week. Households send more or less members to look for a job. And those people looking for jobs find it more or less difficult to find one. The first two reasons for fluctuating employment could perhaps be modeled as the smooth functioning of a market in which the demand and supply of labor respond to changes in market prices. I cannot see any simple way to model unemployment fluctuations as the operation of a competitive market for labor in the usual sense in which economists use that term.

When a person has made the decision to seek a job, the time it takes to find a job depends on the current state of the labor market. If the aggregate demand for commodities is high, a given investment in labor search will succeed in landing a suitable job more swiftly than if demand is low. And if demand depends on animal spirits, the equilibrium unemployment rate will vary with beliefs. In Chapter 6, I make this concept precise by combining a model of labor search and animal spirits with classical economics in a way that preserves the best of both Keynesian and classical ideas.

I have shown, in this chapter, that hours worked, labor force participation, and unemployment display very different characteristics. Although participation and average weekly hours can, plausibly, be described as voluntary decisions, unemployment cannot. It seems clear to me that labor markets do not clear. Can we please stop pretending that they do?

5

FIVE PROBLEMS WITH NEW KEYNESIAN ECONOMICS

Macroeconomics has taken the wrong path. The error has nothing to do with classical versus New Keynesian approaches. It is a more fundamental error that pervades both classical and New Keynesian schools of thought. Macroeconomics took a wrong turn in Cambridge, Massachusetts in 1955 when Paul Samuelson, in the third edition of his textbook, introduced the idea of the "neoclassical synthesis."[1] Everything since then has been the economic equivalent of the scientific theory of phlogiston.

Many economists are exposed to the philosophy of science through Milton Friedman's book *Essays in Positive Economics*.[2] Friedman promoted the views of Karl Popper who argued in *Conjectures and Refutations* that science progresses when theorists make bold conjectures that are confronted by facts.[3] Those conjectures stand until they are refuted by the evidence. Occasionally, economics students are exposed to the ideas of Thomas Kuhn, who talks of paradigm shifts and scientific revolutions.[4] Rarely does the economics curriculum of a PhD program have time to push much further into the methodology of science. That's a pity, because graduate students of economics could benefit a great deal from understanding alternative philosophies.

My colleague Axel Leijonhufvud has argued persuasively that we have much to learn from Imre Lakatos, a philosopher of science who spent much of his career at the London School of Economics.[5] Lakatos, in contrast to Popper and Kuhn, sees science as a set of competing scientific research programs.[6] His approach is a useful one for understanding the current debate among practicing macroeconomists who are facing a series of natural experiments that provide serious challenges to both classical and New Keynesian agendas.

According to Lakatos, all tests of scientific theories are necessarily tests of joint hypotheses. The sciences, both physical and social, are best characterized as interacting communities of scholars. Those scholars adhere to research programs that interpret the evidence through different lenses.

Each research program has a "hard core" and a "protective belt." When an event in nature appears to refute a theory, the scientist must decide which of the possible components of his theory should be rejected to reconcile his worldview with the outcome he observed. Assumptions that make up the hard core of a research program will never be rejected; instead, the scientist will amend one of the assumptions in its protective belt.

The New Keynesian research program is the descendent of Samuelson's neoclassical synthesis. According to that synthesis, the economy is "Keynesian" in the short run, when not all markets have had time to clear; it is "classical" in the long run, when all price adjustment has run its course. These twin propositions form the hard core of the New Keynesian program. According to that program, market economies are self-correcting, and although the adjustment to the long-run equilibrium may take time, that adjustment will, eventually, occur.

Despite its name, the New Keynesian research program is neither new nor Keynesian. The idea that real economic activity may be different from its long-run steady state as a consequence of sticky prices is rooted firmly in the classical monetarist tradition. It originated during the eighteenth century and is summarized by David Hume in his delightful essay "Of Money."[7] Keynes argued, in contrast, in the opening chapters of *The General Theory*, that high unemployment of the kind that persisted during the Great Depression is one of many possible *steady-state equilibria*.[8]

Some might argue that the classical view in which all employment fluctuations are voluntary is clearly false and the New Keynesian approach needs no further defense. I disagree. It is specious to argue that New Keynesian economics is right because classical economics is wrong. Both classical and New Keynesian economics have serious flaws.

In Chapter 4, I explained that classical economics is mistaken in its assumption of continuous market clearing. In this chapter I expand on that point and I provide four additional reasons to reject New Keynesian economics. By "New Keynesian economics," I mean an approach that marries classical economics with Keynes' *General Theory* by adding sticky wages and prices to a model that is built on an RBC core.

Problem 1: Prices Are Implausibly Sticky

In classical economic models, prices move immediately in response to shocks to aggregate demand or aggregate supply. In economic data, they do not. To square economic theory with economic data, New Keynesian economists say that wages and prices are "sticky" and that "frictions" prevent them from moving quickly to clear markets. Let me explain by drawing an analogy with classical mechanics.

If you place a block of wood on an inclined plane, Newton's law of gravity predicts the block should slide down the plane toward the floor. In practice, if the angle of tilt is small, the block will appear to be "sticky" because it is held in place by friction. The greater the friction, the more you need to tilt the plane before the block moves.

The New Keynesians use this analogy to describe markets. Just as Newton's theory of gravity says the block should slide toward the floor when you tilt the plane, so classical economics says wages and prices should increase when you increase the quantity of money. Just as a physical friction prevents the block from moving, so an economic friction prevents prices from moving.

To understand why prices are sticky, New Keynesian economists have developed a theory that explains how firms set prices, and they have added to that theory an economic concept of friction. Before we can understand what New Keynesians mean by friction, it helps to review the classical theory of how prices are set.

In classical economics, prices are chosen to equate the quantity demanded with the quantity supplied of every good in the economy. Importantly, in classical economics, nobody actually sets prices. They are chosen by a deus ex machina with the impressive name of the Walrasian auctioneer. The auctioneer is named after Léon Walras, one of the early contributors to the theory of general equilibrium.

The auctioneer holds an auction in which any good can be exchanged for any other good. This auction takes place every week and, at the auction, the auctioneer stands on a pedestal and announces a list of prices at which each commodity can be bought or sold. For example, the auctioneer might announce that a pound of butter costs $3, a pint of milk costs $1.20, and a loaf of bread is $2.50. Everybody at auction gives the auctioneer a list of how much of each commodity they would like to buy or sell at the announced prices.

The auctioneer adds up the demands and supplies for each good and, if the demands and supply is equal for every good, he stops and exchange takes place. If the demands and supplies are not equal for every commodity, the auctioneer tries again. He raises some prices and lowers others and calls out a new list of prices. Importantly, trade takes place only when the demands and supplies of every good are equal.

New Keynesian economists replace the assumption that firms take prices from an auctioneer by assuming, instead, that firms know how the demand for their goods will change if they raise or lower its price. And they add a friction to their model that prevents the firm from changing the price of its good every week. There are two main variants of this friction.

The first variant, by Julio Rotemberg, assumes that a firm must pay a cost to change its price.[9] Think of this as a cost of reprinting the menu in a restaurant. In Rotemberg's work, the cost of changing the price is proportional to the square of the size of the price change. That assumption is made largely because it leads to a simple formula for the Phillips Curve.

The second variant, by Guillermo Calvo, assumes that a fixed fraction of firms is allowed to change its price in any given week.[10] Every other firm must charge the same price it charged the week before. In the Calvo model, an outside agent, "the Calvo Fairy," chooses at random the fraction that is allowed to change its price.[11] How can we judge if either of these approaches makes sense?

Historically, macroeconomists have constructed highly aggregated models in which they try to explain the behavior of a price index—for example, the consumer price index (CPI), which is an aggregate statistic published monthly by the US Department of Commerce. Classical economic theory predicts that an unanticipated 10% increase in the money supply should be followed by an immediate 10% increase in the CPI. Although there is evidence the CPI will eventually increase by 10%, it takes years, rather than weeks, for the full price adjustment to take place. Economists cite this evidence in support of their assumption that frictions prevent prices from changing quickly.[12]

In recent years, economists have had access to very large micro data sets derived from scanners at supermarket checkouts. These data are incredibly detailed and are broken down to the level of an individual item at a specific location on a specific date. For example: How much did a shopper pay for a twelve-ounce can of Campbell's Tomato Soup in Ralph's Supermarket on the corner of Olympic Boulevard and Barrington Avenue in Santa Monica on August 8, 2015? Economists have studied these data to determine whether the Rotemberg model or the

Calvo model can explain the behavior of the CPI. The answer is not encouraging for New Keynesians.

By measuring the frequency of price changes in the data, researchers have estimated the magnitude of the frictions that would be required to explain the scanner data using either the Rotemberg model or the Calvo model. That approach provides the researcher with an independent estimate of the cost of changing prices and it allows her to fix a key parameter of the New Keynesian theory. Fixing the size of the friction, using micro data, is called *calibrating the model*.

When a model has been calibrated in this way, the researcher can ask if a calibrated New Keynesian model can explain the slow response of the CPI to a change in the money supply we observe in aggregate data. The answer is no. In micro data, prices change frequently, and although many of these changes are temporary, the magnitude of price stickiness implied by the scanner data is much too small to account for the sluggish movement of aggregate prices we observe in response to a monetary shock.[13]

Problem 2: Inflation Is Persistent

Perhaps we should not be concerned about the microeconomic evidence. Maybe we should be looking instead at the behavior of the aggregate price level because there is something in the way that firms coordinate with each other that makes average prices stickier than individual prices. But there is a second problem. It is not just the CPI that is slow to respond to unanticipated changes in the money supply; the rate of change of prices as measured by the inflation rate is also sticky.

To understand the connection between changes in the money supply and changes in the inflation rate, economists construct models of the macroeconomy. The ability of simple New Keynesian models to explain the data can be assessed with a statistical procedure called *regression analysis*. Regression analysis allows us to find out how the current values of a set of macroeconomic variables have changed in past data in response to changes in their own past values. Empirical models constructed in this way are called *vector-autoregressions*.

Economists have derived vector-autoregressions from a classical theory in which all markets clear in every period, and they have shown that the classical theory, with flexible prices, cannot explain the evidence.[14] If we are willing to ignore the micro evidence from supermarket scanner data, a suitably parameterized aggregate New Keynesian model *can* explain why wages and prices are sticky, but it cannot account for a second feature that is uncovered by vector-autoregressions. In the data, it is not just wages and prices that are sticky; the rates of change of wages and prices—that is, wage inflation and price inflation—are also sticky. The stickiness of wage inflation and price inflation is a problem for New Keynesian theory because, according to that theory, the history of inflation is irrelevant from the point of view of a price-setting firm.[15]

To understand why inflation is sticky, Jeffrey Fuhrer and George Moore have modified the theoretical structure of the Phillips Curve.[16] In standard representations of New Keynesian theory, prices are set to reflect expected future inflation. Fuhrer and Moore develop a theory in which workers and firms sign long-term contracts, and workers care about their relative wage. Although the Fuhrer–Moore modification produces a model in which inflation is persistent, it is not clear why the contracts they consider would be signed by rational agents, a point first made by Robert Barro in his critique of the work on labor contracts by Stanley Fischer twenty years earlier.[17]

Problem 3: There Is No Unemployment

The New Keynesian model is adapted from the new classical approach to macroeconomics that was first promoted by Robert Lucas and Leonard Rapping.[18] In this approach, the labor market is treated as an auction in which the money wage adjusts in every period to equate the quantity of labor demanded with the quantity of labor supplied. The New Keynesians adapted this model to allow for monopolistic competition in the goods market, but they did not reject the market-clearing assumption. There is no such thing as unemployment in almost every New Keynesian model that was developed before the 2008 financial crisis.

It is possible to combine New Keynesian models with alternative theories of the labor market, and that agenda is now underway. Mark Gertler and Antonella Trigari have added unemployment to the New Keynesian model, and Gertler, Luca Sala, and Trigari have conducted empirical work to test this augmented New Keynesian theory.[19] They found that the New Keynesian model, augmented with a search theory of unemployment, explains the data about as well as a similar New Keynesian model in which the labor market is an auction.

Although Gertler and Trigari introduce unemployment, their version of search theory maintains the assumption that there is a unique labor market equilibrium. As a consequence, the Gertler–Trigari model, like all other New Keynesian models, preserves the NRH. And, as I demonstrated in Chapter 3, the NRH is false.

In Chapter 6, I describe a theory that is also based on a search theory of unemployment. But, unlike Gertler–Trigari, I drop the assumption that firms and workers bargain over the wage and I replace it with the assumption that beliefs are fundamental.[20] As I explain in Chapter 9, this leads to a model in which there is no natural rate of unemployment and, instead, output and employment are determined by the self-fulfilling beliefs of market participants. My work *can* explain the persistence of unemployment without making arbitrary and unrealistic assumptions about the costs of changing money wages and prices.

Problem 4: Welfare Costs of Business Cycles Are Small

How should we measure the welfare cost of economic booms and recessions? Robert Lucas provided an answer to that question.[21] He suggested that we ask how much consumption a representative person would be willing to forgo to live in a world where business cycles do not occur. The answer to that question in a classical economic model is, at most, one tenth of 1% of steady-state consumption.

The New Keynesian model has the potential to give a different answer. Because the model contains frictions, the employment rate may be greater or lower than the rate that would be chosen by a social planner who did not take account of those frictions. The actual employment rate could be different from the optimal employment rate for many months, and that could, potentially, be very harmful to the representative person.

Three New Keynesian economists—Jordi Galí, Mark Gertler, and David López-Salido—have investigated that issue. They used the same metric for measuring the costs of recessions suggested by Lucas. How much steady-state consumption would the representative person be willing to forgo to live in a world where recessions never happen? The answer was disappointing for the New Keynesian agenda. They showed that the welfare losses that occur in recessions are comparable in magnitude with the welfare losses found by Lucas in his study of classical equilibrium business cycle models.[22] The representative person would be willing to give up just one tenth of 1% of steady-state consumption to avoid booms and recessions.

The reason for this disappointing result can be traced back to Paul Samuelson. The New Keynesians built their theory on the foundation of the neoclassical synthesis. In their model, shocks to the economy cause temporary deviations from a Pareto Optimal steady state. To use the analogy from Chapter 2, the New Keynesian model is a rocking-horse model and the unemployment rate is always close to the natural rate of unemployment.

To explain why unemployment is so painful for so many, we must dispense with the NRH, as I have done in my own work. We need a windy boat model in which the unemployment rate can move far away from its natural rate for many years at a time.

The fact that a model based on the equilibrium assumption cannot generate large welfare losses would not have surprised prominent Keynesian economist James Tobin. Around the time that Edmund Phelps and Milton Friedman formulated the NRH, Tobin quipped: "It takes a lot of Harberger triangles to fill an Okun gap."[23] In other words, the distortions caused by sticky prices are small relative to large movements in the unemployment rate during major recessions. The New Keynesian model cannot explain why we should care about recessions because business cycles, in the New Keynesian model, have trivial effects on peoples' lives.

Problem 5: The Model Cannot Explain Bubbles and Crashes

In *The General Theory*, Keynes stressed the importance of animal spirits as an independent driving force in the economy. In his view, the stock market crash of 1929 *caused* the Great Depression. In my own work, I argue that the stock market crash of 2008 *caused* the Great Recession.[24] New Keynesian economics does not have room for this idea.

The fact that Keynes asserted that nonfundamental market movements caused the Great Depression is not evidence for or against that proposition. The fact that I assert nonfundamental market movements caused the Great Recession is not evidence for or against that proposition. And the fact that many economists assert the 2008 crash was caused by the collapse of a bubble does not make it so. To compare the bubble hypothesis with alternative explanations, we need a theory of bubbles consistent with microeconomic principles in which the bubble theory can be articulated and compared consistently with the alternatives. In my published work, I provide such a theory.[25]

Suppose we accept, for the sake of argument, that speculative bubbles can be observed and that they lead to the misallocation of resources. We might summarize this view by saying markets are irrational. The statement "markets are irrational" could then be interpreted in one of two ways. We might infer, as do George Akerlof and Robert Shiller, that people are themselves irrational.[26] That approach was modeled formally by J. Bradford DeLong and three coauthors in a celebrated paper on "noise traders."[27] Or we might infer, instead, that the aggregate actions of individually rational human beings can sometimes lead to an outcome that is socially irrational.

Shiller provides a summary of his view in the *New York Times*, in which he draws on an argument from neuroscience to stake out the position that human beings are not always rational in the narrow sense in which economists sometimes define rationality.[28] He argues that the economist's conception of human beings as rational is hard to square with the behavior of asset markets.

Although I agree with Shiller that human action is captured inadequately by the assumptions that most economists make about behavior, I am not convinced that we need to go much beyond the narrow rationality assumption to understand what causes financial crises or why they are so devastatingly painful for large numbers of people. The assumption that people maximize utility can get us a very long way.

I am willing to make the assumption that people are rational because, as I argue in Chapter 7, the financial markets would go very badly wrong most of the time even if agents were fully rational. This is the position that Amartya Sen, in his lovely article on rational fools, ascribes to Francis Edgeworth in his book *Mathematical Psychics*.[29]

Edgeworth introduced what he called his first principle of economics, which is that "every agent is actuated only by self interest." As Sen points out, Edgeworth was not naive enough to think that people behave exactly in the way he portrays them. In Sen's words,

> Edgeworth himself was quite aware that [his] first principle of Economics was not a particularly realistic one. Indeed, he felt that "the concrete nineteenth century man is for the most part an impure egoist, a mixed utilitarian."

This raises the interesting question as to why Edgeworth spent so much of his time and talent in developing a line of inquiry the first principle of which he believed to be false.[30]

Sen goes on to provide an answer to his own question, arguing

Edgeworth did not think the assumption to be fundamentally mistaken in the particular types of activities to which he applied what he called "economical calculus": (i) war and (ii) contract.[31]

Like Edgeworth, I believe the rationality assumption is useful to describe much of economic behavior. Unlike Shiller, I do not think we need to move beyond that assumption to explain asset market fluctuations.

In my work, beliefs are driven by an independent fundamental shock, and asset values can take on many different values, including explosive bubbles. In this environment, the collapse of an asset bubble is fully consistent with rational behavior on the part of forward-looking agents, and that collapse can have devastating effects on unemployment and on economic welfare.

In Chapter 6, I show the labor market can go very badly wrong even when everybody is rational; in Chapter 7, I show the financial markets may be characterized by socially inefficient waves of optimism and pessimism. In my model, it is individually rational for people to be optimistic or pessimistic, because those beliefs are self-fulfilling. But even when individuals are fully rational, the labor market and the financial markets may lead to very bad social outcomes.

New Keynesian Economics Is a Degenerative Research Program

Defenders of New Keynesian economics will object that I am setting up a straw man and they will claim the five problems

I have discussed are well known and have been addressed in the literature. Although there is a sense in which that is correct, the defenses necessary to support New Keynesian economics against my five objections are a sign of what Imre Lakatos referred to as a *degenerative research program*.[32]

In 1543, Nicolaus Copernicus introduced the sun-centered theory of the solar system. Ptolemy's theory, which preceded Copernicus, placed Earth at the center of the universe, and that theory was initially better at explaining the motion of the planets than that of Copernicus. But, Ptolemy's theory was successful only through repeatedly more improbable modifications to the concentric circles that described the orbits of the planets.[33]

The modifications that allow New Keynesian economics to explain the data are similar to the addition of concentric circles used to allow Ptolemy's theory to explain new facts. When new evidence contradicts a pillar of the New Keynesian theory, a piece is tacked on to account for the anomaly. A subset of irrational agents accounts for bubbles as in DeLong et al.[34] A concern for relative wages accounts for inflation persistence as in Fuhrer and Moore.[35] Wage bargaining accounts for persistent unemployment as in Gertler and Trigari.[36] These modifications have been relatively successful at explaining data from the 1980s and 1990s. The 2008 financial crisis presents a major new challenge.

Research programs are not refuted, as in Popper, nor are they dramatically overturned, as in Kuhn. They simply attract more new adherents than their competitors. In the language of Lakatos, research programs are progressive or degenerative.

In the normal course of events, a successful research program meets challenges to its hegemony by modifying hypotheses in its protective belt. A progressive research program is one that, occasionally, makes a prediction confirmed by experiment or, in the case of macroeconomics, by history. A degenerative research program is one that struggles with continued refutations by modifying its protective belt continually in ever-more-inelegant ways.

The New Keynesian research program, like the classical program before it, is degenerate. Like Ptolemaic astronomy, it explains new data by adding ever-increasing layers of complexity. And like that theory, New Keynesian economics has not succeeded in making a single prediction that has been confirmed by fresh evidence that was unavailable when the theory was constructed.

Replacing New Keynesian Economics: The Way Ahead

There are those who claim we should return to Keynes' *The General Theory* while rejecting the attempt to build microfoundations. That is the message, for example, of post-Keynesians like Paul Davidson.[37] Although there are attractive elements to that path, I do not believe we should abandon *all* of classical economics. There is much to like in the ideas of demand and supply, and several branches of economics have had notable successes by following the idea that actors are rational and goal oriented. Examples that come to mind are auction theory, which has been used extensively and successfully to sell the rights to the electromagnetic spectrum; and matching theory, which has been used to develop kidney exchanges.[38]

Keynes' central ideas were that there are multiple equilibrium steady-state unemployment rates and the unemployment rate we observe is selected by beliefs. How can we recover these ideas without discarding 300 years of microeconomic principles? My research agenda maintains the notion of unemployment as a steady-state equilibrium and it combines this idea with general equilibrium theory in a new way. The path of combining multiple equilibria with "animal spirits" can explain many of the puzzles thrown out by the Great Recession.

Unlike New Keynesian economists, I do not assume that "frictions" prevent wages or prices from clearing markets. I do not deny wages and prices move slowly relative to quantities. But, that observation does not mean we must assume there are menu costs, contracting costs, or any other artificial barrier to price adjustment. Sticky prices are simply part of a rational expectations equilibrium. Robert Lucas was exactly right when he argued markets are always in equilibrium. But, accepting that proposition does not require us to accept equilibrium is unique, nor must we accept equilibrium is optimal or unemployment is voluntary.

My research program is both neoclassical and Keynesian. As with classical and New Keynesian economics, I construct models of rational actors who interact in markets. In contrast to classical and New Keynesian programs, my approach is built around two propositions absent from the hard core of both of these programs: (1) there is a continuum of possible equilibrium unemployment rates and (2) the unemployment rate that prevails is determined by the "animal spirits" of investors.

For a New Keynesian economist, it is hard to explain why wages and prices have been so sticky that employment still has not fully recovered more than eight years after the onset of the stock market crash. In the theory I construct, that is an expected outcome. High involuntary unemployment is an equilibrium state.

If Keynes were alive today, one thing is certain; he would not be a Keynesian in the sense in which that term is used today. Keynes was notorious for changing his views on a daily basis and was said to be capable of holding several conflicting opinions at the same time. Would he agree with everything I have said in this chapter? Who knows? What is certain is that existing ideas have failed us. For me, that's enough to try something new.

6

WHY UNEMPLOYMENT PERSISTS

THE KEYNESIAN SEARCH MODEL EXPLAINED

The phrase "what goes up must come down" is a pretty good predictor of one of the more important consequences of the law of gravity. It is not a very helpful guide to policymakers interested in preventing the recurrence of major recessions. Although the unemployment rate does go up and down over the business cycle, it never returns to the same place. Policymakers work with a theory that says the economy always reverts to the natural rate of unemployment. But, after every recession, they revise their estimate of what that means.

The reason policymakers must revise their target continually is not because the natural rate of unemployment is moving; it is because there is no tendency for a market economy to return to its natural rate. Unemployment does revert to something, but that something is not the unemployment rate that would be chosen by a benevolent, omniscient social planner. It is an arbitrary rate that depends on the animal spirits of market participants. This chapter explains that idea.

Classical and New Keynesian Explanations for Unemployment

Classical economists argue that in a free market economy the unemployment rate would always be Pareto Optimal. The best thing that a policymaker can do is to design labor market institutions that are minimally invasive and then let the miracle of the free market do the rest. Unemployment rates in Greece and Spain have historically been much higher than the unemployment rate in the United States.[1] Classical economists explain that fact by arguing these countries have poorly designed laws that impede labor mobility.

New Keynesians agree that Greece and Spain have poorly designed laws. For example, regulations in Spain for many years made it very hard for a firm to fire a worker. As a consequence, firms were reluctant to hire workers in the first place, and unemployment was higher on average than it would otherwise have been. To cure that problem, New Keynesians and classical economists agree it is important to design labor market regulations correctly. This is called *supply-side policy.*

Although New Keynesians agree with classical economists that poorly designed supply-side policies may lead to high, inefficient unemployment, they disagree about the reasons why unemployment goes up and down over the business cycle. New Keynesians believe the observed unemployment rate is almost never equal to the natural rate of unemployment because wage and price stickiness prevents the unemployment rate from adjusting to equal its social optimum. They advocate the use of countercyclical monetary and fiscal policies to counteract inefficient swings in the unemployment rate throughout the business cycle. *This is called demand-side policy.*

In my view, classical and New Keynesian economists are right to think poorly designed supply-side policies will lead to excessive unemployment. Greece and Spain have higher unemployment than the United States most of the time because the US labor market is more flexible than the Greek or Spanish labor markets. But, classical and New Keynesian explanations for movements in the unemployment rate throughout the business cycle are both wrong.

New Keynesian economists are right to argue that free markets do not deliver a socially optimal unemployment rate, but they are wrong to point to price and wage stickiness as the source of the problem. The classical economists are right to argue the unemployment rate is always in equilibrium, but they are wrong in their assumption that the quantity of labor demanded is always equal to the quantity of labor supplied. Classical and New Keynesian economists are using the wrong model.

Unemployment, Labor Market Flows, and Search Theory

With the rise of the RBC paradigm during the 1980s, the concept of unemployment disappeared from much of modern mainstream macroeconomics. However, it did not disappear from economics entirely. During the 1970s, microeconomic theorists began to study the properties of markets in which the process of finding a trading partner is costly. This branch of microeconomics is called *search theory*. Search theory recognizes the labor market is a dynamic process. In any given week, some people lose jobs and others find jobs.

Everyone in the United States falls into one of two categories. They are either in or out of the labor force. At the current time, roughly 60% of the US population are either employed or looking for a job. These people are *in the labor force*. The remaining 40% are students, retirees, caregivers, or the independently wealthy. These people are *out of the labor force*.

Those people in the labor force can be either employed or unemployed. In November 2015, 5% of the US labor force was unemployed and the remaining 95% was employed; but these were not the same people from one week to the next.

Every week some unemployed people find jobs and become employed. These people are called *inflows to employment*. Some employed people lose jobs and become unemployed. These people are called *outflows from employment*.

If the inflows are greater than the outflows, the unemployment rate falls over time. If the outflows are greater than the inflows, the unemployment rate increases over time. When the inflows are equal to the outflows, the unemployment rate is constant. During the 1970s, economists developed a new approach—search theory—designed to understand these facts.[2]

The Classical Search Model

Search theory was developed by Peter Diamond, Dale Mortensen, and Christopher Pissarides (DMP). In 2010, they were awarded the Nobel Prize in economics for "their analysis of markets with search frictions."[3] I call the approach of Diamond, Mortensen, and Pissarides the *classical* search model to distinguish it from an alternative model that I developed in my own work. I call my approach the *Keynesian search model.*

In the classical search model, when a firm meets a worker, it bargains over the wage. The bargaining weight expresses the relative power of the worker in her negotiations with the firm. If, for example, the bargaining weight is equal to zero, the worker is paid just enough to induce her to accept the offer. That amount is called the *worker's reservation wage.* If the bargaining weight is equal to one, the worker is paid just enough to make the firm indifferent between hiring her and walking away from the deal. That amount is called the *worker's marginal product.* And if the worker's bargaining weight is equal to one half, the firm and the worker split the difference.

The classical search model is consistent mathematically and has provided several generations of PhD students with elegant problems to solve. But it is not a good description of the data. When the bargaining weight of the worker is chosen appropriately, the classical search model produces the same unemployment rate that would be chosen by a social planner.[4] And in reasonable calibrations of the model, the unemployment rate converges back to this rate quickly. As I showed in Figure 3.3, this is not what happens in the real world.

The Keynesian Search Model

In the Keynesian search model, I drop the bargaining assumption. I assume instead that the firm employs as many people as it needs to meet the demand for its product. And to determine the demand for products, I assume households form self-fulfilling beliefs about the value of their wealth.[5]

Consider a firm in the restaurant business that has a job opening for a waiter. Initially, the restaurant owner might look on the Internet to see what other restaurants are paying for waiters; this might be $15 an hour. If the owner were to offer less than $15 an hour, no worker would apply for a job at that restaurant. If he were to offer more than $15 an hour, the restaurant would go out of business. That latter fact follows because I am able to show that, in Keynesian search equilibrium, every restaurant will be operating with a zero profit margin.

In this example, the restaurant owner decides how many waiters to hire based on the number of customers that frequent the restaurant. If the restaurant is located in a busy downtown location, it may be full every night. If it is located in a sleepy college town, it may be half empty much of the time and only full on weekends. The restaurant in the downtown location will hire more waiters than the restaurant located in the college town.

Classical search theory assumes firms bargain with workers over the wage. Keynesian search theory assumes firms hire as many workers as they need at market wages. Why should you prefer Keynesian search theory over classical search theory?

Superficially, the classical assumption that firms bargain with workers may seem like a better way to close a model. After all, many of us have experienced situations in which we are able to bargain with an employer over our wage. Although that is sometimes true, a worker's bargaining strength is not independent of the demand for the firm's product, as the classical search theorists assume.

In the middle of a depression, a worker who demands a raise may soon find she is not bargaining from a position of strength. When aggregate demand is high, workers will demand a large share of revenues. When aggregate demand is low, workers may demand a large share of revenues but their demands are unlikely to be met. The bargaining weight of a worker is determined by the demand for the product of the firm that employs her, not the other way around.

The Beveridge Curve

Search theorists describe a labor market in which job search is costly and search costs may be borne either by the worker or by the firm. In a labor market in which unemployment is low, a larger share of the search costs is borne by firms. In a market in which unemployment is high, a larger share of the search costs is borne by workers. But what is the empirical evidence that supports these claims?

In 1958, Christopher Dow and Leslie Dicks-Mireaux published an article in which they showed there is a downward-sloping relationship between vacancies and unemployment in UK data.[6] This relationship is now known as the *Beveridge curve*, after UK politician William Beveridge, who was the architect of the post-WWII welfare state in the United Kingdom. In Figure 6.1, I have graphed the Beveridge curve using US data from 2000 through 2013 from the Bureau of Labor Statistics. Using the Keynesian search model, I am able to interpret these data as evidence of what microeconomists call an *isoquant*.

An isoquant is a curve that traces all combinations of inputs that produce the same output. Traditionally, we use isoquants to explain the production of a physical commodity, such as corn. The same idea can be used to explain the production of filled jobs.

What is the process by which people find jobs? In search theory, finding a job is an activity that uses resources. Just as combining labor and capital produces corn, so does combining

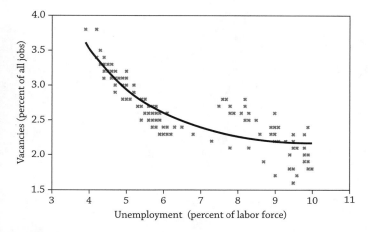

Figure 6.1 The Beveridge Curve in US Data: Job Openings and the Unemployment Rate December 2000 to April 2013.

Source: Bureau of Labor Statistics.

the search time of an unemployed worker with the search time of a recruiting worker produce a filled job. The production function that describes this process is called the *search technology*.

There Are Many Different Ways to Match People with Jobs

A field of corn may be harvested by 100 people with scythes or by one person with a combine harvester. These two possibilities represent different points on the isoquant for the production of one field of harvested corn. Similarly, 40,000 jobs per week can be filled by 800,000 people searching for 200,000 vacancies or by 200,000 people searching for 800,000 vacancies. These two possibilities represent different points on the isoquant for the production of 40,000 filled jobs. These two possibilities are represented in Figure 6.2, which interprets the Beveridge curve as an isoquant.[7]

If the labor force were equal to 10 million people, the first case would result in an unemployment rate of 8% and the

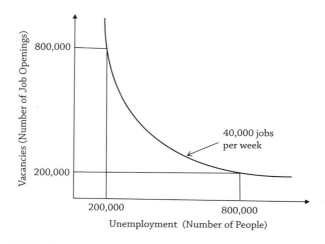

Figure 6.2 The Beveridge Curve as an Isoquant.
Source: Bureau of Labor Statistics and author's calculation.

second in an unemployment rate of 2%. These are not the only two possibilities. There are many different ways of filling a given number of jobs, and each of them is associated with a different unemployment rate and a different point on the Beveridge curve.

The Natural Rate of Unemployment

Reducing the unemployment rate has both costs and benefits. And although there are many ways of filling a given number of jobs, the optimal unemployment rate is not equal to zero. Economists characterize the efficiency of markets by comparing the market outcome with the problem that would be solved by a fictitious social planner who knows the technologies available to produce goods and the preferences of all the people in the economy. The social planner is asked to maximize the welfare of a representative household by choosing the socially optimal unemployment rate. In this book, I refer to this socially optimal unemployment rate as the *natural rate of unemployment*.[8]

In the Appendix at the end of this chapter, I have written a social planning problem in which there is both a search technology and a production technology. I call the output produced *corn* and I ask the question: Which unemployment rate will maximize the steady-state production of corn? The answer is illustrated in Figure 6.3.

This figure plots weekly corn production on the vertical axis against the weekly employment rate on the horizontal axis.[9] For values of the employment rate between 0% and 90%, higher employment leads to greater corn production; but, there comes a point when higher employment leads to lower corn production. For the parameter values I used to construct this graph, it is when 90% of the labor force has a job.

Initially, as we give more people jobs, we produce more corn, but it is not socially optimal for everyone to be employed all the time. People leave jobs to move across the country, to spend

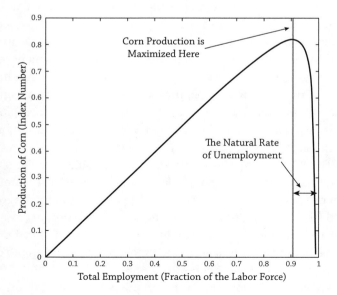

Figure 6.3 The Natural Rate of Unemployment.

Source: Bureau of Labor Statistics and author's calculation.

time rearing children, or to try something new. Firms go out of business and their workers are fired. Because people are constantly separating from employment, there will always be some unemployment. But how much unemployment is optimal?

The social planner could choose to make the unemployment rate arbitrarily small by finding jobs for newly unemployed workers very rapidly. But, to screen unemployed workers and allocate them to a job that fits their needs and makes best use of their skills, the social planner must devote resources to the screening process. Every worker allocated to recruiting is one less worker producing corn. The social planner will keep moving workers from production to recruiting up to the point when the production of corn is maximized. The unemployment rate when that occurs is called the *natural rate of unemployment.*

Why the Market Cannot Find the Natural Rate of Unemployment

The first welfare theorem of economics tells us the social optimum can be achieved anonymously by allocating goods through competitive markets, but is the first welfare theorem true in the real world? Given the very high unemployment rate that prevailed during the Great Depression, and more recently during the Great Recession, that seems unlikely. If I am right, and the market does not find the natural rate of unemployment, we must answer the question: Which of the assumptions of classical economics is wrong?

The New Keynesians provide the following answer. The unemployment rate is not always equal to the natural rate of unemployment because wages and prices are sticky. I agree with the New Keynesians that the unemployment rate is not always equal to the natural rate of unemployment, but I disagree with their diagnosis of the problem. It has nothing to do with wage and price stickiness.

I have a different answer. For markets to work well, prices must send the right signals to firms and workers. And there must be enough prices to guide them into allocating resources correctly to different activities. In the case of the production of corn, the wage and the rental rate of capital adjust to send signals to owners of labor and capital. In the case of the production of jobs, there are no prices to send signals to unemployed workers and corporate recruiters. Because some price signals are missing, the economy can get stuck in an inefficient equilibrium with high involuntary unemployment. [10]

Unemployment, the Belief Function, and Keynesian Search Theory

In a search model, the assumption that the quantity of labor demanded is equal to the quantity of labor supplied does not determine the unemployment rate uniquely. The classical search model introduces an equation, the wage-bargaining equation, to complete the model and determine the wage and the unemployment rate. The Keynesian search model introduces a different equation: *the belief function.*

In the Keynesian search model, as in Keynes *General Theory,* employment is determined by aggregate demand for goods and services, and the belief function is an important component of this model. In a series of books and journal articles, I explained the Keynesian search model in more depth.[11] Drawing on the empirical research of Milton Friedman, Albert Ando, and Franco Modigliani, I developed a new theory in which aggregate demand depends on wealth. And because a person's assets are worth what other people will pay for them, wealth depends on beliefs.[12]

The wealth of a community consists of its stock of houses, factories, and machines, and the skills of its people. A house, a factory, or a machine has value because it generates a stream of profits or rents in future periods. The skills of a nation's people have value because they generate a stream of wage payments in future periods. Houses, factories, machines, and skills are all examples of assets, and the value of an asset depends on incomes and interest rates that people believe will occur in the future.

Consider, for example, a simple model in which all wealth is capitalized in the stock market. In that model, market participants must decide how much they are willing to pay for shares in the companies that are traded on the stock market. I assume they make that decision by using a belief function. The belief function is a rule that predicts future stock market prices based on observations of current and past stock market prices, and on the confidence of households and firms. It is a new fundamental that determines wealth, and should be accorded the same methodological status as technology shocks and preference shocks in conventional DSGE models. When people feel wealthier, they *are* wealthier. Confidence is a self-fulfilling prophecy.

The Keynesian search model, closed with the belief function, has a unique equilibrium unemployment rate. The belief function depends on present and past observables, and on a shock I call "confidence," that encompasses what Keynes called "animal spirits." Keynesian search theory, closed with the belief function, provides a complete explanation of employment, prices, and GDP.[13]

Beliefs and Rational Expectations

Along with the rest of modern macroeconomics, the rational expectations assumption has gotten quite a bit of flak lately. I don't think all of it is deserved. It is not the rational expectations assumption that is at fault—it is the rational expectations assumption in conjunction with the assumption of a unique equilibrium.

In the New Keynesian model, there is a single rational expectations equilibrium. In the Keynesian search model, there are many rational expectations equilibria. Not just one or two or three, but an infinite dimensional continuum of them. That is not a problem. It is an opportunity I exploit to model the idea that beliefs matter.

The belief function is an effective way of operationalizing the Keynesian assumption of animal spirits. It is a forecasting rule that explains how people use current information to predict the future. That rule replaces the classical assumption that the quantity of labor demanded is always equal to the quantity of labor supplied.

You might think that adding a belief function to operationalize animal spirits allows me to dispense with the rational expectations assumption because the belief function could be arbitrary. Not so. Although we do not live in a stationary environment, *our beliefs should be consistent with the outcomes we would observe in a stationary world*. In such a world, beliefs should obey Abraham Lincoln's dictum that "you can fool all of the people some of the time or some of the people all of the time, but you can't fool all of the people all of the time." In my view, *that is* the rational expectations assumption.[14]

Suppose you are building a rational expectations model with a unique equilibrium. In that model, you would not need to model a "belief function" independently. The people in your model would need to forecast the future somehow, and presumably they would use some kind of forecasting rule. But, you would not need to know the parameters of that rule. Whatever rule they use, it would have to be correct "on average."

Stick with the unique rational expectations assumption and suppose the fundamentals change. Perhaps there is a new Fed chairperson or perhaps someone invents a new technology. In a conventional DSGE model, the rule that people use to forecast the future would need to change. That is the point of Lucas' celebrated critique of econometric policy evaluation.[15] The belief function in this world is explained by other features of the model; it is *endogenous*.

Now move to my parallel universe where there is a continuum of rational expectations equilibria. In my universe, the rule that people use to forecast the future is critical. It is the belief function that selects the equilibrium.[16] If people believe there will be high unemployment, that belief will be self-fulfilling.

In my world, ask what happens if the fundamentals change. Perhaps there is a new Fed chairperson or perhaps there is a new technology. In this world, the belief function selects a new equilibrium. Beliefs are fundamental!

Are beliefs really fundamental? I believe so. This is a not a radical idea; it is a radically new way of understanding an old idea. Central bankers have known for a long time that expectations of future inflation are highly persistent. That persistence is often cited as one of the strikes against either the rational expectations assumption or the equilibrium assumption. I believe both of those accusations are misplaced. Persistent expectations are a strike against rational expectations *plus* the uniqueness assumption. It is the uniqueness assumption that needs to go, not the rational expectations assumption, which simply reflects a fact that we have known for a long time: expectations are incredibly persistent. Welcome to my alternate reality!

Conclusion

In this chapter I described a new framework, Keynesian search theory, to explain why unemployment persists and why the market mechanism does not provide incentives for firms to hire unemployed people. Keynesian search theory provides a microfoundation to the aggregate supply curve in Keynes' *General Theory* that is different from the New Keynesian explanation of aggregate supply in a fundamental way.

According to New Keynesian economics, any deviation of unemployment from its natural rate is temporary. We simply need to wait long enough and the magic of the invisible hand will do its job and restore full employment. According to Keynesian search theory, if we wait for the invisible hand to restore full employment we will be waiting until hell freezes over. High persistent unemployment is one of many long-run equilibria.

In his article "A Theoretical Framework for Monetary Analysis," Milton Friedman claimed there is "no fundamental flaw in the price system."[17] I believe he was wrong. The stagnation that occurred in the United States during the Great Depression, in Japan during the "lost decade" of the 1990s, and throughout the western world after the Great Recession, supports that claim.

High, persistent unemployment is not a temporary situation caused by sticky wages and prices. It is a permanent situation caused by incomplete labor markets. The research agenda implied by accepting this idea raises new questions, answers old ones, and provides new ways of thinking not only about economic theory, but also about policy options. Those are the topics I take up in the remaining chapters of this book.

Appendix 6: The Natural Rate of Unemployment

This appendix presents the algebra used to construct the natural rate of unemployment rate graphed in Figure 6.3, where Y is the production of corn, L is the employment rate, U is the unemployment rate, X refers to production workers, V refers to recruiting workers, m refers to new hires, and s is the separation rate.

The number of people in the labor force is normalized to one. There are L employed workers and U unemployed workers. Every worker is either employed or unemployed:

$$L + U = 1. \tag{6.1}$$

Every employed worker is assigned to one of two tasks: production or recruiting. There are L employed workers, X production workers, and V recruiting workers:

$$L = X + V. \tag{6.2}$$

Every production worker produces A units of corn:

$$Y = AX. \tag{6.3}$$

A fraction of workers s separates from their jobs each period. These are the outflows from employment:

$$Outflows = sL. \tag{6.4}$$

A number of new workers m are hired each period by combining V recruiting workers with U unemployed workers in a search technology. These are the inflows to employment:

$$Inflows = m = V^{\frac{1}{2}}U^{\frac{1}{2}}. \tag{6.5}$$

Setting inflows equal to outflows and replacing U with $1-L$ from Eq. 6.1:

$$sL = V^{\frac{1}{2}}(1-L)^{\frac{1}{2}}. \tag{6.6}$$

Eq. 6.6 tells us that when inflows equal outflows,

$$V = \frac{(sL)^2}{1-L}. \tag{6.7}$$

Replacing this expression in Eq. 6.2 and rearranging to find an expression for X gives the following equation, which tells us how many workers will be producing corn in a steady-state equilibrium for any given employment rate L:

$$X = L\left(1 - \frac{s^2 L}{1-L}\right). \tag{6.8}$$

Finally, using the production function for corn, Eq. 6.2, we find an expression for the amount of corn that can be produced as a function of total employment:

$$Y = AL\left(1 - \frac{s^2 L}{1-L}\right). \tag{6.9}$$

Because s is small, the second term in parentheses is small as long as L is not close to one. For most values of L, the first term dominates and the production function is increasing in employment. But, when L gets close to one, the second term in parentheses dominates and reducing the unemployment rate further is counterproductive. I used Eq. 6.9 to draw Figure 6.3.

7

WALL STREET
AND MAIN STREET

In 2013, the Nobel Prize Committee recognized Eugene Fama, Lars Hansen, and Robert Shiller for their work on financial markets. Eugene Fama taught us that asset prices are unpredictable at short horizons. Lars Hansen gave us tools to study their statistical properties, and Robert Shiller taught us that classical economics cannot explain easily the volatility of asset prices.[1] One of these economists, Eugene Fama, is the father of the *efficient markets hypothesis*, a theory that has had a huge impact on the behavior of financial institutions and on the way that we regulate financial markets.

The efficient markets hypothesis has two parts that are often confused.[2] The first, *informational efficiency*, is the statement that, without insider information, it is not possible to make excess profits by buying and selling stocks, bonds, or derivatives. That idea is backed up by extensive research and is a pretty good characterization of the way the world works. The second, *Pareto efficiency*, asserts that financial markets allocate capital efficiently in the sense there is no intervention by government that could improve the welfare of one person without making someone else worse off. That idea is false. Although it is not easy to make money by trading in the financial markets, the financial markets do not allocate capital efficiently.

The argument for free trade in financial assets is the same as the argument for free trade in goods. If I have a good you want, and you have a good I want, we will both be better off if we are able to exchange one good for the other. Economist Vilfredo Pareto formalized that argument in the nineteenth century with the first description of the first welfare theorem of economics—an idea we met in Chapter 1.

Trade in a modern market economy is more complicated than the simple exchange of goods between two people. Every human being on the planet is connected with every other human being by a network of production and exchange that extends from major metropolitan areas such as London, New York, and Tokyo to remote areas like the rain forest in Brazil or the Australian outback. And we are not just connected with human beings who are alive today. By buying and selling financial assets, we are connected indirectly with human beings who are not yet born.

It is clear that free trade between two consenting adults is welfare improving. But the extension to real-world markets is not so clear. In 1983, two University of Pennsylvania economists, David Cass and Karl Shell, showed the first welfare theorem of economics does not apply to financial markets.[3] For those markets to work well, everybody who will be affected by asset price fluctuations must be present to insure against them. Economists call that requirement *complete participation*. Complete participation fails in financial markets because we cannot insure against events that occur before we are born.

Two Asset Pricing Puzzles

In both classical and New Keynesian economic models, aggregate consumption, investment, and employment are chosen by a representative person who tries to make both herself and her descendants as happy as possible. To decide how much that person would choose to save and invest, economists write down a mathematical specification to describe how much she values the present over the future. In a simple specification that works well for many purposes, economists assume that people value the discounted sum of a function of consumption. That function is equal to a constant multiple of monthly consumption raised to a power.[4] When a representative person behaves in this way I say she has *conventional preferences*.

The assumption of conventional preferences works well if we want to model how much we each choose to save as a fraction of our wealth. It does a very poor job of explaining financial data. There are two principal ways in which the assumption of conventional preferences fails to explain financial data. The first failure is called *the excess volatility puzzle*; the second failure is called the *equity premium puzzle*.

The excess volatility puzzle was identified by Robert Shiller, and by Stephen LeRoy and Robert Porter, who pointed out that asset prices are too volatile to be explained by conventional preferences. Asset price fluctuations are not, in themselves, hard to explain. Excessive movements in stock market prices, relative to earnings, *are* hard to explain.[5]

The equity premium puzzle was identified by Raj Mehra and Edward C. Prescott.[6] They pointed out that if aggregate choices are made by a representative agent with conventional preferences, we would expect the average return to holding the stock market to be roughly the same as the average return to holding US Treasury debt. In a century of US data, the average return to holding the stock market has been 6% greater than the average return to holding US treasuries.

Explaining the Puzzles with Exotic Preferences and Rare Disasters

Macroeconomists and financial economists have followed two principal routes in their attempts to explain these two puzzles. Both routes maintain the representative agent assumption.

The first explanation of the two puzzles is what David Backus, Bryan Routledge, and Stanley Zin refer to as models of *exotic preferences*.[7] In these models, the utility of consumption during any given period is not well described by conventional preferences. Instead, people are much more averse to risk or they have more complicated ways of evaluating future utility.

The second explanation of the two puzzles was proposed by Thomas Rietz and Robert Barro.[8] They argue the representative agent expects the economy will experience occasional *rare disasters*. To explain why a representative consumer is willing to hold bonds that pay a very low return, a disaster must be associated with a collapse in the value of the stock market at the same time that US Treasury bonds continue to pay out as promised. Obvious candidates are the Great Depression or the Great Recession, during which the US government remained solvent but many private institutions failed.

The most plausible explanations of the excess volatility puzzle and the equity premium puzzle combine these two features. If the representative agent has exotic preferences, and if there are occasional rare disasters, modern finance theory can explain many of the features of asset prices we observe in data as the choices of a representative agent.

Complete and Incomplete Markets

The representative agent assumption is a powerful device used to great effect by macroeconomists since the inception of the RBC model during the 1980s. However, it carries with it an assumption that is often overlooked. If the same person makes all decisions, there is no need for options, derivatives, or equity markets because these markets simply define the price at which the representative agent is just willing to hold an asset that no one is willing to supply. Trade never occurs because there is no one to trade with.

To be fair to finance theory, the theories constructed to explain asset prices are more sophisticated than this. Much of the asset pricing theory developed during the past fifty years does not assume there is a representative agent. It assumes only that nobody can make profits by buying and selling assets unless they are willing to accept additional risk. When people can trade assets contingent on any future event, we say there are *complete markets*. In economic models in which there are complete markets, the first welfare theorem applies and there is no reason for government to regulate trade in the asset markets.

During the 1990s, the theoretical results of financial economists found their way onto Wall Street, and financial services companies began to trade real-world securities based on the predictions of the complete markets model. Economists argued that free trade in the asset markets is necessarily a good thing, and that argument formed the rationale for the Gramm–Leach–Bliley Act, passed in 1999, that deregulated the financial markets and that, many believe, was responsible for the 2008 financial crisis.

There is a vast body of literature on what happens if we cannot trade assets indexed to every possible contingency that may occur. When this is the case, we say the financial markets are *incomplete*.[9]

Some economists have argued the financial markets are obviously incomplete. Others claim the fact that there are some events against which we do not insure is unimportant quantitatively because rational human beings will agree to make all the contingent trades important to their welfare. Whatever your view on the plausibility of the assumption of complete markets, there is a second fundamental problem that would be present even if every living human being could trade assets contingent on all future events. We cannot trade in asset markets that open before we are born. When some people cannot trade in the asset markets, for whatever reason, we say that there is *incomplete participation*.

Incomplete Participation and Excess Volatility

After the Great Fire of London in 1666, Nicolas Barbon introduced the first fire insurance scheme in 1680.[10] This obvious improvement was widely adopted. However, fire insurance is only possible if a homeowner buys the insurance before his house burns down in a fire.

Financial crises are like fires. If your first job occurs in a year following a financial crisis, you will not just suffer a temporary setback: you will enjoy lower earnings for the rest of your life than your brother or your sister who was lucky enough to be born in a boom.[11] If each of us had the opportunity to trade in a financial market that opened before we were born, we would trade assets that would insure us against the possibility of being born into a state of poverty. Those trades would involve buying assets that pay off in recession states, and selling the market short in states of prosperity. And by engaging in those trades, market traders would eliminate inefficient movements in asset prices that lead to booms and busts.

In a 1983 article, Cass and Shell distinguished uncertainty that influences the economy in a fundamental way from uncertainty that does not.[12] I refer to those two types of uncertainty as *fundamental* and *nonfundamental shocks*. Cass and Shell constructed an abstract theoretical model in which there is incomplete participation in asset markets, and they showed, in their model, that nonfundamental shocks can cause excessive swings in asset prices.

An example of a fundamental shock in the real world is the discovery of a new oil reserve, or the election of a socialist or a conservative government. An example of a nonfundamental shock would be the opinion of an influential journalist that has no foundation in fact and is not informed by any real-world event.

The results of Cass and Shell provide an explanation for Shiller, and LeRoy and Porter's findings of excess volatility. Asset prices are excessively volatile because they are influenced by nonfundamental shocks that cannot be insured away by the unborn. In Cass and Shell's theory, these shocks are Pareto inefficient and government can and should try to prevent them.[13]

Incomplete Participation Is Important in the Real World

It is one thing to show that, because of incomplete participation, nonfundamental shocks can matter in an abstract general equilibrium model. It is quite another to make the case that this is a quantitatively important problem in the real world. My work makes the case that incomplete participation does not just matter in theory; it also matters in practice.[14]

To evaluate the claim that nonfundamental uncertainty matters in the real world, we need a model that can be matched with data in which there are more than two periods and in which the parameters of the model are matched to realistic facts. It would not be very interesting if the only way to generate large, inefficient asset price fluctuations would require us to assume 50% of the population is born every week.

In my academic research, I expanded the representative agent model to allow for people with finite lives that differ in their preference for current over future consumption.[15] As in the real world, it is important that people use money as a unit of account. Using standard assumptions from general equilibrium theory, I have shown that stock prices go up and down because people believe they will, and that the magnitude of these fluctuations is large.

When the market crashes, the price level falls and the real value of both private and government debt goes up. American economist Irving Fisher, writing in the 1920s, called this process *debt deflation*.[16] Debt deflation is not a problem for existing generations because they can offset its consequences by writing contracts with each other. But it *is* a problem for future generations. Our children and our grandchildren do not own government debt, but they *are* responsible for its repayment.

Nonfundamental shocks to the asset markets reallocate wealth between generations, and the effects of this reallocation are important quantitatively. Nonfundamental shocks do not just matter in theory; they also matter in the real world.

Some Empirical Evidence That Markets Are Not Pareto Efficient

I have provided a purely theoretical reason to doubt the claim that free trade in financial markets improves the welfare of all. Is there any empirical evidence to help decide whether they are efficient in practice? I believe there is.

In Figure 7.1, I plot Robert Shiller's measure of the cyclically adjusted price earnings ratio, the CAPE, beginning in January 1890 and ending in December 2014. This chart shows the CAPE has been as low as five in 1919 and as high as forty-four in 1998.[17]

It is one thing to point out the asset markets are volatile and quite another to attribute their movements to animal spirits. How do we know asset price movements are not just the rational response of market participants to their forecasts of future changes in fundamentals? Surely large price movements should be expected in a healthy and growing economy.

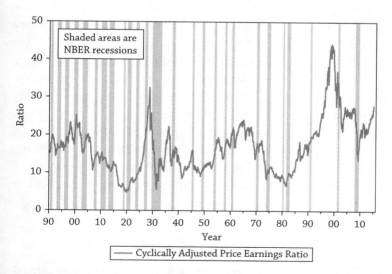

Figure 7.1 The Price-to-Earnings Ratio in the United States from 1890 to 2015. NBER, National Bureau of Economic Research.

Source: Shiller (2015) and NBER.

High prices are a signal that a new innovation has occurred and we are due for a period of prosperity.

It is true that sometimes asset price movements are a signal to be welcomed. The railroad boom of the late nineteenth century, electrification during the early twentieth century, and the growth of the Internet during the early years of the twenty-first century are all examples of innovations expected to cause a big increase in the value of the stock market. They would not be expected to cause a big swing in the CAPE. Large increases in asset values are caused by the expectation of large increases in earnings; yet, it is clear from the evidence I present in Figure 7.1 that it is the price-to-earnings ratios that are volatile, not just asset prices themselves.

If asset price fluctuations were simply a matter of the gains and losses of big banks, then perhaps we should be unconcerned. In good times, the owners of the banks would be richer than in bad times. What's a $100 million loss to a billionaire? But financial fluctuations do not just affect the city of London and Wall Street; they affect all of us through feedback effects on the real economy.

Philip Oreopoulos, Till von Wachter, and Andrew Heisz have shown the lifetime earnings of school leavers whose first job occurs in a recession is 10% to 15% lower than the lifetime earnings of those who enter the labor market in a boom.[18] Fluctuations in financial wealth cause fluctuations in the lifetime prospects of young people because a financial crisis impacts the unemployment rate and that impact has persistent effects that can last as long as fifteen years after the crisis is over.[19]

The Great Depression and the Great Recession: A Comparison

In *The General Theory,* Keynes argued economic cycles are caused by fluctuations in the confidence of investors. He called those fluctuations *animal spirits* and he developed a theory to explain why changes in confidence cause changes in unemployment.

Keynes observed the 1929 stock market crash was followed by the Great Depression. Since Keynes wrote *The General Theory*, we have observed more than eighty years of data. Those data confirm that the fact the Depression was preceded by a market crash was not an unusual event. Persistent drops in stock market wealth are always followed by increases in the unemployment rate.

Figure 7.2 shows what happened to the real value of US assets during the Great Depression. The unmarked line, measured on the left scale, is the value of the stock market in real units; the line with boxes, measured on an inverted scale on the right axis, is the unemployment rate. The chart shows the crash in the value of financial assets preceded the increase in the unemployment rate. In my book *Expectations, Employment and Prices*, I provide a theory that interprets that connection as a causal link.[20]

Figure 7.3 shows the data on the real value of the stock market and the unemployment rate for 2002 through 2010. This chart shows that the 2008 financial crisis was remarkably

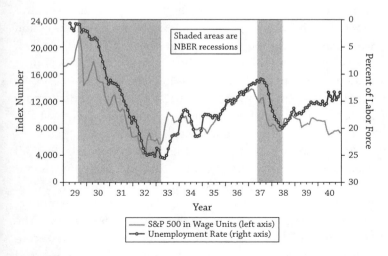

Figure 7.2 Wealth and Unemployment in the United States during the Great Depression. NBER, National Bureau of Economic Research.

Source: Bureau of Labor Statistics, US Department of Commerce, Standard and Poor's, and author's calculations.

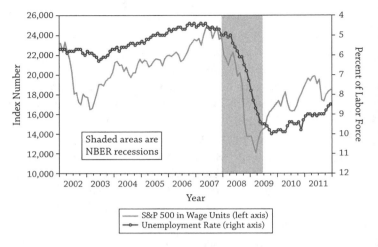

Figure 7.3 Wealth and Unemployment in the United States during the Great Recession. NBER, National Bureau of Economic Research.

Source: Bureau of Labor Statistics, US Department of Commerce, Standard and Poor's, and author's calculations.

similar to the Great Depression. Both were preceded by a dramatic drop in the value of paper assets. The Great Depression was triggered by the stock market crash of 1929. The Great Recession began with a decline in house prices in 2006; but, it did not turn into a full-scale rout until the stock market crash that followed the Lehman Brothers bankruptcy of September 2008. In both cases, the transmission mechanism from wealth to the real economy was the same.[21]

As people lost confidence in the financial markets, they all tried to sell assets at the same time. This financial panic caused a loss in wealth that triggered a fall in consumption spending by households. Firms could no longer sell all they were producing and, in response, they cut prices and laid off workers. The newly unemployed workers cut spending further and the economy spiraled down to a new equilibrium at which the reduced earnings produced by each surviving firm were just sufficient to validate the lower value of assets that triggered the crash.

The Stock Market and Unemployment in Normal Times

I have shown that the Great Depression and the Great Recession were both preceded by a big drop in the value of stock market wealth. But perhaps that is an anomaly. Maybe, in normal times, there is no such connection. To investigate that possibility, I looked at the connection between the real value of the stock market and unemployment three months later.[22]

In Figure 7.4, I plot the value of the S&P 500 measured as a ratio to the money wage, and the unemployment rate. The S&P 500 is marked with circles and is graphed on the left axis. The unemployment rate is measured by the solid line and is graphed on the right axis on an inverted scale.[23] I showed in my published work that each of these variables is nonstationary. They do not display any tendency to return to a single number after a shock. And although they each wander aimlessly up and down, they do not wander too far from each other. Variables that can wander like this are said to have a

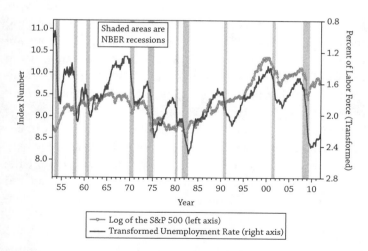

Figure 7.4 Unemployment and the Stock Market Since 1953. NBER, National Bureau of Economic Research.

Source: Bureau of Labor Statistics, US Department of Commerce, Standard and Poor's, and author's calculations.

unit root; variables that wander, but stick together, are said to be *cointegrated*.

What can we learn from the fact these variables are related to each other? To see if the connection between wealth and unemployment holds in normal times, I tried to explain changes in the unemployment rate and changes in the S&P 500 by past values of changes in these variables and by the relationship that ties them together in the long run.[24] I found something remarkable. The equation that links changes in the unemployment rate and changes in the stock market to their own past values has remained stable throughout the entire postwar period. That fact has important real-world consequences.

In Figure 7.5, I illustrate how we could have used what we knew about postwar movements in the stock market and the unemployment rate to guide us in what to expect during the Great Recession. The solid line is the unemployment rate; the lines with circles and crosses are two different forecasts of the unemployment rate. In both cases, those forecasts are made using information available up to and including the fourth quarter of 2008. And the forecasting equations are the same ones a policymaker would have estimated, using information available from the end of WWII up to and including the third quarter of 1979, when Paul Volcker took over as chair of the Fed.

In Figure 7.5, the line with circles is a forecast of future unemployment that uses only the history of the unemployment rate. The line with crosses also uses information from the stock market. This forecast is accurate five quarters ahead and it predicts the depth of the Great Recession by using information from the stock market crash that occurred after the bankruptcy of Lehman Brothers in September 2008. This figure shows there is substantial information in the stock market that helps to predict future recessions. The relationship between these two variables has remained structurally stable for seventy years.

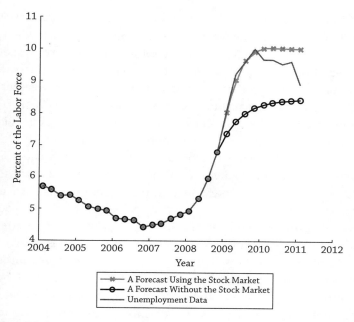

Figure 7.5 Forecasting the Great Recession.

Source: Bureau of Labor Statistics, US Department of Commerce, Standard and Poor's, and author's calculations.

Causation and Control

The fact that information from the financial markets helps to predict the unemployment rate does not *necessarily* imply that if we could control the asset markets through government intervention, we would be able to control the unemployment rate. That point is made clearly by Clive Granger, who distinguished between causation and control.[25]

According to Granger, variable X Granger-causes variable Y if there is information in the past values of X that helps to predict the future values of Y. That does mean that variable X causes variable Y in the same sense that a physicist means by that term. Both X and Y might be caused by a third variable the economist cannot observe.

For example, suppose you turn on the television every day at 6.30 p.m. to watch the weather report. You observe that whenever the weather forecaster predicts it will rain tomorrow, that forecast almost always turns out to be correct. A statistician would say the weather forecast Granger-causes the weather. That information is useful, because it enables you to dress appropriately the next day. But, it is not much help if your goal is to control the rain. *Causation* is not the same as *control*.

Suppose, alternatively, you observe that when a careless person discards a cigarette butt in a dry forest, that event is often followed by a forest fire. In that case, there is a clear causal chain and it would seem reasonable to infer that, if you were to prevent people from smoking in forests in the middle of a drought, you would reduce the incidence of forest fires.

In my work, I show that the stock market Granger-causes the unemployment rate. That is not the same as saying that, by controlling the value of the stock market, government could prevent recessions. To make the case for control, one needs an economic model that provides a plausible mechanism to explain why there is a causal chain from changes in the stock market to changes in economic activity. Some economists, when observing that the stock market Granger-causes unemployment, would argue that the stock market is like a weather forecaster. I disagree. The stock market is like a discarded cigarette butt in a forest. Animal spirits caused the stock market crash of 2008. And the stock market crash *caused* the Great Recession.

The Stock Market Crash Caused the Great Recession

Consider the following two explanations for the Great Recession. In the first explanation, market participants received a signal in fall 2008 that a fundamental event was about to occur that would depress the value of stock market earnings and increase the value of unemployment for an extended period of time. That news raised the likelihood of corporate bankruptcies and increased the cost of credit for low-quality corporate borrowers. An example of such an event would be a court ruling that increased union bargaining power and was perceived to lead to significant future labor market disruptions and loss of output. I call this the *fundamental view of the market*.[26]

In the second explanation, the Great Recession was triggered by the collapse of a housing bubble. After the Great Depression, Congress introduced financial regulations that helped promote financial market stability for more than thirty years. During the 1990s, these regulations were relaxed and financial institutions began to promote low-cost mortgages to borrowers with limited credit. A rush of speculation in the housing market caused house prices to spiral upward in an unsustainable bubble. When house prices began to fall in 2006, the bubble burst and the fall in house prices caused a drop in the equity value of the banks that had promoted and packaged high-risk mortgages.

Although nothing fundamental had changed in the economy, the price of houses began to fall. That fall triggered a drop in the value of the paper wealth of financial institutions as market participants began, correctly, to believe a recession was on the horizon. Shares traded at much lower prices because the house price appreciation that had supported high share prices was no longer there. As the face value of paper assets dropped, households curtailed their spending, causing firms to lay off workers. The reduced level of economic activity resulted in a self-fulfilling drop in the value of earnings per share that validated the initial pessimistic belief. I call this the *animal spirits view of the market*.

According to the fundamental view of the market, an attempt to restore confidence by US Treasury or central bank intervention will be self-defeating. If government buys shares or low-quality corporate bonds, paid for by borrowing, it will lose money in the long run because asset market intervention cannot effectively counteract the fundamental cause of the market crash. According to the animal spirits view of the market, restoration of confidence through asset market purchases is an effective way to prevent a market crash from causing a recession. These two views cannot be distinguished ex ante, although they clearly have different policy implications.

Why should we prefer one explanation over the other? According to the fundamental view of the market, standing in 2008, investors must have anticipated rationally that a very bad event was about to happen that would depress the value of future earnings. The anticipated future collapse caused the stock market crash.

According to the animal spirits view of the market, the direction of causality is different. A loss of confidence in the value of paper assets, triggered by a speculative bubble in the housing market, caused a drop in household wealth. That fall in wealth caused households to consume less and firms to lay off workers, and the loss of confidence became self-fulfilling. It is because I cannot see a reasonable candidate for the future fall in fundamentals that I am not personally persuaded by the fundamental view.

Some have argued that the housing bubble was itself caused by bad economic policy. If the Federal Reserve had been more vigilant in preventing the growth of the subprime mortgage market, the housing bubble might never have occurred. Although that argument has merit, there is no reason why the crash in asset values that occurred in 2008, after the Lehman Brothers bankruptcy, should have caused a six-percentage-point increase in the unemployment rate. If you are going upward in a balloon that is out of control, the solution is not to prick the balloon and release the gas. It is to install a release valve, let out the gas slowly, and engineer a smooth and gentle descent to earth. My thesis, in this book, is that government can install a release valve in the economy by buying and selling shares in the stock market, paid for by issuing short-term Treasury securities.

The animal spirits view of the market provides a causal chain that connects movements in the stock market with subsequent changes in the unemployment rate. If this theory is correct, and I personally find it persuasive, the stock market crash of 2008 *caused* the Great Recession.

Conclusion

In this chapter I provided a theory of financial crises. I call this the *animal spirits view of the market*.[27] According to the animal spirits view of the market, most, if not all, of the persistent movements we see in price-to-earnings ratios are symptomatic of a fundamental flaw in financial markets. Free trade in financial assets does not lead to the efficient allocation of capital across time because unborn generations are unable to participate in markets that open before they are born.

The animal spirits view of the market explains what caused the Great Recession. Like the Great Depression before it, the Great Recession was caused by a crash in the value of paper assets generated by self-fulfilling beliefs.

I provided evidence that changes in the stock market Granger-cause changes in the unemployment rate. A sustained drop in the value of stock market wealth is followed, three months later, by an increase in the unemployment rate. Furthermore, the relationship between the stock market and the unemployment rate has been persistent and stable in seventy years of data. If the real value of the stock market drops by 10%, and remains low for three months, the unemployment rate will increase by three percentage points above the rate that would otherwise have prevailed.

The animal spirits view of the market explains the link between the stock market and the unemployment rate in terms of a causal chain. The signature events that support this theory are the Great Depression and the Great Recession. In 1929, the stock market lost 80% of its value and the unemployment rate increased from 1% to 22% in the space of three years. In 2008 the stock market lost 50% of its value and the unemployment rate went from 4% to 10% in the space of two years. My research documents that the connection between stock market wealth and the unemployment rate is not restricted to these two events. It is stable and persistent.

Paul Samuelson, writing in his *Newsweek* column in 1966, is famously quoted as saying that "the stock market predicted nine of the last five recessions." That quote has stuck in the collective memory of the economics profession, but it is misleading. Day-to-day movements of the stock market do not predict recessions, even if they are very large. Week-to-week movements do not predict recessions. However, large movements of the stock market that persist for three months not only predict recessions, they cause them.

8

THE NEW KEYNESIAN
MODEL EXPLAINED

How does the economy work? What is the role of monetary policy? How are we to understand the impact of central banks on inflation and unemployment? These are fundamental questions that must be addressed if we are to have a hope of improving the institutions that regulate our lives.

Economists use models to help answer these questions. A model is a system of equations that describes the relationships among variables such as inflation, unemployment, and the interest rate. Some of the models used by central bankers involve hundreds of economic variables. But however complex they become, all these models are built around a core New Keynesian model that has only three equations. In this chapter, I describe how this model works and I explain how it is used by monetary policymakers to justify their decisions to raise or lower the interest rate.[1]

The Goals of Monetary Policy

Monetary policymakers are concerned primarily with keeping inflation low and stable. As a secondary objective, some countries also direct their central banks to maintain a high and stable level of economic activity. The United Kingdom is a country where control of the inflation rate is the primary objective of policy, and maintaining full employment and maximum growth of real GDP is a secondary objective. The Federal Reserve System has a dual mandate of price stability and maximum employment whereas the European Central Bank has a single objective: a low and stable inflation rate.

Economists measure economic activity in two different ways. First, they establish a benchmark that reflects what they think the economy could produce if there were no idle resources. Using unemployment as a measure of economic activity, the benchmark is the natural rate of unemployment. Using real GDP as a measure of economic activity, the benchmark is potential GDP.[2] Potential GDP is defined as the real value of the goods and services that could be produced if the economy was operating at full employment. The gap between realized GDP and potential GDP is called the *output gap*.

When unemployment is higher than its natural rate, the output gap is negative; when it is lower than its natural rate, the output gap is positive. The connection between the unemployment rate and the output gap is called *Okun's Law*, named after the American economist Arthur Okun, who first studied the connection between these concepts.[3]

Sometimes, New Keynesian economists use the output gap as a measure of economic activity; other times, they use the unemployment rate. I use both in this chapter.

The Methodology of DSGE Models

The equations of the New Keynesian model describe connections between the interest rate, the inflation rate, and the unemployment rate or the output gap. These equations are *dynamic* and *stochastic*, and each of them describes an equilibrium relationship in the sense of *general equilibrium* theory. It is an example of a dynamic stochastic general equilibrium model, or DSGE model.

The word *dynamic* means past values and beliefs about future values of economic variables influence their current values. The word *stochastic* means random shocks hit the economy in every period. The label *general equilibrium* refers to the fact that each equation is derived from assumptions about the behavior of rational human beings interacting in markets.

The methodology of DSGE models has been attacked following the 2008 crisis, and some critics have claimed DSGE methodology was responsible for a policy failure that contributed to the crisis.[4] That criticism is partly right. Economists failed to recognize that the economic stability which followed the adoption of inflation-targeting regimes during the 1990s was temporary, and widespread acceptance of the efficient markets hypothesis led to deregulation of the financial markets. This left the system vulnerable to financial instability. But, these were failings of the New Keynesian DSGE model. They were not grounds to give up on the entire DSGE agenda.

Not All DSGE Models Are Wrong

Reliance on the New Keynesian DSGE model by central bankers was damaging because it gave policymakers a false sense of security. The New Keynesian model is an example of a self-stabilizing system. After a shock to one of its equations, the interest rate, the inflation rate, and the unemployment rate in the model return to their steady-state values. But as I showed in Chapter 3, the unemployment rate, in the US data, does not return to any fixed number.

The 2008 recession was larger than previous post-WWII recessions, but the response of the inflation rate and the unemployment rate was, at least initially, similar qualitatively to previous episodes. The Fed responds to a typical recession by lowering the interest rate. From 1990 through 2007, that policy was effective and it helped to reduce the severity of recessions. But after every recession, the interest rate was lower than at the end of the previous recession. Inflation, the unemployment rate, and the interest rate all drifted down over this period.

The Great Recession was different from previous post-WWII recessions because the money interest rate reached zero and could not be lowered further. However, even in the absence of the Fed lowering the interest rate, if the New Keynesian model is correct, wage and price declines should have restored full employment eventually. And, although that process may be slow, it is difficult or impossible to explain why it has taken eight years for the economy to recover to prerecession levels using the same New Keynesian model that was effective in understanding the Great Moderation.

. . . *But the New Keynesian DSGE Model* Is *Wrong*

Some have rushed to defend New Keynesian economics by pointing out recessions are inherently unpredictable. That is true. But, as Nassim Taleb has pointed out, the market movements that followed the Lehman Brothers crash in September 2008 were, if conventional theory is to be believed, a seven-standard deviation event.[5] According to conventional theories, this was about as likely to occur as the failure of tomorrow's sunrise.

What can we learn from the failure of economic theory to predict the Great Recession? Should we give up on the New Keynesian model? In my view, the answer to that question is a resounding yes. But, that does not imply that we should give up on all DSGE models. Although the New Keynesian model is an example of a self-stabilizing system, not all DSGE models are self-stabilizing.

In Chapter 9, I combine the two market failures I described in Chapters 6 and 7 in an alternative DSGE model: the Farmer Monetary Model.[6] In that model, because the labor market is incomplete, a high, inefficient unemployment rate can persist forever. And because participation in the financial markets is incomplete, the economy may be subject to large persistent swings in economic activity that have nothing to do with fundamentals. By putting these two ideas together, the Farmer Monetary Model provides an alternative narrative of the experience of inflation, interest rates, and the output gap during the post-WWII period.

The Equations of the New Keynesian DSGE Model

The three equations of the New Keynesian model are the New Keynesian Investment Equals Savings (IS) Curve, the Taylor Rule, and the New Keynesian Phillips Curve. Each of these equations describes a relationship conjectured to hold among past values, current values, and expected future values of the interest rate, the inflation rate, and the output gap.

Economists distinguish the real interest rate from the money interest rate. The money interest rate is the rate you earn on a savings account denominated in dollars. The real interest rate adjusts this money rate for expected changes in the purchasing power of money.

The New Keynesian IS Curve

The first equation of the New Keynesian model is called the *New Keynesian IS Curve*, where IS stands for investment equals savings. It is a channel through which changes in the real interest rate cause changes in the desires of households and firms to increase or decrease their purchases of goods and services.

When households expect their income to be higher in the future, they try to spend some of that money today. If everyone tries to spend more at the same time, firms cannot produce enough goods immediately to satisfy the increased aggregate demand. To choke off part of that demand, the real interest rate increases.

An increase in the real interest rate has two effects. First, some households will choose to save more and spend less. Second, some previously viable investment projects will now seem too expensive, given the increased cost of funds. For both these reasons, if the real interest rate goes up, investment and consumption fall because future goods become more valuable relative to current goods.

Because the New Keynesian IS Curve describes how the quantities demanded of private agents respond to a change in the interest rate, shocks to the curve are referred to as *aggregate demand shocks*. An example of an aggregate demand shock is an unanticipated change in the demand for investment goods caused by more or less pessimistic expectations on the part of entrepreneurs.

The Taylor Rule

The second equation of the New Keynesian model is called the Taylor Rule, named after American economist John Taylor. The Taylor Rule explains how the central bank sets the money interest rate. A central bank that follows the Taylor Rule will raise the interest rate in response to higher inflation or an increase in the output gap. Taylor showed an equation of this form provides a good fit to the post-WWII US data.[7]

New Keynesian theory asserts that output fluctuations are caused by random shocks to aggregate demand and aggregate supply. By studying the behavior of the New Keynesian economic model, New Keynesian economists have shown output—the interest rate and inflation—at least in their model, are all less volatile if the central bank follows the Taylor Rule with a sufficiently aggressive response to inflation. Viewed in this way, the Taylor Rule is a normative prescription that instructs the central bank policymaker on how to respond to shocks of both kinds.

The New Keynesian Phillips Curve

The third equation of the New Keynesian model is the New Keynesian Phillips Curve. This equation explains how current inflation responds to expected future inflation and the output gap. It is based on the assumption that firms try to maximize profits but they are unable to adjust their price in response to constantly changing conditions. Instead, they reset the price of the goods they produce on an infrequent basis in response to current and expected future marginal costs and marginal revenues.

The concepts of marginal cost and marginal revenue are central to the economic theory of profit maximization by firms. Marginal cost is the cost of producing one more unit of output; marginal revenue is the revenue produced from selling that unit. In neoclassical theory, a firm will increase the number of units it produces until marginal revenue is equal to marginal cost. Marginal revenue decreases as the firm sells more because households will buy fewer units if their price goes up. Marginal cost increases as the firm produces more because the firm must compete with other firms for limited factors of production to produce additional units.

In one common version of the New Keynesian theory, price adjustment is not instantaneous because firms must wait to change their price until they win a price-setting lottery—an event referred to as a "visit from the Calvo fairy." It is so named after a paper by Guillermo Calvo, who first developed an ingenious way to build price stickiness into an otherwise classical model.[8] The Calvo Fairy is a not a literal description of how firms operate in the real world. It is a metaphor that captures, in an elegant way, the fact that price changes do not occur instantaneously.

Because the New Keynesian Phillips Curve describes the price at which firms are willing to supply a given quantity of goods, shocks to the New Keynesian Phillips Curve are referred to as *aggregate supply shocks*. Positive aggregate supply shocks are passed on to consumers through higher prices. An example of a positive aggregate supply shock is an unanticipated increase in the price of oil caused by a change in the policy of the OPEC cartel.

The Invisible Man in the Chariot

To solve any DSGE model, the investigator must disentangle the linkages and write down a set of equations, one for each variable, that explains how it evolves in response to random shocks to the system and to past values of all the other variables in the system. This set of equations is called the *reduced form* of the DSGE model.

The variables of the New Keynesian model are the output gap, inflation, and the interest rate, and, if policy is well designed, these three variables will all display the same persistence as that of the shocks that drive the model.[9] In the US data, the output gap, inflation, and the interest rate are all highly persistent. It would be possible to explain why economic variables are persistent by assuming the shocks that drive the economy are themselves persistent, but that is a not a very satisfactory theory. It would be a bit like building a theory of planetary motion by assuming that an invisible man in a chariot is pulling the Earth around the sun.

To avoid the tautological explanation that unemployment is persistent because shocks are persistent, the New Keynesians make additional assumptions about behavior. For example, they claim the interest rate is persistent because policymakers respond not just to inflation and the output gap, but also to the lagged interest rate. They say persistence in output growth arises because the representative agent forms habits that make it costly for him to adjust his consumption too quickly, and persistence in inflation arises because of a concern for relative wages.[10]

These modifications are plausible and they go some way towards helping the model to explain endogenous persistence. But they do not go far enough. There is a more fundamental problem that cannot be fixed by adding any degree of persistence to a model that assumes the unemployment rate converges to its natural rate. There are components of the shocks to the output gap, inflation, and the interest rate that are permanent.

The Interest Rate, the Inflation Rate, and the Unemployment Rate in US Data

In a 2007 paper I coauthored with Andreas Beyer of the European Central Bank, we studied the connection between the interest rate, the inflation rate, and the unemployment rate in US data.[11] Although our study used the unemployment rate, it is relevant to my previous discussion of the New Keynesian model because the output gap and the unemployment rate are connected by Okun's Law.

In Figures 8.1 and 8.2, I updated the data from Beyer and Farmer.[12] Figure 8.1 is a plot of inflation and the interest rate, and Figure 8.2 is a plot of the unemployment rate and the interest rate. The inflation rate is the twelve-month percentage growth rate of the CPI; the interest rate is the average rate in the Federal Funds market.

I added two separate trend lines to each plot. The upward-sloping line is the trend in the Federal Funds rate for 1970 through 1980. The downward-sloping line is the trend in the Federal Funds rate for 1983 through 2005. I broke down the data in this way because there is clear evidence, both in the data

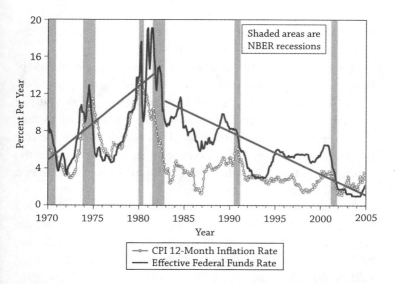

Figure 8.1 Inflation and the Interest Rate in US Data. CPI, consumer price index; NBER, National Bureau of Economic Research.

Source: US Department of Commerce, NBER, and author's calculations.

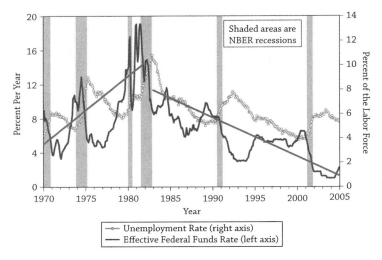

Figure 8.2 Unemployment and the Interest Rate in US Data. NBER, National Bureau of Economic Research.

Source: US Department of Commerce, NBER, and author's calculations.

and in the historical record, that monetary policy operated differently during these two subperiods.

It is apparent from these figures that the unemployment rate, the inflation rate, and the interest rate are all highly persistent time series. Time series that are highly persistent can be analyzed using standard statistical methods as long as they show a tendency to return to a fixed number. If a series has this property, and if its variance is constant from one period to the next, we say that it is *stationary*. The interest rate, the inflation rate, and the unemployment rate do not obey this property.

Formal tests I conducted with Andreas Beyer confirm that unemployment, inflation, and the interest rate are not stationary variables.[13] However, although unemployment, inflation, and the interest rate are all nonstationary individually, we can find weighted sums, called *linear combinations*, of these variables that *are* stationary.[14] Series that display this property are said to be *cointegrated*, a term coined by economist and Nobel Laureate Clive Granger.[15]

Nonstationary time series do not show any tendency to revert to a fixed reference point. The fact that the unemployment rate, the inflation rate, and the interest rate all display this property provides empirical support for my claim that the economy is not self-stabilizing. Although the unemployment rate, the inflation rate, and the unemployment rate do not revert to any fixed value, the fact that they are cointegrated means they cannot drift too far apart from each other.

The inflation rate, the unemployment rate, and the Federal Funds rate act like three drunks wandering down the street, tied together by a rope. By tugging on the rope, the Fed can nudge the inflation rate or the unemployment rate temporarily in one direction or another, but it cannot control both unemployment and inflation permanently at the same time.

The Geometry of Monetary Economies: Balls or Cigars?

The reduced form of the New Keynesian model is a set of three equations (called *difference equations*) disturbed by random shocks.[16] In Chapter 2, using a metaphor from Norwegian economist Ragnar Frisch, I described the economy as a rocking horse, hit repeatedly in an unpredictable manner by a child with a club. The New Keynesian model is a mathematical formalization of this metaphor.

The difference equations represent the mechanism of the rocker. The random shocks represent the child with the club. If the shocks could be turned off, the New Keynesian model predicts the inflation rate, the unemployment rate, and the interest rate would converge back to a unique point; and they would stay there.

We cannot turn off the shocks, but we can ask: What properties should we look for if this model describes the data? The answer is that none of the variables should move too far from its rest point. Suppose we construct a three-dimensional graph on which we could plot the unemployment rate on the first axis, the inflation rate on the second axis, and the interest rate on the third. Each month, we would observe a value for each of these variables and we would represent those values as a point in a three dimensional space.

As time progresses, we would add more and more points to our graph. Because the economy is hit by random shocks, these points will not all be at the same place. As long as the shocks are not too large, none of our three variables can wander too far from its steady-state value. The New Keynesian model predicts the points will cluster into a ball, centered on the steady state.

That is not what we see in data from the real world. Data from the US economy, when plotted on a three-dimensional graph, do not cluster around a point. Instead, they cluster around a line. The object you see if you plot these data is a long, fat cigar, not a tightly packed ball. Stationary data cannot wander too far from a point. Nonstationary cointegrated data cannot wander too far from a line.

Temporary Versus Permanent Shocks: The Unit Root of the Matter

What happens to GDP and unemployment after a shock? The answer to that question depends on whether the shock is temporary or permanent. This issue is not just a statistical curiosity; it has important implications for economic policy. Shocks can have purely temporary effects, purely permanent effects, or a combination of both temporary and permanent effects. When economic data have a permanent component, however big, we say that it has a *unit root*.[17]

When we recognize that some shocks to the economy are permanent, we must take a stand on *why* they are permanent. The New Keynesians assume permanent shocks are caused by movements in the natural rate of unemployment. If that is the case, there is nothing we can or should do about them. The unemployment rate remained elevated six years after the Great Recession was officially declared over because people were choosing voluntarily to consume more leisure.[18]

I do not think that is an accurate description of reality. My alternative to the New Keynesian model is the Keynesian search model. That model explains permanent shocks to the unemployment rate as inefficient shifts from one unemployment equilibrium to another. If I am right, we can and should try to counteract permanent shocks to the unemployment rate by active intervention in which the central bank, acting as an agent for the treasury, buys or sells shares in the stock market to smooth out financial fluctuations.

Temporary Shocks

Figure 8.3 illustrates what happens to unemployment and GDP per person after a temporary shock that raises unemployment. The dashed line on the top panel of this figure represents the natural rate of unemployment. I assume the economy begins from a steady state, where unemployment is at its natural rate. The actual path of the unemployment rate is represented by the solid line coincident with the natural rate of unemployment before date 0.

At date 0, a shock to aggregate demand causes the unemployment rate to increase above its natural rate. This shock might be, for example, a decrease in exports or a temporary reduction in government purchases. After the shock hits, unemployment increases by more than the initial increase and it continues to rise for several periods. This increase would occur in a version of the New Keynesian model where there are endogenous propagation mechanisms—for example, habit formation in preferences and sticky inflation caused by wage contracts. After reaching a peak greater than the initial shock, unemployment begins to fall and, eventually, it returns to the natural rate of unemployment.

The lower panel of Figure 8.3 shows what happens to GDP per person during this episode. The upward-sloping dashed line is potential GDP per person. This grows at a constant rate dictated by exogenous technological progress. The upward-sloping

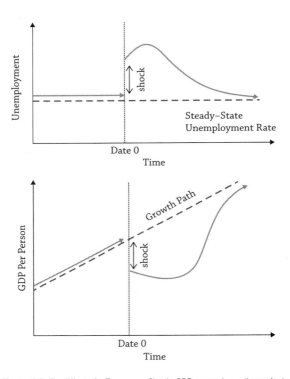

Figure 8.3 The Effect of a Temporary Shock. GDP, gross domestic product.

solid curve is actual GDP per person. Initially, this is coincident with the trend growth path of the economy; but, when the shock hits the economy at date 0, the growth rate of GDP per person drops and continues to drop for a period that corresponds to the increase in unemployment from the upper panel of the figure. Eventually, when unemployment begins to decrease, the growth rate of GDP per person recovers and GDP per person returns to its trend growth path.

The important message to take from Figure 8.3 is that temporary shocks do not alter the natural rate of unemployment and they do not alter the growth path of potential output. According to the classical and New Keynesian models, *all* demand shocks are temporary shocks such as the one depicted in Figure 8.3.

Permanent Shocks

Temporary shocks are not the only kinds of shocks that hit the economy. Some shocks are permanent. The upper panel of Figure 8.4 illustrates what happens to the unemployment rate in response to a permanent shock.

The two dashed lines on the upper panel of this figure represent the steady-state unemployment rates before and after the shock. At date 0, the shock causes an increase in the unemployment rate. This is described by the solid curve that increases to a peak and then converges back to a new level. Because the shock is permanent, unemployment does not converge back to the same place from which it started. Instead, it converges to a new steady state which may be higher or lower than the original unemployment rate.

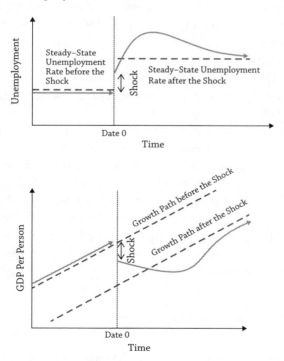

Figure 8.4 The Effect of a Permanent Shock. GDP, gross domestic product.

The lower panel of Figure 8.4 shows what happens to GDP per person during this episode. The two dashed upward-sloping lines represent the trend growth rate of GDP before and after the shock. The solid line is the realized value of GDP per person.

Before the shock hits, the economy is growing at a constant rate. At date 0, the economy is hit by a shock and the growth rate of GDP per person falls by an amount that depends on the value of the shock. The growth rate of GDP continues to decrease further for a period that corresponds to the time during which the unemployment rate is increasing. Eventually, the growth rate of GDP per person begins to increase, and the growth rate of GDP per person returns to the same value it had before the shock.

Unlike the temporary shock depicted in Figure 8.3, when a shock is permanent, GDP per person does not converge back to the same growth path from which it started. Instead, the new growth path may be higher or lower. By assumption, however, the new growth path has the same slope as the initial one. This assumption reflects the fact that the decade average growth rate of GDP per person has not shown any discernible trend in more than a century of US data.

What might *cause* a permanent shock to the unemployment rate? In the classical and New Keynesian models, a permanent shock must be caused by a shift in the natural rate of unemployment. It is, by definition, a supply-side shock. This is not a good description of reality. In the Keynesian search model I described in Chapter 6, a permanent shock to the time path of GDP per person might also be caused by a shift from one equilibrium unemployment rate to a new higher equilibrium unemployment rate.

Data from the Great Recession Show Some Shocks Are Permanent

Which of these figures best describes the US economy? Before 1982, most economists modeled the economy as a collection of stationary variables. Stationarity means economic variables are random variables generated the same way at every point in time. Observing a value for the inflation rate in 2001 is just like observing a value for the inflation rate in 2002. In each case, we are drawing a ball from an urn. And it is the same urn in every case.

Some variables, such as the unemployment rate, were assumed to be stationary around a constant number. Other variables, such as real GDP per person, were assumed to be stationary around a fixed time path. In both cases, the economist has a fixed rule for understanding how the mean and the variance of the economic variables she is observing should be changing over time. A model in which all the variables are stationary is depicted by the scenario in Figure 8.3.

In 1982, Charles Nelson and Charles Plosser wrote an influential article in which they demonstrated GDP is not stationary.[19] It is better described by a statistical model with a unit root. A variable with a unit root shows no tendency to return to a fixed number or to a fixed time path. The responses of nonstationary variables to shocks are described by the scenario in Figure 8.4.

For much of the postwar period, shocks to the permanent component of GDP per person were relatively small and hard to discern with the naked eye. The Great Recession was different. Figure 8.5 plots quarterly real GDP per person in the United States for an eleven-year period that includes the Great Recession.[20]

Compare Figure 8.5 with Figure 8.3, which depicts the theoretical impact of a temporary shock to GDP, and with Figure 8.4, which shows the theoretical effect of a permanent shock. It is clear from a comparison of these graphs that the data are described better by a theory in which there is a permanent component to the movements over time of GDP per person.

Conclusion

After a recession, real GDP per person shows no tendency to return to its previous growth path and the unemployment rate shows no tendency to return to a constant level.

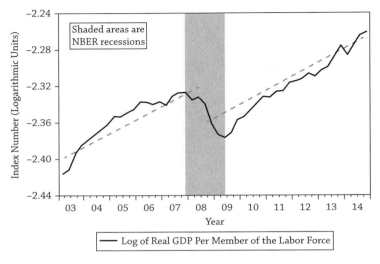

Figure 8.5 Real Gross Domestic Product (GDP) per Person. NBER, National Bureau of Economic Research.

Source: US Department of Commerce and author's calculations.

According to both the classical and New Keynesian models, permanent shocks to the unemployment rate reflect permanent shifts in the natural rate of unemployment. The natural rate of unemployment and the path of potential GDP are changing constantly as a consequence of shifts in the ability of the economy to use resources efficiently. If this explanation is correct, there is nothing the policymaker can or should do about permanent shifts in the unemployment rate.

The Keynesian search model has a different explanation for these facts: the permanent component of changes in the unemployment rate reflects a shift from one inefficient Keynesian equilibrium to another. If this explanation is correct, policymakers should do everything in their power to restore the economy to the socially optimal unemployment rate.

The New Keynesian model was developed to provide a working theory of how central bank actions affect the economy.

It has provided a guide to policymakers for the past thirty years, not because every central bank governor believes every detail of the model, but because it was the only game in town. The classical model developed by RBC economists does not provide a useful alternative because it has no money and because versions of the model that *do* add money have no role for active policy.

In Chapter 9, I take the Keynesian search model I developed in Chapter 6 and I add money. I call the result of this marriage the *Farmer Monetary Model*. The Farmer Monetary Model provides an internally coherent explanation for the effects of monetary policy on inflation and unemployment, and can explain the Great Moderation and the Great Recession in a single step.

Appendix 8: The Equations of the New Keynesian Model

This appendix lays out the equations of the New Keynesian model and explains how to solve these equations for the reduced form. I have made the computer code available on my website (www.rogerfarmer.com).

The variables the New Keynesian model explains are the money interest rate, GDP per person, the inflation rate, and the expectations at date t of the inflation rate and GDP per person at date $t + 1$. Table A8.1 defines symbols for each of these variables. For the exposition in this chapter, I assume potential GDP is constant. The extension to the model in which GDP per person grows at a constant rate is straightforward.

The New Keynesian model is characterized by the eight parameters defined in Table A8.2. These parameters are assumed to be constant.

The model is driven by two fundamental shocks and it contains two nonfundamental shocks that are solved for endogenously after imposing the rational expectations assumption. The shocks are defined in Table A8.3.

Table A8.1 Variables of the New Keynesian Model

Variable Symbol	Variable Name
i_t	The money interest rate at date t
y_t	The log of GDP per person at date t
π_t	The percentage change in the consumer price index between dates $t-1$ and t
$E_t[\pi_{t+1}]$	The expectation at date t of the inflation rate between t and $t+1$
$E_t[y_{t+1}]$	The expectation at date t of log GDP per person at date $t+1$

Table A8.2 The Parameters of the New Keynesian Model

Parameter Symbol	Parameter Name
ρ	Discount rate of the representative agent
α	Risk aversion coefficient of the representative agent
$\bar{\pi}$	Inflation target
$\bar{y}$	The log of potential GDP per person
λ	Inflation coefficient of Taylor Rule
μ	Output gap coefficient of Taylor Rule
κ	Output gap coefficient of Phillips Curve
$\bar{i}$	Interest rate target

Table A8.3 Fundamental and Nonfundamental Shocks

Shock Symbol	Shock Name
u_t^1	The fundamental shock to aggregate demand at date t
u_t^2	The fundamental shock to aggregate supply at date t
w_t^1	The nonfundamental inflation forecast error
w_t^2	The nonfundamental GDP forecast error

Table A8.4 The Equations of the New Keynesian Model

Equation in Symbols	Equation Name
$y_t = E_t[y_{t+1}] - \alpha(i_t - E_t[\pi_{t+1}] - \rho) + u_t^1$	The NK-IS Curve
$i_t = \overline{i} + \lambda(\pi_t - \overline{\pi}) + \mu(y_t - \overline{y})$	The Taylor Rule
$\pi_t = \dfrac{1}{1+\rho} E_t[\pi_{t+1}] + \kappa(y_t - \overline{y}) + u_t^2$	The New Keynesian Phillips Curve
$w_t^1 = \pi_t - E_{t-1}[\pi_t]$	Definition of the inflation forecast shock
$w_t^2 = y_t - E_{t-1}[y_t]$	Definition of the GDP forecast shock

Table A8.4 defines the equations of the model. The first three are symbolic representations of the New Keynesian–Investment Equals Savings Curve, the Taylor Rule, and the New Keynesian Phillips Curve, and the last two are definitions of the endogenous forecast errors.

By defining matrices A, B, C, Ψ, and Π, and vectors of variables X, U, and W, the model can be written more compactly as a vector-valued difference equation. These matrices and variables are defined as follows:

$$X_t = \left[\pi_t, y_t, i_t, E_t[\pi_{t+1}], E_t[y_{t+1}]\right]^T$$
$$U_t = \left[u_t^1, u_t^2\right]^T, \quad W_t = \left[w_t^1, w_t^2\right]^T$$

Here, the superscript T is the transpose operator:

$$A = \begin{bmatrix} 0 & 1 & \alpha & -\alpha & -1 \\ -\lambda & -\mu & 1 & 0 & 0 \\ 1 & -\kappa & 0 & -\dfrac{1}{1+\rho} & 0 \\ 1 & 0 & 0 & 0 & 0 \\ 0 & 1 & 0 & 0 & 0 \end{bmatrix}$$

$$B = \begin{bmatrix} 0 & 0 & 0 & 0 & 0 \\ 0 & 0 & 0 & 0 & 0 \\ 0 & 0 & 0 & 0 & 0 \\ 0 & 0 & 0 & 1 & 0 \\ 0 & 0 & 0 & 0 & 1 \end{bmatrix}, \; C = \begin{bmatrix} \alpha\rho \\ \bar{i} - (\lambda\bar{\pi} + \mu\bar{y}) \\ -\kappa\bar{y} \\ 0 \\ 0 \end{bmatrix}$$

$$\Psi = \begin{bmatrix} 1 & 0 \\ 0 & 0 \\ 0 & 1 \\ 0 & 0 \\ 0 & 0 \end{bmatrix}, \; \Pi = \begin{bmatrix} 0 & 0 \\ 0 & 0 \\ 0 & 0 \\ 1 & 0 \\ 0 & 1 \end{bmatrix}$$

Armed with these definitions, the New Keynesian model is expressed as

$$AX_t = BX_{t-1} + \Psi U_t + \Pi W_t + C. \tag{8.1}$$

This is the *structural form* of the model. To find the reduced form, we write Eq. 8.1 as

$$X_t = A^{-1}BX_{t-1} + A^{-1}\Psi U_t + A^{-1}\Pi W_t + A^{-1}C, \tag{8.2}$$

and we seek a bounded solution to Eq. 8.2. There will be a unique bounded solution to this equation whenever two of the eigenvalues of $A^{-1}B$ are outside the unit circle. If $\mu = 0$, this occurs if $\lambda > 1$. When $\mu \neq 0$, the condition for uniqueness is a little more complicated.

When a unique solution exists it takes the form

$$\begin{cases} \pi_t = c_1 + \delta_{11}u_t^1 + \delta_{12}u_t^2 \\ y_t = c_2 + \delta_{21}u_t^1 + \delta_{22}u_t^2 \,, \\ i_t = c_3 + \delta_{31}u_t^1 + \delta_{32}u_t^2 \end{cases} \tag{8.3}$$

where the reduced form parameters c_i and δ_{ij} are functions of the structural parameters defined in Table A8.2.

9

THE FARMER MONETARY MODEL EXPLAINED

When the Fed raises the interest rate, the unemployment rate increases and, sometime later, the inflation rate falls. The causal mechanism from changes in the money interest rate to changes in inflation and the unemployment rate is called the *monetary transmission mechanism*. Monetary policymakers rely implicitly on a theory of the monetary transmission mechanism when they decide how to set the interest rate.

John Taylor, of the Taylor Rule, has argued that central banks should rely on an explicit formula that adjusts the interest rate mechanically in response to inflation and the output gap. Ben Bernanke, former chair of the Federal Reserve, disagrees.[1] These are family squabbles over degree, not substance. Every decision made by central bank policymakers is based on a mental model that is more or less formal and more or less complete. Although they may disagree over details, Taylor and Bernanke are both following the same mental model: New Keynesian economics.

Monetary Fairy Tales

According to New Keynesian economics, an increase in the money supply lowers the money interest rate and causes output to increase above trend and unemployment to fall below its natural rate. The immediate effect on the output gap and the unemployment rate occurs because frictions prevent wages and prices from adjusting quickly to their equilibrium levels.

After a period of time, when all wages and prices have had time to adjust, all changes in the money supply work their way into higher wages and prices, the output gap returns to zero, and unemployment returns to its natural rate. When a change in the stock of money in circulation does not influence economic activity in the long run, we say *money is neutral*.

Monetary neutrality is a fairy tale that economists have been telling themselves since the late eighteenth century, when David Hume gave a beautiful rendition of it in his delightful essay "Of Money."[2] But like all good fairy tales, it is pure fiction. Money is not neutral, even in the long run. Changes in the money interest rate have permanent effects on output and employment by shifting the economy from one long-run equilibrium to another. This chapter formalizes that idea.

The Equations of the Farmer Monetary Model

I have been critical of the New Keynesian model, but it takes a model to beat a model. If we are to reject New Keynesian economics, what are we to put in its place? Here, I describe my alternative.

The theory I describe first appeared in a conference volume in honor of Edmund Phelps.[3] To distinguish it from the work described in Chapter 6, in which I modeled unemployment in a model without money, I refer to the theory I explain here as the *Farmer Monetary Model*. In the Farmer Monetary Model, any unemployment rate can persist as a permanent, steady-state equilibrium and any steady-state inflation rate can coexist with any steady-state unemployment rate.

When I worked on this topic initially, I referred to my work as the *Old Keynesian model*, but events overtook me. A number of blogs appeared in which other writers started using the term *Old Keynesian model* to refer to a version of the IS-LM model of Alvin Hansen and Sir John Hicks.[4] Roman Frydman, one of the editors of the volume in which my work appeared, encouraged me to use the term *Farmer Monetary Model* to distinguish it from both the New Keynesian and Old Keynesian alternatives.

The Farmer Monetary Model has three equations: the Farmer Monetary IS Curve, the Taylor Rule, and the belief function. In the rest of this chapter, I describe each of these equations and use them to explain features of the US data the New Keynesian model cannot.

The Farmer Monetary Model IS Curve

The first equation of the Farmer Monetary Model is the Farmer Monetary IS Curve. It is similar to the New Keynesian IS Curve but, in contrast to the New Keynesian IS Curve, the Farmer Monetary IS Curve provides an endogenous explanation of why shocks to aggregate demand are persistent.

In the simplest New Keynesian model, the interest rate, GDP, and inflation move around in response to shocks to aggregate demand and aggregate supply. In the New Keynesian model, these variables do not display persistence. If GDP is 20% above trend this quarter, the basic New Keynesian model predicts it will be back on trend next quarter. In the real world, that is not what happens. If GDP is 20% above trend this quarter, it will most likely remain above trend next quarter. GDP, the inflation rate, and the interest rate on Treasury bills are all highly persistent.

The interest rate, adjusted for expected changes in the inflation rate, is called the *real interest rate*. The real interest rate can be measured in different ways. One measure is the inflation-adjusted interest rate on Treasury bills. That measure is computed by subtracting the expected inflation rate from the Treasury bill rate. For example, if Treasury bills are paying 5% and you expect prices will increase, on average, by 3% this year, the annualized expected real interest rate on Treasury bills is 2%.

We can compute the expected real interest rate for holding any asset. Just as there is an expected real interest rate for holding Treasury bills, so there is an expected real interest rate for holding five-year Treasury bonds and an expected real interest rate for holding equities. These rates are different from the real Treasury bill rate because the price of Treasury bonds and the average price of stocks are expected to be different in a year's time. The expected return you earn from holding an asset for one year is equal to the interest or dividend paid on the asset, plus the expected appreciation, or depreciation, in the asset's price.

The expected real rate on Treasury bills, the expected real rate on Treasury bonds, and the expected real rate on the stock market are all persistent in the data. To match this fact, the New Keynesian model assumes the IS curve is subject to persistent random shocks to the rate at which the representative agent discounts the future. These persistent *discount rate shocks* play an important role in the New Keynesian explanation for the Great Recession, but I have not yet seen a plausible and internally coherent economic explanation of where these shocks arise.

Persistent movements in the expected real interest rate in real-world data are reflected in persistent swings in consumer debt, house prices, and stock market wealth. The repeated pattern of asset price booms, the buildup of consumer debt, and the subsequent asset price crash is what Claudio Borio, of the Bank for International Settlements, calls the *financial cycle*. He refers to macroeconomic models without financial cycles as "Hamlet without the Prince of Denmark."[5] The New Keynesian model developed before the 2007 financial crisis cannot explain why some people borrow and other people lend because the representative agent is the only person in the model. It is a performance of Hamlet without the Prince.

Not everyone agrees with my assessment of the New Keynesian agenda. In a recent article, Marco Del Negro, Marc

Giannoni, and Frank Schorfheide claim to explain the Great Recession with a "standard DSGE model" that was "available prior to the recent crisis."[6] I am skeptical of their claim because, in their model, the principal driver of financial cycles is a persistent, unexplained preference shock. I would prefer an explanation in which persistence is part of the propagation mechanism. That is what I provide in my work.

In the Farmer Monetary Model, shocks to the real interest rate are persistent because people with different savings rates borrow and lend to each other, and because the identity of people trading in the asset markets changes as old people die and young people are born. An asset price bubble, like the one we saw in the 2000s, causes people to borrow and build up equity in houses or stocks. When the bubble bursts, the debt hangover takes borrowers many years to pay off.

In a recent popular book, Richard Koo developed a theory of "balance sheet recessions."[7] In his view, financial crises occur because some households and firms borrow too much and their net asset positions become unbalanced. Leverage in the expansion is excessive. My work explains why excess leverage occurs in a world of rational people. The people who participate in the markets are rational; the market equilibrium is not. According to my explanation, persistent asset price movements are Pareto inefficient because of incomplete participation in asset markets. Because equilibria are Pareto inefficient, an active macroprudential policy that stabilizes asset price movements will make everybody better off.[8]

The Taylor Rule

The second equation of the Farmer Monetary Model is the Taylor Rule, an explanation of central bank actions. According to the Taylor Rule, the central bank raises the interest rate in response to higher inflation and an increase in the output gap. This is the same equation that appears in the New Keynesian model described in Chapter 8.

The Farmer Monetary Model Belief Function

The third equation of the Farmer Monetary Model is the belief function. This equation replaces the Phillips Curve of New Keynesian theory. It explains how people form beliefs about the future value of their wealth and how much they decide to spend on goods and services.

I dispensed with the New Keynesian Phillips Curve because I find the microfoundations of this equation to be weak and unconvincing, and because the relationship between inflation and unemployment in the data has shifted over time. I presented the case against the Phillips Curve in Chapter 3.

Although I have dispensed with the Phillips Curve, I recognize the need to explain why changes in the interest rate precede changes in the unemployment rate. If the Fed were to raise the money interest rate on overnight loans, an increase in the unemployment rate would soon follow. The evidence from patterns of interest rates and unemployment in past data supports this conclusion overwhelmingly.

Correlation is not causation. New Keynesian economists believe an unanticipated increase in the money interest rate *causes* an increase in the unemployment rate. They cite the fact that nominal shocks have real effects, as evidence that prices are sticky, and they build price stickiness into their model by assuming some firms are not allowed to change their price in response to changes in aggregate demand.

I agree with the New Keynesians that an unanticipated increase in the money interest rate will cause an increase in the unemployment rate, but the assertion that because changes in nominal variables have real effects, therefore prices must be sticky, is a non sequitur. It is true money prices and money wages do not move rapidly in the data, but prices and wages are not sticky because firms face costs of reprinting their price lists, as some New Keynesian economists assume. They are sticky because beliefs about nominal variables are persistent.

When we decide how much to save and how to allocate our savings across different assets, we must form a guess about the resources that will be available to us in the future. The only reliable evidence we have to make such a guess is what has happened to us in the past. In principle, we could form detailed forecasts of the relative prices of all future goods. In practice, we use rules of thumb. To model this idea, I assume households and firms form expectations of nominal income growth by guessing that next period's nominal income growth will equal this period's nominal income growth. I call this relationship the *belief function*.[9]

Why this very simple functional form for beliefs? In a piece published in 2012, I estimated the Farmer Monetary Model and I used a theory proposed by Milton Friedman in his work on the consumption function to explain beliefs.[10] Friedman argued that people do what economists do; they predict the future using evidence from the past. He modeled that in an elegant way with a simple formula that he called "adaptive expectations."

If expectations are adaptive, beliefs about future income growth are formed by combining past beliefs with observed realizations in a way that may be more or less responsive to current data. In my empirical work using US data, I modeled expectations using a simple version of Friedman's adaptive expectations hypothesis.[11] I assumed people predict future nominal income growth by extrapolating from past nominal income growth and I found that a model, closed with that assumption, outperforms a model closed with the New Keynesian Phillips Curve. I call my simple adaptive forecast rule *the belief function*.

The Belief Function as a New Economic Fundamental

It's one thing to point out that nominal GDP growth is persistent and quite another to elevate an equation linking future to current nominal GDP growth to the status of a new fundamental equation, but this is exactly what I propose. In Chapter 6, I provided a Keynesian search model in which any unemployment rate can persist as the steady-state equilibrium of an economy in which all the people who populate that economy are rational and everybody has rational expectations of future prices. In that Keynesian search model, there are multiple stationary equilibrium unemployment rates. The existence of multiple rational expectations equilibria presents the theorist with a dilemma: he has failed to close the model.

For that reason, some have criticized the multiple equilibrium agenda. I reject that criticism. What sets the Farmer Monetary Model apart from previous classical or New Keynesian models is that, in my work, beliefs are fundamental. Beliefs have the same methodological status as preferences or technology in more familiar DSGE models.[12] And in a rational expectations model in which the belief function is fundamental, there is a unique equilibrium.

One might think that my insistence on modeling a belief function explicitly is irrelevant if I also require that expectations are rational.[13] In a model with a unique equilibrium, that argument would be correct; but, in a model with multiple stationary rational expectations equilibria, it is the belief function that selects which rational expectations equilibrium will prevail.

The Belief Function and Rational Expectations

During the 1960s, economists distinguished between the value of a future price and the expectation of what that price would be. For example, we might call the future price, P, and our belief about that price, P^E. Because we have added a new distinct variable, we must add another equation. We must explain *why* households and firms believe that P will be equal, next period, to P^E.

Initially, economists modeled expectations using adaptive expectations. When expectations are adaptive, households and firms adjust their expectation of the future price by combining their previous belief with new information.

The adaptive expectations assumption was swept away when Robert Lucas showed how to introduce random elements into economic models in a way that is consistent with rational choice.[14] He claimed prices are different from expected prices because all economic variables are random. We cannot know the future with certainty, but we *can* make educated guesses. And although we would not expect the realization of the price in every period is always equal to our best guess, that guess should not be biased systematically. According to the rational expectations hypothesis, we may not know the future price with certainty, but we do know the urn from which it is drawn.

The replacement of adaptive expectations with rational expectations was heralded as a triumph of economic science. Previous models of expectations had posited an ad hoc adaptive rule. Rational expectations replaced this ad hoc rule with a scientific theory of beliefs. Rational agents, acting in a stationary environment, would soon come to learn the truth. Whenever they see event X they should expect the price would be equal to a number $P(X)$. And because X is a random variable, so is $P(X)$.

Slipped into the theory of rational expectations, unnoticed by all but a few, was the assumption that the rational expectations equilibrium is unique. That assumption is very far from being innocuous. Uniqueness of equilibrium is a very special property that does not hold in general, even in the canonical model of microeconomics developed by Kenneth Arrow and Gerard Debreu.[15] But at least in the Arrow–Debreu model, there are only finitely many equilibria.

An economic model might predict that, if the Fed behaves in a certain way, the only equilibrium outcome would be an inflation rate of 3%. In that case, we would say that equilibrium is unique. It is more common for there to be multiple possible outcomes associated with a given policy. For example, if the Fed acts in a certain way, it might be that the inflation rate could be 3%, but it could also be 7%. In that case, we would say that there are two equilibria.

The case of multiple equilibria is inconvenient, but it does not invalidate standard arguments economists use to predict the outcome of a change in policy. Whichever equilibrium prevails in practice, a small change in economic policy should lead to a small change in the outcome. If the equilibrium inflation rate is 3%, then a policy tightening might cause it to increase to 3.1%. If it is 7%, the same policy tightening might cause it to increase to 7.1%. But, when one recognizes that people die and new people are born, and who can deny that fact, the situation becomes different.[16] In these models (called *overlapping generations models*) there are often infinitely many equilibria. If an inflation rate of 3% in 2011 is an equilibrium, and an inflation rate of 7%, in the same year, is also an equilibrium, then so is any inflation rate between 3% and 7%.

How should we deal with that inconvenient truth? We must ask: How would a rational human being act if placed into an environment where, according to the economist, there are multiple possible ways in which it would be rational for him to act? And to answer that question, we need to return to the economics of the 1950s. Rational human beings do exactly what economists would do when faced with a forecasting problem; they extrapolate from what they have observed in the past.

More on Balls and Cigars

The Farmer Monetary Model, like the New Keynesian model, is a DSGE model and to find the predictions of the model, we must first find its reduced form. Like the New Keynesian model, the reduced form of the Farmer Monetary Model is a system of equations that describes how the current values of the interest rate, the inflation rate, and the output gap depend on their own past values and shocks to the equations of the model.

The reduced form of the New Keynesian model is a set of equations called a *vector-autoregression*. The word *vector* means a list of variables. The word *autoregression* means these variables depend on their own past values. The nature of their dependence on the past is uncovered by a statistical technique called *regression analysis*.

A vector-autoregression contains two parts that match Ragnar Frisch's description of an impulse and a propagation mechanism that we met in Chapter 2. The impulse is captured by a set of random variables called *shocks*, which are assumed to hit the system during every period. These shocks are like Frisch's child with the club. The propagation mechanism is captured by the coefficients of the equations that define the vector-autoregression. These are numbers that are assumed to be constant. They are the economic analog of the structure of Frisch's rocking horse.

Suppose we were to shut down all the shocks in a DSGE model and ask: How do the variables behave? In the New Keynesian model, the interest rate, the inflation rate, and the output gap would return relatively quickly to their steady-state values. At the steady state, the output gap is zero and the unemployment rate is constant and equal to its natural rate. These facts reflect the fact that the New Keynesian model incorporates the NRH. The other variables of the New Keynesian model would return to unique values defined by the structure of preferences and technology.[17]

What of the Farmer Monetary Model? Here, things are different. If we shut off the shocks and try to solve for the steady state, we are left with only two equations with which to explain three variables. The Taylor Rule and the Farmer Monetary IS Curve give us two steady-state equations in these variables, but the belief function does not deliver a third. This equation asserts that the current growth rate of nominal GDP is equal to the expected future growth rate of nominal GDP. In a stationary state, this could be true for any growth rate and for any inflation rate. The fact that we have two equations to determine three variables implies the model has a continuum of possible steady-state values.

Economists have a name for dynamic models that do not converge to a steady state; they are called vector error correction models or VECMs. The time path of the variables of a VECM is well defined for any initial value, but the system does not converge to a unique point. Where it ends up depends on where it started.[18] When a VECM is hit by a sequence of shocks, the variables wander with no tendency to return to a point. But, their wanderings are not aimless; they can never wander too far from each other.

In Chapter 8, I distinguished between data that cluster around a ball and data that cluster around a cigar. The data resemble a long fat cigar; they do not resemble a ball. That behavior is captured by a VECM and that is why the Farmer Monetary Model is a better fit to the facts than the New Keynesian model.

Explaining Data with the New Keynesian and Farmer Monetary Models

Economists predict the future path of the inflation rate and the output gap by simulating the future using a model estimated from past data. The Fed uses the Federal Reserve Board, FRB/US model, the Bank of England uses COMPASS, and the European Central Bank uses the New-Area-Wide Model. All these systems of equations have the New Keynesian model at their core. It is important, not only for the purpose of prediction, but also as a guide to policymakers, that the model by which they are informed is the right one.

The New Keynesian and Farmer Monetary Models make very different predictions about the behavior of the inflation rate and the unemployment rate over the business cycle. To figure out which one is better, I compared both models with economic data and investigated their properties. I showed that the Farmer Monetary Model, closed with a belief function, does a better job of explaining the data.[19] Why might that be?

A good explanation of the data requires a model in which there is not just one source of persistence; there must be two. In the Farmer Monetary Model, the real interest rate is persistent because people spend less when they are heavily in debt and it takes time for their debts to be repaid. The unemployment rate is persistent because there is no stabilizing force returning unemployment to its natural rate. The Farmer Monetary Model provides a better description of the data than the New Keynesian model because the real interest rate and the unemployment rate are both highly persistent and, in the US data, the unemployment rate is not just persistent, it is nonstationary.

I do not want to claim too much for the ability of data to distinguish one theory from another. A researcher who is wedded to the New Keynesian model could explain the data equally well by adapting the protective belt of his theory while maintaining the key assumptions of the neoclassical synthesis and the NRH. For example, a New Keynesian could drop the assumption that the natural rate of unemployment is constant and replace it with the assumption that the natural rate of unemployment is a random walk. That is the route taken by Robert J. Gordon in a recent paper that defends the ability of a backward-looking version of the Phillips Curve to explain the data.[20] Although past data can be explained quite well by a model in which the natural rate of unemployment is a random walk, it is not, in my view, a plausible description of the slow recovery from the Great Recession.

The Farmer Monetary Model assumes the economy may drift arbitrarily far away from the natural rate of unemployment because of persistence in the way people form beliefs. The New Keynesian model can explain the same data only by assuming the natural rate of unemployment has changed. If one were to choose this route to rescue the New Keynesian model, one would be forced to conclude youth unemployment in Greece was still more than 50% in 2015 because the social planner chose to leave large numbers of young people unemployed. Temporary high deviations of unemployment from its natural rate can be explained by sticky prices—persistent high deviations cannot.

Two Important Differences between the New Keynesian and Farmer Monetary Models

The differences between the New Keynesian model and the Farmer Monetary Model are not just a difference of degree. They are differences of substance. There are two substantial differences, one of which is more significant than the other.

First, the Farmer Monetary Model contains an explanation for fluctuations in the real interest rate grounded in microeconomic theory. I explain why this variable is persistent and I explain why movements in the real interest rate are Pareto inefficient and should be counteracted by active policy.

Second, the Farmer Monetary Model denies the NRH. It replaces the Phillips Curve with the assumption that beliefs about future expected nominal growth are equal to current realized nominal income growth. To make sense of the assumption that beliefs are fundamental, I draw on the theory of multiple equilibrium unemployment rates I explained in Chapter 6. In the Farmer Monetary Model, any quantity of goods demanded will be supplied and, as in Keynes' General Theory, the unemployment rate adjusts to produce a sufficient quantity of goods to meet aggregate demand.

The first of these differences is not inconsistent with New Keynesian economics. A committed New Keynesian could take the theory of incomplete participation in asset markets that I described in Chapter 1 and graft it onto the New Keynesian model, closed with a Phillips Curve. Seen in that light, my work on incomplete asset market participation is a complement to a large body of literature that studies asset market frictions. It provides a compelling reason to explain why the Fed should be concerned not just about the inflation rate, but also about asset prices.

The second difference in my work, denial of the NRH, is fundamental. I claim there is a structural problem with New Keynesian theory. The economy is not self-correcting as the New Keynesian model implies. My reason for making this claim is that it is difficult, if not impossible, to find evidence for a stable Phillips Curve in data without resorting to the assumption that the natural rate of unemployment is itself moving in unpredictable ways over time. That may be a palatable assumption during the period of the Great Moderation, when the US unemployment rate remained below 7.5%; however, it is much harder to square with episodes of long depressions.

Conclusion

The ebb and flow of the markets is like the ebb and flow of the tides. Tenth-century Norse ruler King Canute is reputed to have sat on the seashore and commanded Neptune to cease the movements of the waves. On discovering his folly, Canute proclaimed the power of kings to be worthless and he hung up his crown. Although I commend the good king for recognizing his impotence, it would be a mistake for central bankers to draw the same lesson from their failure to prevent the Great Recession.

The asset markets are volatile because most of the people who are affected by asset price fluctuations are unable to trade in the markets for a simple reason. The markets open before they are born. The fact that individuals cannot trade in markets would not matter if there were no operative transfer between current and future generations, but there is such a transfer. When the price level falls, the value of government debt increases. That debt is held by existing generations. It is repaid by our children and our grandchildren.

During the 2008 financial crisis, the Federal Reserve bought large quantities of long-dated and risky assets, and it is widely believed those purchases were instrumental in lessening the severity of the recession. Before leaving office in 2014, the then-chair of the Fed, Ben Bernanke, was asked if he was confident in advance if this policy, dubbed *quantitative easing* or *QE*, would be effective. Mr. Bernanke replied: "The problem with QE is it works in practice, but it doesn't work in theory."

I explained in Chapter 7 why QE works in theory. The central bank, acting in conjunction with the Treasury, can influence asset prices because they are able to make the trades that the unborn would make if they could participate in prenatal financial markets. In Chapter 11, I provide a detailed proposal for how to put that idea into practice.

Appendix 9A: A Parable of a Financial Crisis

This appendix uses the model I developed in this chapter to provide a parable of a financial crisis.

Real economies are populated by many different types of people. To move beyond the representative agent, but still maintain a tractable model, I suppose there are two types of people: patient and impatient.

People of both types are born and die but only those currently alive in a given year are able to participate in the asset markets. To make a rational choice about how much to borrow and how much to lend, patient and impatient people must form a guess about the income they will earn throughout the course of their lifetimes. That guess is summarized by what Friedman called *permanent income*.[21] It is the discounted present value of future income. I assume both types have the same permanent income.

During every period, permanent income may go up by X dollars with probability p or it may go down by Y dollars with probability $(1-p)$. I assume

$$pX + (1-p)Y = 0.$$

In words, everybody expects that next period's permanent income will be the same as this period's permanent income.

But people are not certain about the realization of their permanent income. Things might get better or they might get worse.[22]

Because patient and impatient people will save a different amount of their permanent income, each group will benefit from trading with the other in the asset markets. What will those trades look like?

Because there are only two events in any given period, complete insurance requires only two assets: equity and debt. The first is a claim to permanent income. I call this claim *equity*. Equity pays an excess return of X in one state and Y in the other. The second is a promise to pay $1 next period for certain. I call this claim *debt*. Debt has a zero excess return in both states. Because they have different propensities to save out of permanent income, patient and impatient people will take different positions in these two assets.

There is a third player in the financial markets: government. Government is a net borrower but it does not hold equity. Government debt is, instead, backed by its ability to levy taxes on current and future generations.

Much of macroeconomics is based on the unrealistic assumption that government debt does not represent net wealth to the economy. Government debt is not net wealth in models where there is a single representative agent because the value of debt is offset exactly by the net present value of tax obligations. If government borrows today and uses the proceeds of the loan to lower taxes, it must raise taxes at some date in the future to repay the loan. In the representative agent world, this action simply redistributes the timing of taxes.

The real world is not well described by a single representative agent. Not only do people differ in their impatience, as I assume in this parable, they are born and they die. Government debt is net wealth because, if government borrows and distributes the proceeds to those of us alive today, our children and our grandchildren will be saddled with higher taxes to repay the debt. That fact explains why a decrease in the dollar value of next period's permanent income will have real consequences for the people alive today. It represents a transfer of the tax burden of the debt from current to future generations. Irving Fisher called this transfer *debt deflation*.[23]

In my parable, I assume away all financial frictions. When a person is born, he may trade in a complete set of financial markets. He is completely insured over all possible future realizations of shock to his permanent income. And, permanent income depends on the entire history of shocks. If a person is lucky enough to be born at a time when permanent income is high, he will enjoy a permanently high claim on the resources of the economy for the rest of his life. If he is born in a recession, he will be condemned to a lifetime of poverty.

Permanent income, in this parable, is synonymous with the stock market. I asserted the stock market goes up by X dollars with probability p and it goes down by Y dollars with probability $1 - p$. What enforces those movements?

Patient and impatient people read the financial press and they are aware a particular financial journalist, I call him Mr. W, is good at forecasting the economy. Mr. W writes only two types of articles: optimistic pieces and pessimistic pieces. In the past, every time Mr. W has written an optimistic piece, the value of the stock market has increased by X dollars; every time he has written a pessimistic piece, it has fallen by Y dollars. The people of this economy expect this track record to continue. Furthermore, everybody yet to be born will learn from their parents that they too should believe the writings of Mr. W.

Mr. W is an optimistic type of fellow who predicts the market will increase most of the time. When Mr. W's articles are optimistic, I say the economy is in normal times.

In normal times, equity earns an excess return of X. The relative net wealth of borrowers, who invest their borrowing in the stock market, will increase at the expense of lenders. These are periods when we see bull markets, increasing GDP, and falling unemployment rates. Periods of booming asset markets and increasing nominal GDP are periods of falling unemployment because central banks channel part of nominal GDP growth into an increase in real aggregate demand and part into persistent increases in expected inflation.

But all good things come to an end. The excess returns earned by borrowers during the bull market will be followed eventually by a reversal of sentiment. Mr. W will, eventually, write a pessimistic piece and, when this happens, the stock market will drop by Y dollars. The fact that Mr. W is an optimistic fellow means that p is close to one. Booms are persistent because market participants are optimistic about the economy most of the time. And because booms are persistent, the crash, when it occurs, will be large. Y is bigger than X by the amount $p/(1-p)$.

In this narrative, the crash is rational and anticipated by everyone in the markets—only its timing is uncertain. Borrowers earn an excess return of X when the economy was growing and they incur a loss of Y in a crash.

Why do we care about a market crash if there is a complete set of insurance markets?

A crash is bad for two reasons. First, new generations who are born in a recession are worse off because the present value of their lifetime income is lower than if they had been born into a boom. Second, in the presence of incomplete labor markets, central banks are unable to stabilize real economic activity completely. When nominal income falls, part of that fall is translated into a reduction in the aggregate demand for goods and services, and an increase in the unemployment rate.

Appendix 9B: The Equations of the Farmer Monetary Model

This appendix lays out the equations of the Farmer Monetary Model for comparison purposes with the New Keynesian model from Chapter 8.

The variables the Farmer Monetary Model explains are the money interest rate, GDP per person, the inflation rate, and the expectations at date t of the growth rate of nominal GDP between periods t and $t + 1$. Table A9B.1 defines symbols for each of these variables. For the exposition in this appendix I assume the central bank targets a constant level of potential GDP per person.

The Farmer Monetary Model is characterized by the seven parameters defined in Table A9B.2. These parameters are assumed to be constant.

The model is driven by two fundamental shocks and it contains one nonfundamental shock solved for endogenously after imposing the rational expectations assumption. The shocks are defined in Table A9B.3.

Table A9B.1 Variables of the Farmer Monetary Model

Variable Symbol	Variable Name
i_t	The money interest rate at date t
y_t	The log of GDP per person at date t
π_t	The percentage change in the consumer price index between dates $t - 1$ and t
$x_t = \pi_t + y_t - y_{t-1}$	The growth rate of nominal GDP per person between dates $t - 1$ and t
$E_t[x_{t+1}]$	The expectation of growth in nominal GDP per person from t to $t + 1$

Table A9B.2 Parameters of the Farmer Monetary Model

Parameter Symbol	Parameter Name
ρ	Discount rate of the representative agent
$\bar{\pi}$	Inflation target
$\bar{y}$	The log of central bank's GDP target
λ	Inflation coefficient of Taylor Rule
μ	Output gap coefficient of Taylor Rule
η	Persistence of real interest rate shocks
$\bar{i}$	Interest rate target

Table A9B.3 Fundamental and Nonfundamental Shocks

Shock Symbol	Shock Name
u_t^1	The fundamental shock to aggregate demand at date t
u_t^2	The fundamental shock to beliefs at date t
w_t	The nonfundamental nominal GDP forecast error

Table A9B.4 Equations of the Farmer Monetary Model

Equation in Symbols	Equation Name
$i_t = E_t[x_{t+1}] - \eta(i_{t-1} - E_{t-1}[x_t]) + \rho + u_t^1$	The FM-IS Curve
$i_t = \bar{i} + \lambda(\pi_t - \bar{\pi}) + \mu(y_t - \bar{y})$	The Taylor Rule
$E_t[x_{t+1}] = x_t + u_t^2$	The belief function
$w_t = \pi_t + y_t - y_{t-1} - E_{t-1}[x_t]$	Definition of the nominal GDP forecast shock
$x_t = \pi_t + y_t - y_{t-1}$	The growth rate of nominal GDP per person between dates $t-1$ and t

Table A9B.4 defines the equations of the model. The first three are symbolic representations of the Farmer Monetary Investment Equals Savings (FM-IS) Curve, the Taylor Rule, and the belief function; the fourth equation is the definition of the single endogenous forecast error; and the fifth equation is a definition of x_t.

By defining matrices A, B, C, Ψ, and $\amalg\!\!\amalg$; and vectors of variables X, U, and W, the model can be written more compactly as a vector-valued difference equation. These matrices and variable are defined as follows:

$$X_t = \left[\pi_t, y_t, i_t, E_t[x_{t+1}]\right]^T$$

$$U_t = \left[u_t^1, u_t^2\right]^T, \quad W_t = w_t.$$

Here, the superscript T is the transpose operator. Using the definitions of x_t and w_t, we can rewrite the FM-IS Curve and the belief function as follows:

$$i_t + \eta\pi_t + \eta y_t - E_t[x_{t+1}] = \eta i_{t-1} + \eta y_{t-1} + \rho + u_t^1 + \eta w_t \qquad (9.1)$$

$$\pi_t + y_t - E(x_{t+1}) = y_{t-1} - u_t^2 \qquad (9.2)$$

$$A = \begin{bmatrix} \eta & \eta & 1 & -1 \\ -\lambda & -\mu & 1 & 0 \\ 1 & 1 & 0 & -1 \\ 1 & 1 & 0 & 0 \end{bmatrix}$$

$$B = \begin{bmatrix} 0 & \eta & \eta & 0 \\ 0 & 0 & 0 & 0 \\ 0 & 1 & 0 & 0 \\ 0 & 1 & 0 & 1 \end{bmatrix}, C = \begin{bmatrix} \rho \\ i - (\lambda\bar{\pi} + \mu\bar{y}) \\ 0 \\ 0 \end{bmatrix}$$

$$\Psi = \begin{bmatrix} 1 & 0 \\ 0 & 0 \\ 0 & -1 \\ 0 & 0 \end{bmatrix}, \Pi = \begin{bmatrix} \eta \\ 0 \\ 0 \\ 1 \end{bmatrix}$$

Using these definitions, the Farmer Monetary Model is expressed in Eq. 9.3:

$$AX_t = BX_{t-1} + \Psi U_t + \Pi W_t + C. \qquad (9.3)$$

This is the *structural form* of the model. To find the reduced form, we write Eq. 9.3 as

$$X_t = A^{-1}BX_{t-1} + A^{-1}\Psi U_t + A^{-1}\Pi W_t + A^{-1}C, \qquad (9.4)$$

and we seek a bounded solution. There will be a unique bounded solution to this equation whenever one of the eigenvalues of $A^{-1}B$ is outside the unit circle. The roots of this equation are 0, 1, η, and $\lambda/(\lambda - \mu)$. Because the first three roots are on or inside the unit circle, uniqueness requires that

$$\left|\frac{\lambda}{\lambda - \mu}\right| > 1. \tag{9.5}$$

The unique equilibrium has a very different reduced form from the New Keynesian model. It is described by the equations

$$\begin{cases}
\pi_t = c_1 + \gamma_{12}y_{t-1} + \gamma_{13}i_{t-1} + \gamma_{14}E_{t-1}[x_t] + \delta_{11}u_t^1 + \delta_{12}u_1^2 \\
y_t = c_2 + \gamma_{22}y_{t-1} + \gamma_{23}i_{t-1} + \gamma_{24}E_{t-1}[x_t] + \delta_{21}u_t^1 + \delta_{22}u_1^2 \\
i_t = c_3 + \gamma_{32}y_{t-1} + \gamma_{33}i_{t-1} + \gamma_{34}E_{t-1}[x_t] + \delta_{31}u_t^1 + \delta_{32}u_1^2 \\
E_t[x_{t+1}] = c_4 + \gamma_{42}y_{t-1} + \gamma_{43}i_{t-1} + \gamma_{44}E_{t-1}[x_t] + \delta_{41}u_t^1 + \delta_{42}u_1^2
\end{cases} \tag{9.6}$$

Recall the reduced form of the New Keynesian model was the system of Eq. 8.3, which I reproduce here as Eq. 9.7:

$$\begin{cases}
\pi_t = c_1 + \delta_{11}u_t^1 + \delta_{12}u_t^2 \\
y_t = c_2 + \delta_{21}u_t^1 + \delta_{22}u_t^2 \\
i_t = c_3 + \delta_{31}u_t^1 + \delta_{32}u_t^2
\end{cases} \tag{9.7}$$

There are two important differences between these two reduced forms. The most important difference is that $E_{t-1}(x_t)$, which represents beliefs about the growth rate of nominal GDP per person, is a state variable. Beliefs are generated by a random walk, hit by the belief shock u_t^2.

The second difference between these systems is the money interest rate is a state variable, which is persistent and mean reverting. Models in this class can be estimated using standard software packages such as DYNARE, using the method described in "Solving and Estimating Indeterminate DSGE Models", (Farmer, et al. 2015).

10

KEYNESIAN ECONOMICS WITHOUT THE CONSUMPTION FUNCTION

I began thinking about multiple equilibria as of a way of understanding Keynesian economics more than thirty-five years ago. My early work was part of an exciting new agenda that began during the 1980s at the University of Pennsylvania and at CEPREMAP and École Polytechnique in Paris.[1] The important ideas that developed at that time were that multiple equilibria matter, and that animal spirits and self-fulfilling prophecies are important independent drivers of business cycles.

The early work on self-fulfilling prophecies, however, was affected by some of the same problems that beset New Keynesian economics. Researchers who worked on multiple equilibria, animal spirits, and self-fulfilling prophecies adopted the assumption of Robert Lucas, that all markets are always in equilibrium all of the time. I made that same assumption in some of my own work because I felt it was important to choose your battles. It was hard enough to persuade other economists that beliefs matter, without trying, simultaneously, to fight on a second front. With the benefit of hindsight, it was a mistake to accept Lucas' argument for continuous labor market clearing.

I have always been uncomfortable with the idea that there is a unique steady-state unemployment rate,[2] and in 2005 I began to think about how to combine the idea that animal spirits drive business cycles with models where there are multiple steady-state unemployment rates.[3] That research culminated in the ideas I described in Chapter 6, and it forms a dividing line between what I call first- and second-generation models of endogenous business cycles.[4] The ideas I describe in this chapter were first developed in my 2008 paper "Aggregate Demand and Supply."[5]

Knocking over the Rocking Horse

In first-generation endogenous business-cycle models, animal spirits are one of many impulses to the business cycle. Using Ragnar Frisch's metaphor, animal spirits are one more disturbance that causes the child with the club to pound on the rocking horse. In that regard, it is no different from labor stoppages, new inventions, hurricanes, or unanticipated monetary shocks. The rocking horse always returns to the same rest point. In second-generation endogenous business-cycle models, the animal spirits shock is so violent that it can knock over the horse.

When I began work on the connection between animal spirits and steady-state unemployment rates, I thought I would be creating a new foundation for Keynesian economics. An outcome of my research would be that a policy of large-scale fiscal expansion, of the kind advocated forcibly by some prominent New Keynesian economists, would arise naturally in a Keynesian model with sound microfoundations. I realized, after much hard thought, I was wrong. This chapter describes how I came to that conclusion.

I break my argument into two parts. First, I deal with the *theory* of fiscal policy in the Keynesian model. How is it *supposed* to work? I describe an important concept that has dominated the political debate for the past eight years: the Keynesian theory of the multiplier. Second, I deal with empirical evidence for and against the effectiveness of fiscal policy. This topic has generated more heat than light. Most of the arguments that fiscal policy is effective have more to do with the political priors of the protagonists than with hard scientific evidence.

The Keynesian Cross and the Multiplier

Figure 10.1 goes by the name of the *Keynesian cross*. On the horizontal axis, I plotted income—the value of all wages, rents, and profits earned from producing goods and services in a given year. On the vertical axis, I plotted expenditure—the value of all expenditures on goods and services produced in the economy in a given year. And because all the goods produced generate income for someone, income and expenditure are also equal to GDP.[6] In Table 10.1 I express this idea as an equation called the *circular flow of income*.

Figure 10.1 contains two upward-sloping lines. The dash-dot line labeled $X = Y$, plots all points for which income is equal to expenditure. In Keynesian economics, this line is an aggregate

Table 10.1 The Circular Flow of Income

Income = Expenditure = GDP

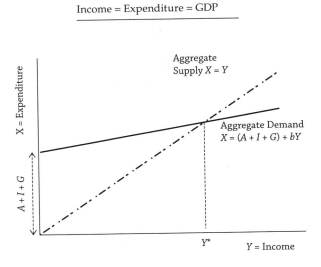

Figure 10.1 The Keynesian Cross.

supply curve. It represents the assumption that whatever is demanded will be supplied. In Chapter 6, I provided a Keynesian search theory, based on the behavior of profit-maximizing firms, that explains the theoretical foundation for this assumption.

The solid line plots planned expenditure on the vertical axis against income on the horizontal axis. This is the Keynesian aggregate demand curve.[7] As we move up the aggregate demand curve, every horizontal movement to the right, of $1 in income, is met by a vertical increase of b dollars in planned expenditure. The increase in planned expenditure is less than the increase in income because consumers spend a fraction b of every additional dollar of income. The fraction b is called the *marginal propensity to consume*. A represents the part of consumption independent of income, I is investment, G is government purchases, X is planned expenditure, and Y is income.

If income is always equal to expenditure, what makes the intersection of the two lines special? The answer lies is in the distinction between expenditure and *planned* expenditure. Included in the definition of investment expenditure is the unplanned accumulation of inventories. If Toyota builds 100,000 cars in Kentucky, but only 60,000 are sold, the 40,000 unsold cars are counted as unplanned investment. The 60,000 sold cars are counted as durable consumption goods.

If investment is greater than planned investment, inventories will fall, firms will hire more workers, and income will rise. If investment is less than planned investment, inventories will rise, firms will lay off workers, and income will fall. The intersection of aggregate demand and aggregate supply is the only point where income equals planned expenditure and it is the only point where firms have no incentive to change the number of people they employ.

There is no necessary reason why the point where the intersection of the aggregate demand and aggregate supply curves should be associated with full employment, and most of the time it won't be. If investors decide spontaneously to build fewer factories, the aggregate demand curve will shift down and equilibrium income will fall. If investors decide spontaneously to build more factories, the aggregate demand curve will shift up and equilibrium income will rise. Because higher income means more people employed, an increase in investment, as a result of optimistic expectations, will cause a reduction in the unemployment rate.

If investment increases by $100,000, how much will equilibrium income increase? Will it also increase by $100,000? Or will it increase by more? The answer is the amount of the increase in income depends on the value of the multiplier. The *multiplier* is the percentage increase in equilibrium income for a given percentage increase in investment expenditure.

For example, if the multiplier is 2, every dollar of new investment will generate an increase of $2 of extra income. Higher investment expenditure will generate new jobs, and the newly employed people will buy goods and generate even more new jobs.[8] The multiplier is the ratio of the final increase in income to the initial increase in investment.

The Multiplier and the Great Depression

Keynes used the theory of the multiplier to provide an explanation of the Great Depression. Figure 10.2 is a graphical depiction of his explanation. The upward-sloping solid line represents aggregate demand in 1929 before the stock market crash. The upward-sloping dashed line represents aggregate demand in 1932, after the stock market crash. The dashed line is lower than the solid line because between 1929 and 1932, investment expenditure fell precipitously. How big were government purchases, investment, and GDP in the data?

Table 10.2 shows the magnitude of the crash between 1929 and 1932. I am measuring GDP, investment, government purchases, and consumption using the money wage as my unit of measurement, and I divided the entire series by the size of the labor force. When I measure variables this way, I say they are measured in wage units per person.[9]

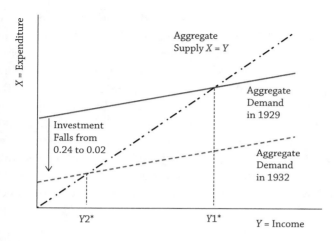

Figure 10.2 Keynes' Explanation for the Great Depression.

Table 10.2 Investment Spending in the Great Depression

Year	GDP	Investment	Government Purchases	Consumption
1929	1.5	0.24	0.14	1.12
1932	1.02	0.02	0.15	0.85

In 1929, GDP in wage units per person was equal to 1.5. In practical terms, this means the value of all the goods and services produced in the United States in 1929 was 1.5 times the value of the labor used to produce it. The additional 0.5 wage units represent the contribution of land and capital to the production of goods.

Between 1929 and 1932, investment expenditure fell from 0.24 wage units to 0.02 wage units. That drop in investment is represented in Figure 10.2 by the downward shift in the aggregate demand curve. As the aggregate demand curve shifted downward, the intersection of aggregate demand and aggregate supply moved to the left. Table 10.2 shows GDP fell from 1.5 wage units in 1929 to 1.02 wage units in 1932. This is represented on Figure 10.2 by the shift from the point labeled $Y1^*$ to the point labeled $Y2^*$ where the star notation indicates that this is an equilibrium point.

Table 10.2 also shows the fall in GDP between 1929 and 1932 was larger than the fall in investment. GDP fell by 0.48 wage units, but investment fell by only 0.22 wage units. According to the Keynesian theory of the multiplier, this is because consumption depends on income. As investment fell, so consumption also fell. Every dollar of reduced consumption expenditure led to an additional decrease in income of b dollars, where b is the marginal propensity to consume. In the data, b is equal to 0.54.

The Wartime Recovery from the Great Depression

Keynes did not just provide an explanation for the Great Depression. He provided a way for government to restore full employment. Government must replace the lost investment spending with government spending. Figure 10.3 shows how this is supposed to work. The dashed line in this figure is aggregate demand in 1932 during the depth of the Depression. The upper solid line is the aggregate demand curve in 1945, after the increase in government purchases that financed

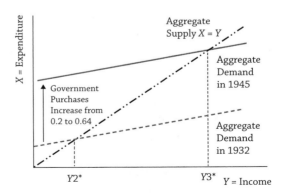

Figure 10.3 Keynes' Remedy for the Great Depression.

Table 10.3 Government Spending in WWII

Year	GDP	Investment	Government Purchases	Consumption
1938	1.24	0.1	0.2	0.93
1945	1.53	0.07	0.64	0.82

WWII. Government purchases increased steadily during the 1930s. But the increase was dwarfed by the size of government as the United States entered the war.

Table 10.3 shows that, in 1938, on the eve of the war, government purchases in wage units were equal to 0.2 and they increased to 0.64 wage unit in 1945. This increase in the size of government in the economy was massive and unprecedented. It represented an increase of 32% of GDP in just seven years.

Government purchases as a percentage of GDP went from 16% in 1938 to 48% in 1945. This huge increase in the size of government heralded the end of the Great Depression.

Figure 10.4 plots real GDP and government purchases per person beginning in 1929 and ending in 1950. The solid line, measured on the right scale, is GDP and the dashed line, measured on the left scale, is government purchases. The gray shaded areas, and the vertical line in 1945, are recessions. This figure shows government purchases did not increase substantially until the outbreak of WWII in Europe in 1939.

In 1935, Franklin Delano Roosevelt's administration passed the Emergency Relief Appropriations Act in an attempt to create jobs. Figure 10.4 shows that this Act had little or no effect and, before 1940, there *was* no stimulus. Government purchases did increase during that period, but it was not until the United States ramped up expenditures to pay for WWII that the economy fully recovered from the Depression.

Was the increase in government expenditure a good thing? Is it a policy that we should make use of to combat recessions

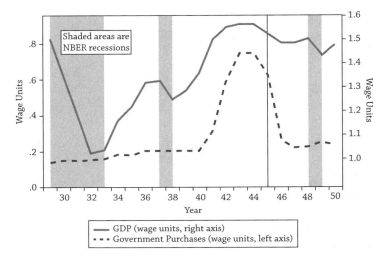

Figure 10.4 Gross Domestic Product (GDP) and Government Purchases per Person from 1929 to 1950. NBER, National Bureau of Economic Research.

Source: US Department of Commerce and author's calculations.

in normal times? I do not believe so. A massive fiscal expansion made a lot of sense in WWII when the United States was involved in a major World War. It makes less sense in peacetime. The increase in the size of government in wartime was enough to restore full employment. But the spending that had been carried out in 1929 by the private sector was carried out in 1945 by the government. The United States cured the unemployment problem by putting unemployed people into the US Army.

The Keynesian Consumption Function Is Not There in the Data

Natural scientists test their theories by experimenting. They hold all but one variable constant and then vary that one variable to trace its effects. Economists cannot do this. As much as we would like to experiment with fiscal and monetary policy, to see what happens, there are very good reasons not to play games with people's lives. This is why the evidence from big

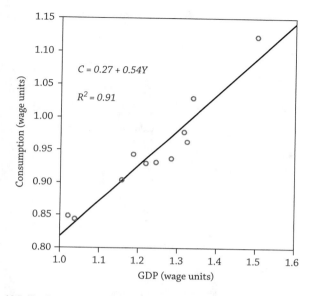

$C = 0.27 + 0.54Y$

$R^2 = 0.91$

Figure 10.5 The Consumption Function during the Great Depression (1929–1939). GDP, gross domestic product.

Source: US Department of Commerce and author's calculations.

events such as WWII, the Great Depression, and the Great Recession are so important. They are large *natural* experiments.

In Figure 10.5 I plotted consumption against GDP for 1929 through 1939. This graph shows clearly that consumption moves with GDP, and the marginal propensity to consume, which is the slope of this graph, is approximately 0.54. This graph suggests the Keynesian theory of the multiplier is on track.

I have added a measure, called the R^2 *coefficient*, to the graph. R^2 is a number that measures how well a straight line explains the data. The value of R^2 varies between zero if a theory has no explanatory power and one if the fit is perfect. For the data in Figure 10.5, the R^2 value is 0.91, reflecting the fact that the model explains 91% of the data. The consumption function fits the data well during the Great Depression.

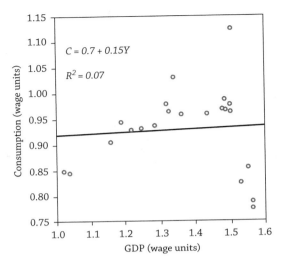

Figure 10.6 The Consumption Function from 1929 to 1950.

Source: US Department of Commerce and author's calculations.

What about the effect of government purchases during WWII? In Figure 10.6, I supplied additional data to Figure 10.5 from WWII. What we should see, if Keynesian theory is correct, is that these additional data points lie around the same line I fitted to the data from the Great Depression. The huge movements in government purchases during the war should cause independent movements in GDP. These independent movements in GDP should cause consumption to vary in response.

The facts are very different. Figure 10.6 shows the consumption function that had remained stable during the Great Depression falls apart when we add in data from WWII. An R^2 value of 0.91 in Figure 10.5 turns into an R^2 value of 0.07 in Figure 10.6, implying the consumption function explains only 7% of the movements in the data.

Consumption Depends on Wealth, Not on Income

During the 1950s and 1960s, economists began to evaluate the ability of the consumption function to explain data. They used two methods to estimate the marginal propensity to consume. One method used a cross-section of incomes at a point in time. The second method used data on aggregate consumption and aggregate income over a number of years. The outcome of that research was that consumption is explained better by wealth than by income.

The conclusion that consumption depends on wealth was arrived at independently by monetary economist Milton Friedman and Keynesian economists Franco Modigliani and Albert Ando.[10] Friedman called his theory "permanent income," and Ando and Modigliani referred to their work as "the life cycle hypothesis." These were not people who agreed on much else. Friedman was a lifelong opponent of active intervention by government; Ando and Modigliani, in contrast, were champions of active government stabilization policy.

The permanent income hypothesis suggests a way of reconciling the evidence from Figures 10.5 and 10.6. The drop in investment and the decrease in consumption that occurred during the Great Depression were both triggered by the stock market crash. In my view, consumption did not fall because it depends on income; it fell because consumption depends on wealth.

The Treasury View

During the 1920s, the staff of the UK Treasury argued that unemployment could not be cured by increased government expenditure.[11] Winston Churchill, speaking to the House of Commons in 1929, put it this way:

> The orthodox Treasury view ... is that when the Government borrow [sic] in the money market it becomes a new competitor with industry and engrosses to itself resources which would otherwise have been employed by private enterprise, and in the process it raises the rent of money to all who have need of it.[12]

In other words, increased government purchases crowds out private expenditure.

Some people might argue the Treasury view leaves no room for demand management to restore full employment.[13] This argument is false. The Treasury view asserts government competes with private companies in the asset markets—a proposition that is undeniable. The questions we must ask are: How does increased government expenditure influence the aggregate demand for goods and services? And: Is crowding out important or is crowding out negligible?

Keynesians have long recognized that a given increase in government purchases will have a different effect on employment if it is financed by taxes rather than by borrowing. It also matters if government purchases are spent on investment goods or on consumption goods, and if the government borrows by issuing three-month treasuries or by issuing twenty-year bonds.

If the government is competing with private households and firms for funds, we might expect any increase in government purchases to cause a reduction either in consumption or investment by the private sector. This suggests a test of the Treasury view against the Keynesian theory of the consumption function.

If we maintain the assumptions of the simplest Keynesian model, changes in investment and government purchases are caused by factors independent of those that cause changes in aggregate consumption. When investment falls, we would expect to see consumption decrease. This proposition is borne out by Figure 10.5. We should also see that, when government purchases increase, consumption increases. That proposition is false, as I showed in Figure 10.6.

The Treasury view provides a possible explanation of these facts. It asserts government competes with the private sector for funds, and that when government purchases increase, consumption should fall. In the extreme case, when government purchases are close substitutes for private consumption, we

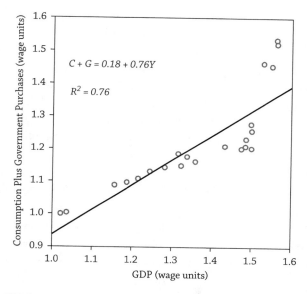

Figure 10.7 Consumption and Government Spending, 1929 to 1950. GDP, gross domestic product.

Source: US Department of Commerce and author's calculations.

would expect to see a closer relationship between consumption plus government purchases and GDP than between consumption and GDP. Figure 10.7 shows this is exactly what we see in data from 1929 through 1950.

On the vertical axis of Figure 10.7, I plotted the sum of government purchases and consumption per person, both measured in wage units. On the horizontal axis, I plotted GDP. If we abstract from foreign trade, government purchases plus consumption plus investment are equal to GDP. This fact implies the only reason the points on Figure 10.7 do not all lie along the diagonal is because of movements in investment we assume are exogenous. The figure shows that, as GDP increases by $1, consumption plus government purchases increase by 76¢.

In Figure 10.7, I indicate the slope of the best line through these points. And although the fit of this equation is not perfect, it has an R^2 value of 0.76, which is much higher than the private consumption function for the same period plotted in Figure 10.6. The assumption that the sum of government purchases plus consumption is related to income by a straight line explains 76% of the data between 1929 and 1950. The assumption that consumption alone is related to income by a straight line explains only 7%.

Rationing in Wartime Does Not Invalidate My Argument

Paul Krugman has pointed out there was rationing during WWII.[14] He implies we should ignore the evidence that consumption and government expenditure moved in opposite directions during this period because markets were hampered by rationing. I am skeptical of the claim we should discount evidence that does not accord with our prior beliefs, but I will give Krugman the benefit of the doubt and discard the wartime years from the sample.

In Figure 10.8, I plotted the data from Figure 10.7, but I have eliminated the war years. On the vertical axis of this figure, I plotted consumption plus government expenditure per person, measured in wage units; on the horizontal axis, I plotted GDP. Recall we are assuming investment and government expenditure move independently. The hypothesis we are testing is whether changes in either of these variables causes a movement in consumption.

My maintained assumption is changes in government purchases cause changes in consumption purchases, not the other way around. If this argument is correct, the correct relationship between consumption and GDP is represented by Figure 10.5, not by Figure 10.8.

If consumption depends on income, but government purchases do not, by adding government purchases to consumption and plotting their sum against GDP, as I have done in

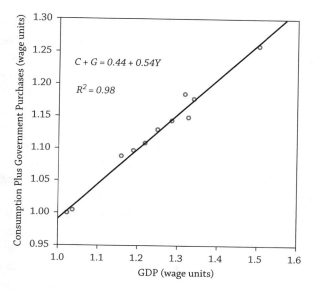

Figure 10.8 Consumption and Government Spending, 1929 to 1939. GDP, gross domestic product.

Source: US Department of Commerce and author's calculations.

Figure 10.8, I have constructed a misspecified model. I have added an irrelevant random variable—government purchases—to the correct left-hand-side variable: aggregate consumption. Statistical theory implies that the R^2 value for this misspecified model should be less than for the correctly specified equation plotted in Figure 10.5.

The facts are different. By adding government purchases to consumption, the points lie closely around a straight line with a slope equal to 0.54. The R^2 value of the fit of consumption plus government purchases against GDP is 0.98 as opposed to 0.91 for the graph of consumption against GDP depicted in Figure 10.5. We cannot explain these facts by arguing that WWII was special because of rationing. Instead, we must conclude the Treasury view beats the Keynesian multiplier hypothesis in a straight horse race.

There Is Nothing Special about Zero Interest Rates

A claim that is often made by those who cling to the Hicks–Hansen view of Keynesian economics is that the multiplier is larger when the interest rate is equal to zero. This argument comes from their interpretation of Keynesian theory. The graphical analysis promoted by Alvin Hansen and John Hicks implies that a fiscal stimulus, caused by an increase in government expenditure, will be larger when the interest rate is being held at 0% by central bank policy, than when the central bank raises or lowers the interest rate in response to market conditions.

In normal times, higher government expenditure will lead to lower private expenditure because increased aggregate demand leads to higher expected inflation and the central bank responds by raising the interest rate. The reduction in private expecnditure, caused by an increase in the interest rate, is called *crowding out*. When the central bank pegs the interest rate at zero, private expenditure is not crowded out by increased government expenditure because the central bank does not allow the interest rate to increase. That, at least, is the New Keynesian argument.

There are two problems with this argument. One is empirical; the other is theoretical. The empirical case against the greater effectiveness of fiscal stimulus when the interest rate is fixed at zero is the evidence I presented in this chapter. From 1935 to 1947, the Treasury-bill rate in the United States never went above 0.7%. The Great Depression and WWII were periods when, like today, the interest rate was stuck, effectively, at zero.[15]

The theoretical case against the effectiveness of fiscal stimulus at the zero lower bound is that there is more than one interest rate and not all interest rates are at zero.[16] There is an interest rate on overnight loans, an interest rate on thirty-year Treasury bonds, and an interest rate on loans of every maturity in between. If the government borrows by issuing ten- or twenty-year bonds, as some have advocated, it still has the potential to crowd out corporate borrowers who are borrowing long term to finance private investment projects. There is nothing special about zero interest rates.

The Politics of Multipliers

For the past seven years, I have been attending academic conferences where economists have been grappling with the current financial crisis: in Boston, Montreal, Amsterdam, London, Cleveland, Sydney, Toronto, and Atlanta. One question addressed at all these conferences is: How big is the multiplier? The answer: We don't know for sure, but we have learned a few things. Here is what I said about the views expressed at these conferences in a 2010 article for the *Financial Times*, Economists' Forum:

> Half of the papers [at these conferences] are about the quantitative effects of fiscal policy. If government spending goes up by $1, how much will income go up? The answer varies from zero to three depending on the assumptions made by the economist to disentangle cause and effect. Administration economists claim that the multiplier is 1.5. Well, at least we got it right on average!

I couldn't resist adding an "oldie but goldy" statistician joke:

> Two statisticians go deer hunting. One fires off a shot and misses by ten feet to the left. The second fires off a shot and misses by ten feet to the right. They both shout out triumphantly, "We hit it!"

I went on to add the following:

> Suppose that a government official is building a bridge and he needs to know the elasticity of steel because if he gets it wrong by 20% or more the bridge will fall down.

The official asks two engineers. One claims that it's 20 and the other says, no, it's 40. No problem says the official, I'll take the average. Don't laugh. That's how we're running fiscal policy.[17]

There is no consensus on the size of the multiplier because everything in economics is changing at the same time.

Consider, as an example, the case of Greece. The Greek economy has suffered a much deeper recession than any other country in the European Union. The Greek government has also raised taxes and reduced expenditure more than any other European country—a policy referred to as *fiscal austerity*. Can we infer the policy of austerity caused the deep recession? Or was it caused by some other factor that also forced the Greek government to raise taxes? If we observe that two variables X and Y are correlated, we cannot infer that X caused Y. Disentangling the causal links is called the *identification problem*.

Identification is at the heart of disagreements between economists about the size of the multiplier. And those disagreements are very real. Here is a direct quote from Harvard economist N. Gregory Mankiw:

In a TV interview last month, Vice President Joe Biden said the following:

"Every economist, as I've said, from conservative to liberal, acknowledges that direct government spending on a direct program now is the best way to infuse economic growth and create jobs."[18]

Back to Mankiw:

That statement is clearly false. As I have documented on this blog in recent weeks, skeptics about a spending stimulus include quite a few well-known economists, such as (in alphabetical order) Alberto Alesina, Robert Barro, Gary Becker, John Cochrane, Eugene Fama, Robert

Lucas, Greg Mankiw, Kevin Murphy, Thomas Sargent, Harald Uhlig, and Luigi Zingales—and I am sure there are many others as well.

You can include me on that list. Mankiw goes on to say the following:

> Regardless of whether one agrees with them on the merits of the case, it is hard to dispute that this list is pretty impressive, as judged by the standard objective criteria by which economists evaluate one another. If any university managed to hire all of them, it would immediately have a top-ranked economics department.

Quite. The divisions among economists on this issue are not divisions between Keynesian and classical economists. Greg Mankiw coauthored a volume of readings that kicked off the New Keynesian agenda.[19] And although many of the other economists on this list are identified with classical economics, this does not invalidate their ability to make informed judgments about the evidence.

The Economics of Multipliers

Economists disagree about the size of fiscal multipliers because the evidence is inconclusive. There are two main approaches to identify fiscal multipliers. One approach goes by the imposing name of *structural vector autoregressions* (SVARs). The SVAR approach starts from a theoretical model. The model imposes a causal structure on the contemporaneous linkages between changes in government purchases and changes in GDP. Using the theoretical model to identify the shocks, the economist measures the size of the change in GDP for a given change in government purchases. Olivier Blanchard, former research director of the IMF, is a leading proponent of this approach.[20]

A drawback of the SVAR approach is that, if the model is wrong, so is the inference about the size of the multiplier. One promising alternative was suggested by Christina and David Romer.[21] They suggest sifting through historical documents and drawing inferences from those documents about the reasons for a change in government purchases or taxes. An important conclusion that has arisen from their work is that the multiplier associated with a cut in taxes is large and significant. In contrast, Valerie Ramey has shown, also using a narrative approach to identify shocks, that fiscal expenditure multipliers are less than one. In other words, when the government spends more, the private sector spends less.[22]

The Romer and Romer finding that tax multipliers are large is notable because it contradicts the simple Keynesian model. According to the Keynesian cross analysis illustrated in Figure 10.2, government will have a larger impact on employment if it spends money directly than if it gives money to households and allows them to spend it. The reason, in Keynesian theory, is the household will save part of the transfer it receives, but the government will spend all of a given fiscal stimulus directly on goods and services.[23]

Why are tax multipliers large but spending multipliers small? A classical economist might argue the reason is that taxes distort incentives. Economists' models contain lump-sum taxes in which a flat sum is levied on every person independent of their income. In practice, taxes are levied as a fraction of income with a fraction that is greater the more you earn. When the tax rate is high, a person is less likely to work because a fraction of her earnings is taken by government. An argument of this kind is called a *supply-side argument* because it implies taxes reduce the supply of labor.

I am personally skeptical of the supply-side argument. If supply-side effects were at play, we would expect to see a big increase in the labor force participation rate in response to a reduction in the income tax rate, as workers choose to supply more labor in response to an increase in their after-tax wage.

But, as I showed in Chapter 4, the labor force participation rate is governed by demographics and it does not increase much, if at all, during booms. A more compelling argument, in my view, is that a reduction in the tax rate will increase consumption and cause firms to employ more workers because it raises the value of after-tax wealth.

The evidence of Romer and Romer and Valerie Ramey and her coauthors is consistent with the findings I reported from WWII. And all the evidence is consistent with the view that employment fluctuations are caused by movements in aggregate demand, as long as we recognize and accept that consumption is a function of wealth, not of income.

The Economics of Austerity

Following the Great Recession of 2008, journalists, academic economists, and bloggers have been engaged in a heated debate about the economics and politics of fiscal policy. The question at the heart of this debate is: Should governments be concerned about the ratio of government debt to GDP?

In a 2012 article I coauthored with Dmitry Plotnikov, we asked: Does fiscal policy matter?[24] As with many questions in economics, the answer is: It depends.

A recession is a period when GDP per person falls below trend. Because government debt is repaid over a period of decades, it does not fall during recessions. This causes a problem for national treasuries similar to the problem you would face if you lost your job at a time when your credit card was maxed out and you had just taken out a mortgage on a new house.

Governments do not want to reduce their expenditures during recessions. To the contrary, governments want to increase their expenditures during recessions because they must pay unemployment insurance benefits for a growing number of unemployed people. At the same time, tax revenues fall. The outcome of increasing expenditures and falling revenues is that the ratio of government debt to GDP increases. How should governments deal with this situation?

If government were a private household, it would be forced to spend less or to find a way of earning extra income. To the extent recessions are temporary, the same argument does not apply to governments.

There have been recent calls in Germany and in the United States for constitutional changes and, in the United Kingdom, for parliamentary legislation, to restrict the ability of national treasuries to borrow. In the United States, this would take the form of an amendment to the Constitution that would require the federal government to balance its budget. There are three reasons why that is a very bad idea.

The first argument for why government should not be required to balance its budget is that governments, like private companies, own capital. Roads and bridges, national parks, museums, and public buildings are essential to the functioning of a modern economy. And there are good reasons why they should be provided by government rather than by the private sector.

When the government builds a road, a bridge, or an airport, the newly created public capital serves the needs not only of the current generation, but also of future generations for decades into the future. Because its benefits extend through time, roads, bridges, and airports should not be paid for out of current tax revenues. They should be paid for by borrowing, which allows for future generations to compensate current generations for the resources used to construct the roads, bridges and airports in the first place.

This argument explains why the normal state of affairs is one in which government is in debt to the private sector and the taxes paid by one segment of the population are used to pay interest to a different segment.

The second argument for why government should not be required to balance its budget is one that is peculiar to recessions. Governments provide unemployment benefits because private markets for unemployment insurance do not exist. They do not exist because of a problem that economists call *moral hazard*—that is, taking risks when someone else bears the cost of the risk-taking.

When we accept government has a responsibility to provide unemployment insurance for those people who lose their jobs in a recession, we must ask: Who should pay for the transfers to the unemployed? The answer is the same as the answer to the question: Who should pay to construct a new airport? The cost of the insurance should be borne, not only by existing generations, but also by future generations.

The third argument for why government should not be required to balance its budget is the existence of government debt increases the set of trading opportunities between people of different generations. To decide on an optimal fiscal policy we need a criterion to judge what is a good policy and what is not. A policy that maximizes the consumption opportunities available to an average person, whenever they are born, is called the *golden rule*. If government pursues a golden rule policy, economists have shown it should set fiscal policy to equate the interest rate, adjusted for inflation, to equal the growth rate of GDP.[25]

A policy of a balanced budget will, in general, conflict with the golden rule. If the interest rate is equal to the growth rate, the value of government debt will be either greater than or less than the value of public capital. It will never, except by chance, be equal to zero.

Keynesian Economics without the Consumption Function

Keynesian economics has two parts: a theory of aggregate supply and a theory of aggregate demand. Traditionally, Keynesians have focused on the theory of aggregate demand. The central part of that theory is the consumption function, and an implication of the theory of the consumption function is that an increase in government expenditure will cause GDP to increase by a multiple of the initial increase in spending. That theory is wrong. Consumption depends on wealth, not on income.

But although I reject the Keynesian theory of aggregate demand, I provide a foundation—Keynesian search theory— to the Keynesian theory of aggregate supply. This new theory is rooted firmly in the microeconomic theory of behavior. According to Keynesian search theory, everything demanded will be supplied and any unemployment rate can be an equilibrium unemployment rate.

By providing a microfounded explanation to the theory of aggregate supply, I integrated Keynesian economics with the microeconomic theory of general equilibrium in a new way. By rejecting the Keynesian theory of aggregate demand, I was forced to reevaluate traditional Keynesian policy responses to high unemployment. More government expenditure is not the right way to prevent a depression.

Figure 10.9 illustrates the implications of a theory of Keynesian economics without the consumption function. The aggregate demand curve does not slope upward with income;

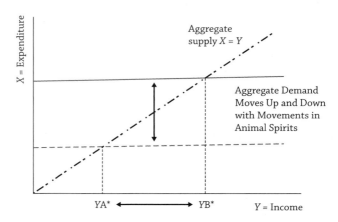

Figure 10.9 Keynesian Economics without the Consumption Function.

Source: US Department of Commerce and author's calculations.

it is a horizontal straight line. The position of this line depends on the beliefs of market participants about the value of their financial assets. As the value of financial assets fluctuate, driven by self-fulfilling beliefs, so the aggregate demand curve moves up and down between the solid horizontal line and the dashed horizontal line. As people feel more or less wealthy, they buy more or fewer goods. Firms hire more or fewer workers and real GDP fluctuates between point YA^* and YB^*.

The Fear Factor

In the representation of Keynesian economics constructed by John Hicks and Alvin Hansen, there is a single interest rate. That is a gross simplification. In the real world, there is a spectrum of interest rates for borrowing at different horizons and there are many kinds of financial contracts that split risk in different ways. In a recession, the spread between risky rates and risk-free rates widens.

In the current crisis, we are in a situation in which government can borrow money for three months for almost nothing, and it can borrow money for ten or twenty years for very low rates. Private companies can also borrow at these low rates, but they choose not to do so. Corporations in the United States are holding trillions of dollars in liquid assets, cash, and government bonds they are not investing in machines and factories. Why?

Companies are choosing to hold on to liquid assets because they are afraid of volatility in the future. If a computer gaming company borrows at 5% for ten years and invests in a new game, it is betting it can sell the software it produces at a profit. That game might take two years to develop. The price at which it will sell its game depends on the general level of prices two years from now. But, with interest rates at the lower bound, the Fed has lost is ability to control the inflation rate. Companies are worried, rightly, that there will be another recession in the near future—and that is very bad for business confidence.

The Case for Infrastructure Investment

A conservative will be suspicious of an increase in government investment expenditure conducted to counter a recession because it is much easier to expand the role of government than to shrink it. The creation of a large new government enterprise, they might argue, is not the best way for society to allocate resources. Once the recession is over, we will be left with a new government agency and a less efficient economic system.

A possible counter-argument is that government does not need to set up a separate corporation. It could put out tenders to private companies to bid for the chance to build new roads, railways, and bridges. Would that policy increase employment?

That depends on how the additional expenditure is financed. If the government prints money, or if it finances its expenditure by issuing three-month Treasury bills, a large-scale infrastructure investment is likely to expand employment. But, if it issues new bonds at ten- or twenty-year horizons, the Treasury will be competing with private companies for funds and it will drive up yields at the long end of the yield curve.

When one recognizes that the maturity structure of government debt matters, it is a short step to recognize that it is *only* the maturity structure that matters.[26] Animal spirits affect financial markets by changing the risk premium. A high risk-premium does not reflect an irrational fear; it is a self-fulfilling prophecy waiting to happen. And it is a fear that can be alleviated by taking risk onto the public balance sheet by interventions in the asset markets to stabilize the costs of long-term and risky financing.

So should we go ahead and repair the US infrastructure? Of course we should. But the decisions regarding which projects are appropriate to pursue, and which are not, are ones that should be made using standard cost–benefit principles. Those projects that have a positive net present value, using an appropriate social rate of discount, are ones that should be pursued.

We should not be building bridges to nowhere just because we cannot think of another way to reduce unemployment.

Conclusion

In this chapter, I made a case against traditional fiscal policy based on evidence from the Great Depression and WWII. These two episodes provide a dramatic natural experiment that helps us to distinguish alternative viewpoints.

What of more recent evidence? If you get your information from reading blogs and opinion pieces, you could be forgiven for thinking that the weight of scientific evidence lines up with Keynesian economics. A number of vocal columnists and bloggers have claimed repeatedly that there is overwhelming evidence that supports the proposition that increased government purchases can restore full employment. This simply is not so.[27]

Keynesians such as Paul Krugman or Lawrence Summers who rely on insights from the Hicks–Hansen IS-LM model see evidence for the effectiveness of fiscal policy because they have a very strong prior belief this is the way the world works. I disagree. In a recent paper coauthored with Konstantin Platonov, we show how to rebuild the IS-LM model in a way that incorporates Keynes' insight that high involuntary unemployment is one of many possible steady state equilibria of a capitalist market economy.[28] The model we build there has different policy conclusions from the Hicks-Hansen interpretation of *The General Theory*. I share the view of Krugman and Summers that the unemployment rate is often high and inefficient. I do not share their view that the solution to this problem is more government expenditure.

11

HOW TO PREVENT
FINANCIAL CRISES

Keynes did not just provide a theoretical framework to understand what went wrong during the Great Depression; he provided a policy recommendation to prevent a similar event from reoccurring. Although the theory I present in this chapter is based on Keynesian ideas, it has significant differences from Keynes' General Theory. These differences suggest a refinement of the policies Keynes advocated to maintain full employment. In this chapter, I explain the policy recommendation that arises from my work: active intervention in the stock market by the central bank, acting as an agent of the treasury, with the goal of maintaining full employment.

A decade after the publication of *The General Theory*, governments throughout the world began to operate active stabilization policies through monetary and fiscal mechanisms. Those policies were effective and led to a protracted period of economic stability, but the value of financial assets continued to be highly volatile and, in 2008, a new financial crisis hit.

Central banks in America, Europe, and Asia lowered the interest rate on overnight loans in an attempt to provide much-needed cash to financial firms that could no longer raise short-term financing. That response is precisely why central banks were created in the first place, and it is a prescription for combating financial panic that dates back to the English economist Walter Bagehot, who wrote a famous treatise on central banking in 1873.[1]

The 1929 crash and the 2008 panic are not the only times in recent history when there was a large drop in the paper value of financial assets. The largest ever one-day percentage fall in the US stock market occurred on Black Monday, October 19, 1987, when the stock market fell by 22.6%. That event was not followed by a depression. Why?

In 1987, the Federal Reserve under Paul Volcker slashed the interest rate on overnight loans and flooded the US economy with liquid assets. That action was successful at preventing the crash from having a major effect on the real economy. The crashes of 1929 and 2008 were different because, in 1933 and in 2008, the standard channel of monetary response—lowering the interest rate on short-term loans—was exhausted. When the interest rate was at zero, it could be lowered no further.

In the United States, the Fed lowered the short-term interest rate to one tenth of 1% in autumn 2008. The Bank of England followed suit shortly after, lowering the bank rate to half a percentage point in early 2009. When interest rates reached an effective lower bound, the traditional response of lowering the interest rate was no longer an option.[2] Instead, inspired by the writings of American economist Milton Friedman, central banks engaged in a process of massive and unprecedented monetary expansion.[3]

A large-asset purchase by a central bank, paid for by printing money, is called *quantitative easing*. A change in the asset composition of the central bank, achieved by exchanging short-term central bank assets for long-term government debt or claims to risky assets such as stock market equity or mortgage-backed securities, is called *qualitative easing*.[4] Both policies have been used extensively during the past seven years, and both policies, in my view, have been spectacularly successful.[5] In this chapter, I document this view with evidence from US data and I explain how to prevent future financial crises by making these policies a permanent part of the arsenal of tools available to central banks around the world.

Quantitative and Qualitative Easing

Many economists believe that, although it matters a lot whether government expenditure is funded by borrowing or by printing money, it doesn't matter at all if government borrows by issuing three-month bonds, five-year bonds, or thirty-year bonds. I believe this perception is gravely mistaken. It matters a great deal.

The *size* of the central bank balance sheet matters because it forms the base for the money supply. In normal times, when the interest rate is positive, there is a strong, positive correlation between the inflation rate and the rate of money creation. That correlation led Milton Friedman to argue that inflation is "always and everywhere a monetary phenomenon."[6]

The *composition* of the central bank balance sheet matters because there is incomplete participation in the asset markets. An exchange of short-term debt for long-term debt or other risky assets in the central bank's portfolio transfers nominal income risk from current taxpayers to future taxpayers. The composition of the portfolio matters because our unborn children and grandchildren cannot trade in the financial markets.

In 2009, the balance sheets of the Bank of England, the Federal Reserve, and the European Central Bank increased by a factor of three or more in the space of a few months. That expansion had two components. The first was quantitative easing; the second was qualitative easing. Both policies were successful, the first by preventing deflation and the second by ameliorating what would have been a much deeper crash in the stock market.

Quantitative Easing Prevented Deflation

The Bank of England is charged with maintaining price stability, currently interpreted as 2% inflation. And to the extent it is compatible with the inflation target, it is charged with "supporting the Government's economic policy, including its objectives for growth and employment."[7] The Federal Reserve has a dual mandate to maintain price stability and maximum employment and, although it does not have a single mandate, it has operated in a way that is consistent with inflation targeting for the past thirty years.

Price stability is important because fluctuations in the value of money have unintended consequences. This is true both of unanticipated inflations, which transfer wealth from lenders to borrowers, and unanticipated deflations, which transfer wealth from borrowers to lenders. Deflation is extremely disruptive to economic activity and is associated with bankruptcy and unemployment as firms struggle to repay fixed nominal loans with earnings worth less in monetary units.

Figure 11.1 shows how the Federal Reserve board responded to the financial crisis. The solid line, measured in percent per year on the right-hand axis, measures the expected rate of inflation. The outer boundary of the shaded region, measured on the left-hand axis in millions of dollars, is the size of the Federal Reserve's balance sheet.

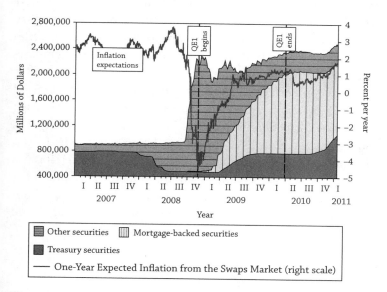

Figure 11.1 Quantitative Easing (QE) and Inflation Expectations in the US: 2007 to 2010.
Source: Federal Reserve Board, Table H.4.1, and author's calculations.

From January 2007 through September 2008, expected inflation fluctuated between 2% and 3.5%. When Lehman Brothers declared bankruptcy in September 2008, expected inflation fell by nearly 800 basis points in the space of two months. By October 2008, it reached a low of −4.5%!

Immediately after the collapse of Lehman Brothers, the Fed began to purchase assets of troubled financial companies, and the Fed's balance sheet, indicated in Figure 11.1 by the envelope of the three shaded regions, increased from $800 billion in August 2008 to $2.5 trillion in January 2009. This initial wave of asset purchases was called *QE1* and it is noted in Figure 11.1 by the region between the two vertical dashed lines. Immediately after the Federal Reserve purchase of $1.3 trillion of new securities, expected inflation went back up into positive territory.

Deflation is damaging to real economic activity because it causes bankruptcies and layoffs. The Fed's actions did not prevent deflation completely, and the CPI inflation rate fell to −2% in July 2009. But, the Fed's actions did turn around inflationary expectations and it is likely QE prevented a much larger deflation, which would have had catastrophic effects on unemployment, had it been allowed to occur.

As a counterfactual, consider what happened during the Great Depression. During that episode, the Fed did not engage in QE; the correction that occurred in the private economy was not pretty. In June 1932, the CPI inflation rate reached −11% and the unemployment rate peaked at 25% a year later. It is my view that the actions of the Fed in the United States and of the Bank of England in the United Kingdom helped to spare both economies from suffering a disaster of similar magnitude after the 2008 financial crisis.

Qualitative Easing Prevented Depression-Era Unemployment Rates

In normal times central banks are very conservative; they buy short-term securities backed by high-quality collateral and, in so doing, they face little or no risk. Central banks pay for asset purchases by creating money, and money is used by households and firms to buy and sell goods. Central banks provide liquidity that "oils the wheels of trade."

In times of crisis, central banks act very differently; they provide a backstop to the financial system that prevents systemic bankruptcies from disrupting economic activity. The 2008 crisis is a good example of this process in action. During the 2008 crisis, central banks throughout the world no longer confined their purchases to safe short-term assets.

The Bank of England began a program of purchasing long-term government bonds, and the Federal Reserve purchased long-term bonds and mortgage-backed securities (MBSs). These long-term assets carry two kinds of risks. When interest rates rise in the future, central banks will take capital losses on their bond portfolios because, as the interest rate rises, bond prices will fall. MBSs face a second risk because the holders of the mortgages may repay early, resulting in a loss to the lender, who must relend money at a lower rate.

Figure 11.2 contains the same information on asset purchases as Figure 11.1, but instead of plotting expected inflation on this chart, the solid line is the value of the stock market. I use this figure to make a point about the effects on markets of the *type* of assets that central banks buy.

The shaded area in Figure 11.2 is broken down into three regions. The solid shaded region is holdings of Treasury securities. In normal times this is *all* the Federal Reserve holds. The area shaded with horizontal lines is other securities, mainly long-term bonds and the assets of the banks that were bailed out by the Federal Reserve. Finally, the area shaded with vertical lines is the Federal Reserve's holding of MBSs.

Notice the coincidence in timing of the Federal Reserve's purchases of risky MBSs with movements in the stock market, shown by the solid line. The turnaround in the stock market that occurred at the beginning of 2009 coincides closely with the Fed's intervention in the MBS market. Furthermore, when asset buying was suspended temporarily during the second

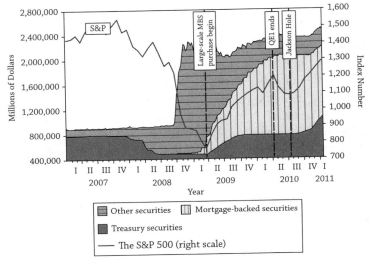

Figure 11.2 Qualitative Easing (QE) and Equity Prices in the US: 2007 to 2011.
Source: Federal Reserve Board, Table H.4.1, and author's calculations.

quarter of 2010, the stock market resumed its downward spiral. It only picked up again when the Federal Reserve announced at the Jackson Hole conference, in the late autumn of the same year, that large-scale asset purchases would resume. This was a big success story for QE.[8]

Figure 11.2 was reproduced from the text of the John Flemming Memorial lecture that I presented at the Bank of England in 2013.[9] It was constructed using weekly data on the composition of the Federal Reserve's balance sheet from 2007 to 2011. In Figure 11.3, I updated the figure to include observations through December 2015. The correlation between Fed purchases of MBSs and the value of the S&P 500 to which I drew attention in 2013 has held up remarkably well.

Figure 11.2 ends in December 2010. QE2, the second wave of large-scale asset purchases, began in September 2010 and ended in June 2011. During that twenty-one-month period, the Fed's balance sheet went from $2.4 trillion to $2.9 trillion

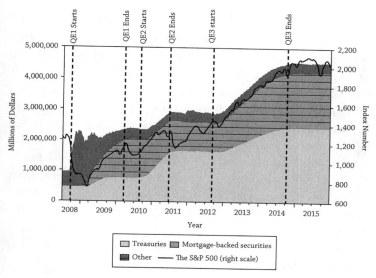

Figure 11.3 Qualitative Easing (QE) and Equity Prices in the US: 2008 to 2015.

Source: Federal Reserve Board, Table H.4.1, and author's calculations.

and the S&P 500 increased from 1,100 to 1,300—an increase of 18%. When QE2 ended, the market fell and, in the space of a month, it had lost almost all the gains that accrued during the period of QE.

In September 2012, the Fed began a third period of QE, again purchasing a significant quantity of MBSs, but also shifting its portfolio toward longer dated Treasury bonds. By the time QE3 ended in November 2014, the Fed's balance sheet had reached $4.5 trillion—more then 25% of US GDP. As with QE2 before it, the increase in the Fed's purchases of MBSs was accompanied by a stock market rally. When QE3 began, in September 2012, the S&P 500 was at 1,400. When QE3 ended, in September 2014, it had climbed to 2,000—a gain of 43% in two years. In my view, these two periods of stock market appreciation were driven, at least in part, by Federal Reserve intervention in the market for MBSs.

Macroprudential Policy and a Sovereign Wealth Fund

I showed, in Chapter 7, that the real value of the stock market is correlated with the unemployment rate. And in Chapters 6 and 7, I provided a theory that interprets this correlation as causal. In the remaining sections of this chapter, I explain how we can design a policy to improve people's lives. My argument is based on two premises. First, most of the fluctuations in the price-to-earnings ratio are Pareto inefficient. They make all of us worse off, and if we could ask our grandchildren what to do about it, they would be cheerleaders for active intervention in the financial markets. Second, there *is* something we can do about it. We can prevent the swings in asset prices that make all of us worse off.

To manage financial market volatility, in 2009 I made the following argument in the online journal VOX.

> In recent years the Fed has used one instrument—the Fed funds rate—to control two targets: inflation and unemployment. I argue that the Fed should add a second instrument—the rate of growth of the price of a stock market index.[10]

To control market volatility, the appropriate political body, Congress in the United States, or Parliament in the United Kingdom, would need to enact legislation defining the characteristics of those assets the central bank would be permitted to trade. Writing in the *Financial Times* in 2009, I explained how this would work.[11] First, politicians would need to decide which asset would be controlled. Rather than buy individual stocks, it would be better to control a broad basket of stocks. I suggested in a second *Financial Times* article that the basket should include "every publicly traded stock, weighted by market capitalization and adjusted on a regular basis to reflect changes in the composition and size of firms."[12] The Fed would then

[b]uy shares in all publicly traded companies at current market prices in proportion to the weights by which they enter the [basket]. To pay for these assets [it] should issue three month bills, backed by the treasury. These securities would trade at the same price as three-month treasury bills since the two classes of assets would be perfect substitutes.[13]

Rather than have the Fed manage the composition of the basket by purchasing individual shares, a better plan is to encourage private financial institutions such as Vanguard or Fidelity to create ETFs with a predefined set of characteristics, and for the Fed to buy or sell private ETFs. Once a market was created, the Fed would "stand ready to buy and sell [the ETF] at a price to be set at regular intervals. Since the price of the ETF needs to be coordinated with interest rate policy, an appropriate body to set the price would be the Fed Open Market Committee."[14]

Writing on his blog in 2013, Miles Kimball proposed a similar idea that he called a US sovereign wealth fund (SWF):

Why not create a separate government agency to run a US sovereign wealth fund? Then the Fed can stick to what it does best—keeping the economy on track—while the sovereign wealth fund takes the political heat, gives the Fed running room, and concentrates on making a profit that can reduce our national debt.[15]

Calling it a *sovereign wealth fund* seemed like a catchy title, and I adopted it when I presented my idea to the UK Treasury Select Committee in 2013.[16] Kimball advocated that the Social Security trust fund should be invested in the stock market—a proposal that was floated by Lawrence Summers when he was deputy secretary of the Treasury.[17] Unlike Kimball and Summers, I am not just advocating that US pension assets be invested in stocks; I am also arguing that the government portfolio should be traded actively to stabilize the financial markets. The case I put forward in Chapter 7 explains why.

SWFs are typically associated with states in which government has positive net assets, such as Norway, which has an SWF worth $800 billion, or the United Arab Emirates, which is not far behind. The existence of an SWF with a large positive value is neither necessary nor sufficient for a sovereign state to stabilize its own financial markets. It is not necessary, because any purchase of shares by a treasury could be financed by short-term borrowing, collateralized by the present value of future tax revenues. It is not sufficient, because simply owning shares does not guarantee financial stability. The SWF portfolio must also be traded actively to meet long-term goals.

To stabilize markets effectively, the assets of an SWF would need to be substantial. But, this does not imply its net asset position should be large, or even that it should be positive. Its assets would consist of shares in an ETF. Its liabilities would consist of sovereign debt. There might be periods when the net asset position of the SWF becomes negative. Unlike a private company, a negative net asset position for an SWF would not imply the fund is insolvent; its liabilities are backed ultimately by the ability of the Treasury to raise taxes on all future citizens. That is a very deep pocket.

The size of an intervention needed to maintain any given price would depend, in part, on the confidence of market participants. The more credible an announcement is, the smaller the intervention required to achieve it. I argued before the Treasury Committee that, in the United Kingdom, an initial purchase of £150 billion would be a good starting point, but it is important the public be aware that no upper bound would be placed on the possible size of an intervention to avoid the possibility that private investors might game the fund. George Soros did this in 1992, when he bet against the ability of the Bank of England to maintain the exchange rate of the pound.[18]

Maintaining the value of an ETF is a very different proposition than trying to maintain a fixed exchange rate in the foreign exchange market. In 1992, the pound was overvalued because the United Kingdom pound was running a more expansionary monetary policy than the currencies of the European countries to which the pound was pegged in the exchange rate mechanism. To maintain parity with the Deutschmark, the Bank of England was forced to sell foreign currency and, eventually, it ran out of foreign currency reserves.

In the case of stock market intervention, there is no analog of running out of reserves. A national treasury has the capacity to borrow against future tax revenues, and the history of government borrowing in the United Kingdom has shown the UK government can borrow at least as much as two and a half times its GDP, as it did during the Napoleonic War and again in 1945 to finance WWII. Borrowing to purchase an asset is very different from borrowing to pay for a war, because the newly created liabilities—government debt—are backed by a newly acquired asset: equity in the ETF. The entire value of publicly traded stocks is less than three times the GDP and, if necessary, an SWF could acquire the entire market. This is a scenario that must not be ruled out in advance if pronouncements by the fund managers are to be deemed credible by the market.

What about the possibility that the financial markets are trading at a value that is too high and the SWF managers believe the market price is in the grip of an unsustainable bubble? Here, the problem is not a quantity constraint; it is a political one. An SWF that has sold all its shares in the ETF can sell the market short by creating artificial assets with the same dividend stream as the ETF. A policy of this kind would prove difficult to implement by a political appointee, and for that reason the day-to-day running of the SWF would need to be in the hands of an independent body. In the United Kingdom, such a body already exists: the Financial Policy Committee. In the following sections, I refer to a body that operates financial policy with the generic title of a financial policy committee (FPC).

Creating a Financial Policy Committee

It is widely believed by economists that monetary policy is effective when it is controlled by an independent committee. The day-to-day setting of interest rates by an independent central bank helps to alleviate the political conflicts that arise when an elected government is tempted to place short-term goals for reelection over the longer term goal of price stability. The same argument applies, a fortiori, with regard to financial policy.

As I argued at a 2013 policy roundtable, the natural body to operate an asset price stabilization fund in the UK context would be the FPC, operating in consultation with the monetary policy committee (MPC).[19] Parliament would set out operational guidelines, but the day-to-day running of the fund *must* be independent of short-term political considerations for the same reasons that informed the creation of an independent Bank of England.

If an FPC were to be created in a sovereign state, modeled on the UK Financial Policy Committee, what should be its mandate? There are two possible answers to this question. The first is that the FPC should be concerned solely with financial stability and should target the price-to-earnings ratio of the ETF. The second, and one that I favor, is that the FPC should target the unemployment rate. The following section explains why.

The Mandate of the FPC Should Be to Maintain Full Employment

The price-to-earnings ratio is very persistent. It is also very volatile and is affected by demand and supply shocks, and also by shocks to animal spirits. After a shock of any kind, the price-to-earnings ratio will return slowly to its long-run average, but it may take as long as fifteen years for it to return halfway to its steady-state value, which, historically, has been roughly seventeen.[20]

The steady-state price-to-earnings ratio is not a concern of financial policy. Fluctuations in the price-to-earnings ratio *are* a concern. These fluctuations cause big changes in the unemployment rate. If, as I have argued, swings in price-to-earnings ratios are caused by animal spirits, government can and should act to prevent them.

Suppose the FPC was able to eliminate inefficient fluctuations in price-to-earnings ratios by trading an ETF for short-term debt. That policy, if targeted correctly, would ensure the price-to-earnings ratio was equal to seventeen. But, the fact that the price-to-earnings ratio is constant does not guarantee full employment. The price-to-earnings ratio could be equal to seventeen with an unemployment rate of 5%, an unemployment rate of 10%, or an unemployment rate of 25%.

Getting the right price-to-earnings ratio does not guarantee full employment because it does not ensure earnings are correct. For every unemployment rate, there is an associated level of earnings and only one of them is the right one. An optimal stabilization policy must allow stock market prices to grow faster than earnings when unemployment is above its natural rate, and it must slow down the growth of asset prices, relative to earnings, when the unemployment rate is below its natural rate.

Although it is true monetary policy alone cannot influence the long-run unemployment rate, the FPC would be operating what is, in effect, a fiscal policy. Through active control of the stock market, the Treasury will make trades on behalf of future generations that they themselves are unable to make. This policy recommendation is based on a coherent theory that reconciles Keynesian and classical economics in a new way, and explains why high involuntary unemployment will persist if we do not act to prevent it.[21]

Some Practical Questions

Would a fund of the kind I propose be costly to the taxpayer? I do not believe so. My theory predicts that the asset price stabilization fund will generate positive revenues for the Treasury because the Treasury can exploit its longevity to take asset positions that private citizens cannot. The market can remain irrational longer than you or I. It can remain irrational longer than George Soros or Bill Gates. It cannot remain irrational for longer than the US or the UK governments.

Historically, the stock market has paid a return that is roughly six percentage points higher than the return on short-term Treasury bonds. That return exists to compensate market participants for the risk involved from excessive stock market volatility. By stabilizing that volatility, the future return on equity will fall, and the return on mutual funds will rise, until returns on the ETF are approximately equal to the return to long-term government debt. Economic theory suggests this return should be stabilized at approximately the growth rate of the real economy.[22]

Critics might argue it is dangerous to inflate an asset price bubble; but a bubble is only dangerous to the real economy if it is allowed to burst. Currently, households and firms that borrowed during the 2000s are paying down debt. That debt was sustainable when the value of collateral was high. It became unsustainable when the value of collateral assets crashed after the financial crisis. By restoring the value of equity, those households and firms currently in debt will be able to redirect their purchasing power to the real economy.

The mandate of the FPC must be not only to raise asset prices when they are too low, but also to lower them when they are too high. A successful financial policy must prevent bubbles as well as crashes. When unemployment falls to a sustainable level, the FPC should act to slow the growth of equity prices. Theory predicts that lower unemployment will be accompanied by additional output of goods and services only up to a point. Pushing unemployment below its natural rate will lead to lower output, relative to trend. Just as monetary policymakers make judgments based on a range of different indicators, so must financial policymakers.

Financial Policy Should Be Coordinated with Monetary Policy

Financial policy is not, nor should it be, independent of monetary policy. It is critically important that central banks throughout the world return quickly to a situation of positive short-term interest rates. This goal is important because when the interest rate is fixed at zero, monetary policymakers have lost control of their only tool for maintaining control of the inflation rate. It is important the central bank has the flexibility not only to raise the interest rate if it perceives inflation is about to return, but also to lower the interest rate if deflation is a bigger threat.

To have the flexibility to lower the interest rate in the future, it must first be raised to a more normal level. This is not happening in the current economic climate because monetary policymakers perceive, rightly, that if they were to increase the interest rate, the stock market would fall and, in three months' time, the unemployment rate would increase. But, if the MPC were to act in concert with the FPC, the negative consequences of an interest rate increase could be avoided. The MPC would announce an interest rate rise and, simultaneously, the FPC would announce a target path for the stock market. Currently, the MPC has lost access to its traditional instrument for controlling inflation. Financial policy, through active trades in the stock market, would give policymakers the option of targeting the real economy independently of the price level.

How would that combined operation work? Imagine that, at the next MPC meeting, Bank of England Governor Mark Carney were to announce the interest rate would be increased to 2%. Simultaneously, the FPC would announce the newly created ETF, currently trading at 100, is too low. As of the date of the MPC meeting, the SWF would stand ready to buy or sell the fund at a price of 120 and, for the next month, they would intervene in the markets to ensure the index would increase daily by 3% at an annualized rate.

The day-to-day running of the SWF would operate much like current monetary policy. Each month, the FPC would form a new judgment regarding the current state of the economy. Suppose that, in the judgment of the FPC, unemployment was too high. The committee would then announce a new value at which it would be willing to purchase shares in the SWF—for example, 130—and a targeted growth rate for the SWF for the next month—for example, 2.5% annualized. By picking the growth path of the ETF, and the money interest rate, the combination of monetary and financial policies would be targeting both the real and the nominal interest rates. And by controlling the value of financial assets, they would determine the unemployment rate.

The International Implications of Financial Market Stabilization

We live in a world of international capital markets, and globalization has led to a big increase in the cross-border ownership of assets during the past fifty years. In 1975, foreigners owned assets equal to roughly 15% of US GDP. Americans owned slightly more foreign assets, but that position reversed in 1985 and the United States is now a net debtor. More importantly, the size of cross-border capital flows has increased substantially and, since 2014, foreign ownership of US assets is now more than 100% of US GDP.[23] In a smaller and more open economy—such as the United Kingdom, for example—the magnitudes are much larger and foreigners own assets worth more then eight times UK GDP.[24]

As a consequence of globalization, a large percentage of the stocks listed on a country's stock exchange are international corporations with operations spread across the globe. It would be foolish to think the UK Treasury could set the dollar price of the financial institution HSBC or the petroleum giant Royal Dutch Shell—two of the largest companies traded on the London Stock Exchange. But, it can control the price quoted in pounds Sterling because the Bank of England is the monopoly supplier of pounds.

Suppose the UK Financial Policy Committee decides that, to boost the demand for UK goods and services, it should increase the value of an ETF that includes Royal Dutch Shell as a large component of its basket. And suppose that foreign investors disagree with their decision. Foreigners will sell dollars and buy pounds to take advantage of what they perceive to be a profit opportunity that has opened up because the UK government is paying more for shares in Royal Dutch Shell than the market thinks they are worth.

If the Bank of England wishes to maintain the value of an ETF and maintain simultaneously the value of the exchange rate of the pound, it will need to prevent foreigners from buying pounds in the free market. This policy, called the *imposition of capital controls*, was a routine component of the operation of international capital markets under the fixed exchange rate system that operated immediately after WWII.[25]

If the Bank of England chooses not to impose capital controls, the pound will appreciate as foreigners trade dollars for pounds to invest in UK stocks. The lesson I want readers to take away from this example is that the central bank of an economy that trades with the rest of the world cannot control simultaneously the value of domestic stocks and the value of its currency. In a world where international financial markets remain volatile, the domestic economy can only be insulated from the animal spirits of participants in foreign asset markets by allowing those animal spirits to cause persistent movements in the exchange rate. A government that chooses to stabilize its domestic financial markets must forgo attempts to stabilize its exchange rate.

Three Contemporary Issues

In this closing section, I take up the question of how my work is related to three issues with which readers of this book are likely to be familiar: (1) Scott Sumner's proposal for nominal GDP targeting, (2) Willem Buiter's proposal for negative nominal interest rates, and (3) Michael Woodford's proposal for forward guidance as an alternative to QE.[26]

Scott Sumner and Nominal GDP Targeting

Beginning in February 2009, Scott Sumner became a powerful voice for the idea that the Fed should target nominal GDP growth. One scheme he has written about on his blog is similar to the proposal I put forward in my 2008 *Financial Times* article, "How to Prevent the Great Depression of 2009."[27] Sumner suggests the Fed should establish a futures market in nominal GDP and that it should trade in that market with the goal of stabilizing nominal GDP growth.

I had assumed, incorrectly, Sumner was proposing central banks should simply adjust the coefficients on their interest rate policies, the so-called Taylor Rule, to raise the nominal interest rate when nominal GDP growth is above target and to lower it when nominal GDP growth is below target. I will refer to that variant of nominal GDP targeting as *growth rate targeting*. An alternative, nominal GDP-level targeting, would make these interest rate adjustments in response to deviations of nominal GDP from a target growth path.[28]

Viewed in this light, nominal GDP targeting, of either variety, is not a particularly new idea, nor does it represent a departure from the body of New Keynesian economics that grew up in the decades since 1983, when Edward C. Prescott sought to banish money from macroeconomic models. Sumner is saying much, much more than that.

The novel aspect of Sumner's proposal—and one I endorse wholeheartedly—is the means he advocates to achieve his goal. Sumner proposes central banks and/or national treasuries should set up markets for nominal GDP futures. Robert Shiller has made a similar suggestion. He proposes national treasuries finance their borrowing by issuing securities that pay off a dividend proportional to nominal GDP. He calls these "Trills," where a Trill is a claim to one trillionth of GDP in perpetuity.[29]

I have suggested central banks trade an ETF to stabilize real economic activity. Hold that thought because the word *real* represents a significant point where Sumner and I differ.

Trading Trills, trading GDP futures, and trading an ETF are all methods of targeting nominal wealth. I do not want to quibble over the exact method, and I readily concede that Trills or GDP futures have advantages over ETFs. The important insight here is that wealth, or permanent income, drives aggregate demand and that expectations cause inefficient fluctuations in aggregate demand that can be stabilized through relatively straightforward interventions.

In the simplest macroeconomic models, GDP measured in wage units is proportional to employment. Sumner points out that money wages move slowly and, as a consequence, stabilizing nominal GDP will stabilize employment, and eventually wages and prices. Like the New Keynesians, Sumner bases his ideas on Samuelson's neoclassical synthesis; the economy is Keynesian in the short run, when prices and wages are sticky, and classical in the long run.

In Sumner's world, the economy homes in on the natural rate of unemployment just as surely as a heat-seeking missile converges to its target. Sumner's intellectual heritage is firmly monetarist. If Milton Friedman were alive today, one might imagine that Sumner would find a supporter for his ideas.

I wholeheartedly endorse Sumner's proposal for open market trades in GDP futures. And, like Robert Shiller, I would like to see the creation of a market for Trills. Unlike Sumner, I do not endorse the proposal to stabilize either the level or the growth rate of nominal GDP. Trades in GDP futures should aim to stabilize the unemployment rate. And here is my biggest difference from Sumner: trades in GDP futures should be seen as a complement to inflation targeting, not as a substitute. A nominal GDP target, in conjunction with an inflation target, would give the Treasury and the central bank the power not just to influence inflation in the long run, but also to influence the unemployment rate.

Willem Buiter and Eliminating the Zero Lower Bound

The second proposal I wish to address is one that Willem Buiter proposed in a 2009 academic paper, in which he suggested eliminating paper currency and moving to a form of electronic money. That proposal is a practical way of allowing central banks to set negative nominal interest rates and it is territory that Japan, Sweden, Denmark, and Switzerland have now entered.[30]

New Keynesian economists want the flexibility to lower the money interest rate below zero because they believe that by lowering the money interest rate, it will be possible to reduce the real interest rate and stimulate aggregate demand. In the IS-LM world, the real interest rate and the unemployment rate move hand in hand. Although I see no harm in proposals for electronic money and negative rates, I do not think the ability to lower the interest rate below zero is the best long-term solution to the problem of aggregate demand management.

My objections are related to my differences with Scott Sumner. In my view, nominal GDP growth is driven by the animal spirits of market participants. A policy of inflation targeting has been in place in most western countries for twenty-five years. It is an effective way to channel nominal GDP shocks either into inflationary expectations or to changes in the unemployment rate. It was fortuitous that during the past three decades these objectives were not in conflict. There is no guarantee that that happy coincidence will continue.

In the New Keynesian world, where the NRH holds, the goal of policy is to stabilize the economy in the short run. The long run will take care of itself. In my view, the problem is deeper. A policymaker who is freed from the lower bound still has two objectives—price stability and maximum employment—but has only one instrument: changes in the nominal interest rate. Even if a policymaker could achieve an inflation rate of 2% by moving the nominal interest rate in a reasonable range, there is no guarantee she would achieve her employment target simultaneously.

In the New Keynesian model, there is a tight connection between the steady-state interest rate, the steady-state inflation rate, and the steady-state unemployment rate. When the policymaker has achieved a target steady-state real interest rate, she has also achieved her steady-state unemployment target. The natural rate of unemployment is associated uniquely with the natural rate of interest.

I do not believe New Keynesian theory is correct. Although there is a unique natural rate of interest, there are multiple possible steady-state equilibrium unemployment rates. Achieving the natural rate of interest does not imply we have attained the natural rate of unemployment automatically.

Michael Woodford and Forward Guidance

In an influential paper presented at the 2012 Federal Reserve Conference in Jackson Hole, Wyoming, Michael Woodford compared policies of QE, in which a central bank changes the composition of its balance sheet explicitly, with an alternative policy he called *forward guidance*.[31]

In Woodford's view, changes in the asset composition of the central bank's balance sheet are unlikely to be successful. To the extent that QE works in practice, it must be by providing information to the public about the central bank's intent with regard to future policy actions. It is a short step to the recommendation that central bank intentions should be communicated directly, a policy that Woodford calls *forward guidance.*

Woodford's paper was highly influential, and it has had a direct impact on the way the MPC at the Bank of England in the United Kingdom, and the Open Market Committee at the Fed in the United States have communicated with the public.

Woodford thinks the composition of the central bank balance sheet does not matter because it does not matter in the canonical New Keynesian model that guides him. The following passage is taken from my 2012 paper "Qualitative Easing: How it Works and Why it Matters":

> In a complete markets environment, the government cannot remove risk. It can simply transfer that risk from the private balance sheet to the public balance sheet. Since the public balance sheet is ultimately backed by the tax liabilities of the private sector, the risk does not disappear; it is simply relabeled. Rational agents . . . readjust their financial positions to undo the central bank intervention and the change in the central bank's balance sheet will have no influence on realized security prices.[32]

The key to the transmission channel of composition effects is the fact that participation in the assets markets is incomplete. That channel is missing from the theoretical model to which Woodford refers and, as a consequence, he concludes the channel is missing in the real world.

In his Jackson Hole paper, Woodford argued that QE may be effective; but, if it is effective, it works by influencing expectations. And Woodford thinks that it would be better to influence expectations directly through forward guidance. I disagree. QE is effective because beliefs are fundamental and changes in the asset composition of the central bank shift risk from current generations to future generations.

My Argument Summarized

Since the United States passed the Employment Act of 1946, US policymakers have been concerned with two variables: the inflation rate and the unemployment rate. After the Great Recession of 2008, it has become increasingly fashionable to voice the concern that the stability of the asset markets is key to achieving both objectives. I have a concrete proposal on how financial stability can be achieved.

It is widely recognized that control of the money supply is key to achieving a low and stable inflation rate. Since the advent of inflation targeting during the 1990s, that has been achieved by setting a target for the inflation rate in the medium term and by raising or lowering the money interest rate in response to deviations of inflation from its target.

Most economists believe the unemployment rate may deviate temporarily from its natural rate. The New Keynesians argue we should make adjustments to the interest rate to help combat these deviations and return the unemployment rate to the natural rate more quickly. Milton Friedman argued against this position, which he called "leaning against the wind." Friedman lost that argument and today policy in central banks is overwhelmingly dictated by the New Keynesian view.

The New Keynesian view is wrong. Deviations of unemployment from its natural rate are not temporary; they are permanent. Government should adjust the money interest rate to achieve an inflation target. And it should adopt a new macroprudential tool, targeting the stock market, to achieve a full employment target.

It has become topical to argue that financial instability is a problem that can be solved by regulation. In 2010, the US Congress passed the Dodd–Frank Act. In the United Kingdom, Parliament passed the 2012 Financial Services Act, which created a new Financial Policy Committee of the Bank of England and a new Prudential Regulation Authority with powers to regulate financial institutions. Will the new regulations passed in the United States and in the United Kingdom help prevent future financial crises? Perhaps. But I am concerned economists have not recognized the extent of the problems we face.[33]

The financial markets are incomplete because people cannot participate in markets that open before they are born. And labor markets are incomplete because there are not enough prices to allocate people efficiently to jobs. I have referred to these two market failures collectively as the *incomplete markets problem.* The way to solve the incomplete markets problem is to create an SWF, funded by government borrowing, with a mandate to trade the stock market actively and to prevent future bubbles and crashes.

Financial crises are not rare events. They have been a regular feature of market economies for as long as we have traded in organized financial markets. Orthodox economic theory tells us free trade in financial markets should lead to Pareto-efficient outcomes that cannot be improved on by government intervention. Orthodox economic theory is wrong. This is why economics must change and in this book I have explained how to change it.

The 2008 financial crisis was preceded by a wave of optimism that carried the seeds of its own destruction. Market participants, buoyed by optimistic expectations, engaged in trades that led to a long period of excess returns. When confidence evaporated, in fall 2008, the market crashed. Fear gripped the markets.

When businesswomen and men are afraid, they stop investing in the real economy. Fear is reflected in low and volatile asset values. Investors come to believe stocks and the values of the machines and factories that back those stocks may fall further. Fear feeds on itself, and the prediction that stocks will lose value becomes self-fulfilling. Active trades in the financial markets would combat this vicious cycle by absorbing the risk private citizens are unwilling to bear.

When the Fed was created in 1913, central bank intervention in the financial markets to control a short-term interest rate was considered to be a radical step. A century later, we have learned that interest rate control is an effective way to maintain price stability, but we have not yet learned how to prevent financial crises. Modern policymakers have been assigned one instrument—control of the money interest rate—and two targets: low inflation and full employment. A single instrument is not sufficient to accomplish both tasks.

Asset market fluctuations are not caused by inevitable fluctuations in productive capacity. They are caused by the animal spirits of human beings. The remedy is to design an institution, modeled on the modern central bank, with both the authority and the tools to stabilize aggregate fluctuations in the stock market.

Since the inception of central banking during the seventeenth century, it has taken us 350 years to evolve institutions to manage prices. The path has not been easy and we have made many missteps. Let us hope the adoption of a new financial policy that can prevent and/or mitigate the effects of financial crises on persistent and long-term unemployment will be a much swifter process than the 350 years it took to develop the modern central bank.

NOTES

Chapter 1

1. I am referring to wealth measured in units of 2008 purchasing power.
2. These data are taken from *The World Factbook* (Central Intelligence Agency, 2015).
3. *An Introduction to the Principles of Morals and Legislation* (Bentham, 2002). Economists formalize this idea by defining a *social welfare function*, which is a weighted sum of the utilities of all the people in a given nation state.
4. There is a branch of economics called *mechanism design* that studies a related question. I made the sweeping assertion that the social planner knows the preferences of all the people in the economy. But how does she know this? We cannot simply ask people what they want because they may have an incentive to lie. Economists distinguish private goods, like food, from public goods, such as access to roads. If we ask a person if he wants access to roads, knowing he will be charged for the roads if he says yes, that person has an incentive to underreport his preference for public transportation services. Mechanism design is about ways of allocating goods that recognize constraints of this nature. In 2007, Leonid Hurwicz, Eric Maskin, and Roger Myerson were awarded the Nobel Prize for their work on this issue.
5. *The Fatal Conceit: The Errors of Socialism* (Hayek, 1988).
6. *The General Theory of Employment, Interest and Money* (Keynes, 1936).
7. Not everyone would agree. The case against the success of Keynesian stabilization policy was made by Christina Romer,

former chair of President Obama's Council of Economic Advisors (Romer, "Spurious Volatility in Historical Unemployment Data," 1986; "The Prewar Business Cycle Reconsidered: New Estimates of Gross National Product, 1869–1908," 1989). In these papers, Romer claimed that the increased stability of the postwar data is an artifact of the fact that it was constructed differently from data that preceded the Great Depression. Nathan Balke and Robert J. Gordon ("The Estimation of Prewar Gross National Product: Methodology and New Evidence," 1989) offer an alternative view. They claim the reduction in volatility that characterizes data after WWII is real. I find the Balke–Gordon argument more persuasive. Although part of the reduction in the volatility of unemployment and real gross national product in the prewar and postwar data may be an artifact of measurement, it is unlikely that all of it is. Romer is currently a professor of economics at the University of California, Berkeley; Nathan Balke is an economics professor at Southern Methodist University; and Robert J. Gordon is an economics professor at Northwestern University.

8. The story of inflation targeting is told by Ben Bernanke, Thomas Laubach, Frederic S. Mishkin, and Adam S. Posen in *Inflation Targeting: Lessons from the International Experience* (1999).

9. Although neo-Austrians such as Ron Paul are a minority voice in American politics, they represent a vocal and influential bloc in the Republican Party. Paul published a book, *End the Fed* (Paul, 2009), which reached number one on the *New York Times* bestseller list.

10. This view is contested by a number of authors and there is an ongoing debate in the literature regarding the cause of the Great Moderation. Critics, notably Christopher Sims and Tao Zha (Sims and Zha, *Were There Regime Switches in US Monetary Policy?* 2006) have proposed instead that the Great Moderation was caused by "good luck"—that is, the shocks that hit the economy after 1980 have been smaller. In my opinion, the "good policy" view is more convincing.

11. *Remarks by Governor Ben S. Bernanke at the Conference to Honor Milton Friedman* (Bernanke, 2002).

12. *The Monetary History of the United States: 1867–1960* (Friedman and Schwartz, 1963).

13. For Hayek's views on socialism and social planning, see *The Road to Serfdom* (Hayek, 1944), which he dedicated to "socialists of all parties."

14. *The Road to Serfdom* (Hayek, 1944).

15. Youth unemployment in Spain reached 56.1% in 2013 and, in Greece, a staggering 62.9% of young people were without jobs (Burgen, "Spain Youth Unemployment Reaches Record 56.1%," 2013).

16. "Online Data Robert Shiller" (Shiller, 2015). The CAPE is a measure of the ratio of stock prices to expected future earnings, where earnings are smoothed over twenty years to eliminate cycles. Financial economists assume that earnings growth in any instant is equal to a positive number; this is called the *drift*, plus a random variable that is equally likely to be positive as negative. A random variable with this property is called a *random walk with drift*. Models in which earnings growth is a random walk with drift, when coupled with simple but plausible theories of behavior, predict that the CAPE should be constant.

17. My book *Expectations, Employment and Prices* (Farmer, 2010a) explains my original concept of "incomplete factor markets" in more depth. The first published version appeared in Farmer ("Old Keynesian Economics," 2008c). Related works that discuss the idea of incomplete factor markets include Farmer ("Old Keynesian Economics," 2006; "Animal Spirits, Persistent Unemployment and the Belief Function," 2012a; "Confidence, Crashes and Animal Spirits," 2012b; "Animal Spirits, Financial Crises and Persistent Unemployment," 2013a. Narayana Kocherlakota ("Incomplete Labor Markets," 2012) uses the term *incomplete labor markets* to refer to the same idea. I have adopted Kocherlakota's term *incomplete labor markets* because the term *incomplete factor markets* requires additional explanation for the general reader who is not familiar with the jargon of economics.

18. "The Stock Market Crash Really Did Cause the Great Recession" (Farmer 2015b). A thirty-year-old person with a portfolio of stocks in a retirement account will not change her purchases every day in response to fluctuations in the value of her pension assets. A sixty-five-year-old couple who recently retired will change their expenditure plans if the value of their pension assets falls by 10% and is expected to remain depressed for five to ten years. For an alternative view of the transmission mechanism from wealth to stock prices, see the article by Jean-Paul Fitoussi et al. (Fitoussi, Jestaz, Phelps, and Zoega, "Roots of the Recent Recoveries: Labor Reforms or Private Sector Forces," 2000) and Edmund Phelps' book, *Structural Slumps* (1994).

19. Although unemployment in the United States is now almost back to prerecession levels, it has taken eight years to get there. And it

is unlikely, in my view, that unemployment would have returned to 5% in the absence of the remarkable monetary stimulus that was engaged in by the Federal Reserve.

20. "The Austerity Delusion" (Krugman, 2015).

21. Sir John Hicks ("Mr. Keynes and the Classics: A Suggested Interpretation," 1937) and Alvin Hansen ("Mr. Keynes on Underemployment Equilibrium," 1936) are jointly credited with the development of the IS-LM model. Paul Samuelson introduced a version of the Hicks–Hansen model to several generations of undergraduates and added an adjustment mechanism to connect the short run with the long run. The neoclassical synthesis first appeared in the third edition of his undergraduate textbook *Economics: An Introductory Analysis* (Samuelson, 1955). For a discussion of the role of Samuelson's text in the history of thought, see "After the Revolution: Paul Samuelson and the Textbook Keynesian Model" (Pearce and Hoover, 1995).

22. Prominent Keynesians of the IS-LM persuasion include University of California Berkeley professor J. Bradford DeLong, Nobel Laureate Paul Krugman, and former US Treasury secretary and Harvard president Lawrence Summers.

23. Friedman developed the *permanent income hypothesis* (Friedman, *A Theory of the Consumption Function*, 1957) and, in related work, Albert Ando and Franco Modigliani ("The 'Life Cycle' Hypothesis of Saving: Aggregate Implications and Tests," 1963) worked on *the life cycle hypothesis*. These theories are complementary. They each deny the importance of current income as the sole determinant of aggregate consumption and they replace income with a concept of aggregate wealth.

24. "The Relationship of Home Investment to Unemployment" (Kahn, 1931).

25. See Farmer ("The Stock Market Crash of 2008 Caused the Great Recession: Theory and Evidence," 2012d; "The Stock Market Crash Really Did Cause the Great Recession," 2015b), Corpe ("Forecasting UK Unemployment Using Stock Market Prices," 2014), and Fritsche and Pierdzioch ("Animal Spirits, the Stock Market, and the Unemployment Rate: Some Evidence for German Data," 2016).

26. Friedman's prescription for economic policy was that the central bank should set the rate of money creation at 5% per year and refrain from trying to influence economic activity. Government attempts to stabilize the economy would, according to Friedman, introduce

additional uncertainty and make it more difficult for private agents to act (Friedman, *A Program for Monetary Stability*, 1960).

27. I have frequently met this comment when presenting my work at academic conferences. It is inspired by Robert Barro's work on the connection between models where choices are made by a representative family, and models of overlapping generations of agents. The equilibria of overlapping-generations models are frequently Pareto inefficient. The reason is subtle and is connected with the double-infinity of people and commodities in these models (Shell, "Notes on the Economics of Infinity," 1971). Barro showed that, under some circumstances, the market failure that arises in these models could be corrected by chains of operative bequests from parents to their children (Barro, "Are Government Bonds Net Wealth?" 1974). Barro's argument does not apply to the Pareto inefficiency caused by incomplete participation in insurance markets.

28. An ETF is an asset that consists of a basket of stocks where the stocks are chosen to reflect some desired characteristic. For example, it is possible to buy an ETF that consists of every stock that makes up the Dow Jones index. The price of the ETF goes up and down in line with the Dow, and the stocks that make up the basket are held in proportion to the weight of their relative value in the market index.

29. See, for example, the article "On a Correct Measure of Inflation" by Alchian and Klein (1973).

30. See the work by Mathias Drehmann, Claudio Borio, and Costas Tsatsaronis ("Anchoring Countercyclical Capital Buffers: The Role of Credit Aggregates," 2011).

31. For a concise history of contemporary economic thought, with a unique twist, read my book *How the Economy Works* (Farmer, 2010b).

Chapter 2

1. "Propagation Problems and Impulse Problems in Dynamic Economics" (Frisch, 1966 [1933]), *Interest and Prices* (Wicksell, 1965 [1898]).

2. *How the Economy Works: Confidence, Crashes and Self-fulfilling Prophecies* (Farmer, 2010b).

3. *Value and Capital* (Hicks, 1946 [1939]).

4. For an elaboration of this argument, see "The Temporary Equilibrium Method: Hicks against Hicks" (De Vroey, 2006).

5. *Economics: An Introductory Analysis* (Samuelson, 1955).

6. *Contributions to Modern Economics* (Robinson, 1978, p. 256).
7. The ideas and development of that school are summarized in a recent research paper by Beatrice Cherrier and Aurélian Saïdi, "The Indeterminate Fate of Sunspots in Economics" (2015) and in my survey paper "The Evolution of Endogenous Business Cycles" (Farmer, 2014c).
8. "Self-fulfilling Prophecies" (Azariadis, 1981), "Do Sunspots Matter?" (Cass and Shell, 1983).
9. "Commercial Crises and Sun-spots" (Jevons, 1878).
10. "Monnaie et Allocation Intertemporelle" (Shell, 1977).
11. The response to Shell's seminar was reported to me by Karl in a personal conversation.
12. I moved to West Philadelphia a couple of years later and I learned of the genesis of these ideas from personal conversations with Costas. His initial surprise at the idea that "sunspots matter" is recorded in an interview that Costas gave to Beatrice Cherrier and Aurélian Saïdi for their survey article "The Indeterminate Fate of Sunspots in Economics" (2015).
13. "Self-fulfilling Prophecies" (Azariadis, 1981).
14. "Self-fulfilling Prophecies and the Business Cycle" (Farmer and Woodford, 1984, 1997). The working paper version of this paper appeared in 1984 (Farmer and Woodford, 1984). It remained unpublished, but influential, for 13 years and was eventually published in 1997 as the first of a series of "classic unpublished papers" in *Macroeconomic Dynamics* (Farmer and Woodford, 1997). Woodford chose not to follow the Penn agenda and went on, instead, to promote New Keynesian economics. His book *Interest and Prices: Foundations of a Theory of Monetary Policy* (2003) is one of the most comprehensive treatments of New Keynesian economics in the field.
15. "Indeterminacy and Increasing Returns" (Benhabib and Farmer, 1994), "Real Business Cycles and the Animal Spirits Hypothesis" (Farmer and Guo, 1994), "Time to Build and Aggregate Fluctuations" (Kydland and Prescott, 1982).
16. *The Macroeconomics of Self-Fulfilling Prophecies* (Farmer, 1993).
17. See "The Indeterminate Fate of Sunspots in Economics" (Cherrier and Saïdi, 2015) for an elaboration of that theme.
18. "The Evolution of Endogenous Business Cycles" (Farmer, 2014c). The book, *A History of Macroeconomics* (De Vroey, 2016), contains a nice summary of my work on second generation models. It is also an excellent summary of the recent history of macroeconomic theory.

19. Papers in the second-generation Endogenous Business Cycle (EBC2) literature include those by Angeletos and La'O ("Sentiments," 2013); Benhabib, Wang, and Wen ("Sentiments and Aggregate Demand Fluctuations," 2015); Brown ("Essays in Macroeconomics and International Trade," 2010); Farmer and Plotnikov ("Does Fiscal Policy Matter? Blinder and Solow Revisited," 2012); Gelain and Guerrazzi ("A DGSE Model from the Old Keynesian Economics: An Empirical Investigation," 2010); Guerrazzi ("Expectations Employment and Prices: A Suggested Interpretation of the New 'Farmerian Economics,'" 2010); Guerrazzi ("Search and Stochastic Dynamics in the Old Keynesian Economics: A Rationale for the Shimer Puzzle," 2011); Guerrazzi ("The 'Farmerian' Approach to Ending Finance-Induced Recession: Notes on Stability and Dynamics," 2012); Heathcote and Perri ("Wealth and Volatility," 2012); Kashiwagi ("Search Theory and the Housing Market," 2010); Kashiwagi ("Sunspots and Self-Fulfilling Beliefs in the U.S. Housing Market," 2014); Kocherlakota ("Incomplete Labor Markets," 2012); Miao, Wang, and Xu ("Stock Market Bubbles and Unemployment," 2012); Michaillat and Saez ("A Model of Aggregate Demand and Unemployment," 2013); Michaillat and Saez ("An Economical Business Cycle Model," 2014); Plotnikov ("Three Essays on Macroeconomics with Incomplete Factor Markets," 2010), Plotnikov ("Hysteresis in Unemployment and Jobless Recoveries," 2014); Schmitt-Grohé and Uribe ("Pegs and Pain," 2011); and Schmitt-Grohé and Uribe ("Pegs, Downward Wage Rigidity and Unemployment: The Role of Financial Structure," 2014).

20. *Expectations, Employment and Prices* (Farmer, 2010a).

Chapter 3

1. Smith's seminal work, *An Inquiry into the Nature and Causes of the Wealth of Nations*, is considered by many to represent the beginning of modern economics (1776).

2. *A Treatise on Political Economy* (Say, 1834).

3. *Industrial Fluctuations* (Pigou, 1927).

4. "The Relationship between Unemployment and the Rate of Change of Money Wages in the United Kingdom 1861–1957" (Phillips, 1958).

5. *Economics: An Introductory Analysis* (Samuelson, 1955).

6. I am using the term *hard core* in the sense of Lakatos (*The Methodology of Scientific Research Programmes*, 1978). I elaborate further on this idea in Chapter 5.

7. Richard G. Lipsey was one of the first to explore the theoretical underpinnings of the Phillips Curve ("The Relation between Unemployment and the Rate of Change of Money Wage Rates in the United Kingdom, 1861–1957: A Further Analysis," 1960). For a history and survey of the importance of the Phillips Curve, see Lipsey and Scarth's (2011) *Inflation and Unemployment: The Evolution of the Phillips Curve*.

8. *The Hunt for Vulcan: … And How Albert Einstein Destroyed a Planet, Discovered Relativity, and Deciphered the Universe* (Levenson, 2015).

9. "Analytical Aspects of Anti-Inflation Policy" (Samuelson and Solow, 1960).

10. "The Counter-Revolution in Monetary Theory," (Friedman, 1970b, page 11).

11. See "The Role of Monetary Policy" (Friedman, 1968) and "Money Wage Dynamics and Labor Market Equilibrium" (Phelps, 1968).

12. Friedman ("The Role of Monetary Policy," 1968).

13. This narrative is based on the work of Jo-Anna Gray ("Wage Indexation: A Macroeconomic Approach," 1976).

14. Friedman introduced adaptive expectations in his book, *A Theory of the Consumption Function* (Friedman, 1957).

15. See "Expectations and the Neutrality of Money" (Lucas Jr., 1972).

16. See "Rational Expectations and the Theory of Price Movements" (Muth, 1961).

17. "Natural Rate Doubts" (Beyer and Farmer, 2007). We were not the first to study the low-frequency properties of these data. Robert G. King and Mark Watson ("Testing Long-Run Neutrality," 1997) looked at bivariate tests of the long-run neutrality of money and found that evidence for the nonneutrality of money is inconclusive. Our study looks at three, not two, time series, and we allow for structural breaks.

18. "The Natural Rate Hypothesis: An Idea Past Its Sell-by-Date" (Farmer, 2013d).

19. The fact that there is an upward-sloping long-run Phillips Curve can be explained in equilibrium models of money. See, for example, Berentsen, Menzio, and Wright ("Inflation and Unemployment in the Long Run," 2011).

Chapter 4

1. Economic models try to explain how many hours the average person spends in paid employment. However, they do not break this up into its three constituent parts: How many people are part of

the labor force, as opposed to those who are retired or stay-at-home caregivers? How many hours a week does each employed person work? And how many people who want to work are actually in paid employment as opposed to being unemployed?

2. *The General Theory of Employment, Interest and Money* (Keynes, 1936).

3. Lucas' first work on this topic was a coauthored article with Leonard Rapping ("Real Wages Employment and Inflation," 1969). Three years later Lucas published an influential single-author paper ("Expectations and the Neutrality of Money," 1972) that introduced the concept of rational expectations. Lucas continued to write a series of papers that used the market-clearing approach and, despite initial resistance from Keynesian economists, the equilibrium approach became dominant in a relatively short period.

4. See Kydland and Prescott ("Time to Build and Aggregate Fluctuations," 1982). The Ramsey growth model is named after Frank Ramsey ("A Mathematical Theory of Saving," 1928). Ramsey was a contemporary of Keynes in Cambridge, England, and he was the first person to introduce the mathematics necessary to study the optimization problem of an infinitely lived family. The term *real business cycles* comes from an article by John B. Long Jr. and Charles Plosser ("Real Business Cycles," 1983).

5. See Hodrick and Prescott ("Post-War U.S. Business Cycles: A Descriptive Empirical Investigation," 1997).

6. "The Monetarist Controversy, or Should We Forsake Stabilization Policies" (Modigliani, 1977).

7. See Mankiw and Romer (*New Keynesian Economics: Vol. 2: Coordination Failures and Real Rigidities*, 1991).

8. *Industrial Fluctuations* (Pigou, 1927). Important contributions to the New Keynesian DSGE agenda were made, among others, by Lawrence J. Christiano, Martin Eichenbaum, and Charles Evans ("Nominal Rigidities and the Dynamics Effects of a Shock to Monetary Policy," 2005); Jordi Galí and Mark Gertler ("The Science of Monetary Policy: A New Keynesian Perspective," 1999); and Michael Woodford (*Interest and Prices: Foundations of a Theory of Monetary Policy*, 2003). The pinnacle of the DSGE approach is summarized in an influential paper by Frank Smets and Raf Wouters ("An Estimated Dynamic Stochastic General Equilibrium Model of the Euro Area," 2003). By adding many different frictions and shocks to a DSGE model, they showed that a New Keynesian DSGE model provides a credible explanation of past data. The problem

with their approach is that the New Keynesian DSGE model must be modified continually by adding new frictions or new shocks to incorporate new facts.

9. In *Expectations, Employment and Prices* (Farmer, 2010a), I present an alternative to the Hodrick–Prescott filter that I call *measurement of data in wage units*.

10. This argument is drawn from my article "The Natural Rate Hypothesis: An Idea Past Its Sell-by-Date," (Farmer, 2013d). It first appeared in the *Bank of England Quarterly Bulletin*.

11. "Changing Trends in the Labor Force: A Survey" (DiCecio, Engemann, Owyang, and Wheeler, 2008).

Chapter 5

1. See Pearce and Hoover ("After the Revolution: Paul Samuelson and the Textbook Keynesian Model," 1995) for a discussion of the influence of Samuelson's textbook.

2. *Essays in Positive Economics* (Friedman, 1953).

3. *Conjectures and Refutations: The Growth of Scientific Knowledge* (Popper, 1963).

4. The leading reference is *The Structure of Scientific Revolutions* (Kuhn, 1962).

5. Axel Leijonhufvud has written many essays and several books on the connection between macroeconomics and the philosophy of science. One of my favorite collections is his book *Information and Coordination: Essays in Macroeconomic Theory* (Leijonhufvud, 1981).

6. The book *Criticism and the Growth of Knowledge* (Lakatos and Musgrave, 1970) contains a delightful collection of essays by leading philosophers of science, including a marvelous chapter by Imre Lakatos. I recommend it highly to anyone with an interest in philosophy and to the discerning graduate student of economics who is looking for a break from his or her latest homework assignment on functional analysis.

7. *Essays, Moral, Political and Literary,* based on the 1777 edition published originally published as vol. 1 of *Essays and Treatises on Several Subjects* (Hume, 1987 [1777]).

8. Economists use the word *equilibrium* to refer to a situation when no person has an incentive to change his or her behavior. When used in a dynamic concept, the variables modeled by a dynamic equilibrium may be changing over time. That is very different from the physicist's use of equilibrium, which means a state that is constant from

one period to the next. To describe the physicist's concept, economists refer to a *steady-state equilibrium*. I discuss these differences in
my book *The Macroeconomics of Self-fulfilling Prophecies* (Farmer, 1993).

9. "Sticky Prices in the United States" (Rotemberg, 1982).

10. See "Staggered Prices in a Utility Maximizing Model" (Calvo, 1983).
Tak Yun (1996) first used the Calvo mechanism in a complete gen-
eral equilibrium model, documented in "Nominal Price Rigidity,
Money Supply Endogeneity, and Business Cycles."

11. I first heard the term *Calvo Fairy*, used as a humorous reference to
Calvo's randomizing device, during a visit to the economics department at Arizona State University seven or eight years ago. I used
the term in a piece in the *Financial Times* in January 2010 (Farmer,
"The Stimulus Plan, Unemployment and Economic Theory: Why
I Don't Believe in Fairies," 2010e). The term has lost some of its edge
since Paul Krugman wrote a piece in the *New York Times* in July
2010 (Krugman, "Don't Know Much About History," 2010), where
he coined the term "confidence fairy" to represent the antihero in a
narrative that makes fun of the idea that confidence matters in the
way that I claim in this book, and that I summarized in my *Financial
Times* article. The idea that confidence is a primary driving variable
is the biggest difference between my view of financial crises and the
traditional Keynesian view that Krugman advocates. If I am right,
expansive fiscal policy to combat a recession is unlikely to succeed
unless it simultaneously restores confidence in the stock market.

12. "Nominal Rigidities and the Dynamics Effects of a Shock to
Monetary Policy" (Christiano, Eichenbaum, and Evans (2005).

13. Peter Klenow and Benjamin Malin (2011) survey the evidence from
supermarket scanner data in "Microeconomic Evidence on Price
Setting." Some progress has been made on models in which people
choose not to keep up with all the information relevant to their decisions because they have a limited attention span. These are referred to by Christopher Sims (2003), in "Implications of Rational
Inattention," as models of *rational inattention*. A related concept,
sticky information, was proposed by N. Gregory Mankiw and
Ricardo Reis (2007) in "Sticky Information in General Equilibrium."
To date, neither of these concepts has been incorporated fully into
New Keynesian theory, although there is some promising research
that attempts to do so. See the survey by Mirko Wiedeholt (2010) in
New Palgrave Dictionary of Economics (Wiederholt, 2010).

14. See, for example, the article "Models and Their Uses" (Sims, 1989).

15. Persistence of the inflation rate is not the only feature of data contradicted by the simplest New Keynesian models. The interest rate and the growth rate of real GDP also display inertia. It is possible to modify the New Keynesian model by adding additional features. For example, preferences may be determined in part by habits in which past consumption matters, as in the work of Andrew Abel ("Asset Prices under Habit Formation and Catching up with the Joneses," 1990) or George Constantinides ("Habit Formation: A Resolution of the Equity Premium Puzzle," 1990). This modification explains why lagged GDP growth may influence current GDP growth. The central bank may take lagged interest rates into account when setting the current interest rate, as argued by Olivier Coibion and Yuriy Gorodnichenko ("Why Are Target Interest Rate Changes So Persistent?" 2012). This modification explains why last period's interest rate may influence the current interest rate. It is harder, in my view, to find a plausible modification to the New Keynesian model that gives a role to lagged inflation while maintaining the core assumption of rational agents.

16. "Inflation Persistence" (Fuhrer and Moore, 1995).

17. This debate is an example of the fact that the same issues in economics are often debated several times as the next generation forgets the knowledge accumulated by the preceding ones. In 1977, Stanley Fischer wrote an article titled "Long-Term Contracts, Rational Expectations and the Optimal Money Supply Rule," in which he explained sticky prices as the outcome of nominal contracts between workers and firms. Robert Barro replied. In a criticism of Fischer, Barro wrote the article "Long-Term Contracting, Sticky Prices and Monetary Policy" (Barro, 1977), in which he pointed out that rational agents would never write the contracts that Fischer simply assumed, because they would leave both parties to the contract worse off.

18. "Real Wages Employment and Inflation" (Lucas Jr. and Rapping, 1969).

19. "Unemployment Fluctuations with Staggered Nash Wage Bargaining" (Gertler and Trigari, 2009), "An Estimated DSGE Model with Unemployment and Staggered Wage Bargaining," (Gertler, Sala, and Trigari, 2008). The Gertler–Trigari model is based on theoretical work by Robert Hall and Paul Milgrom (2008), "The Limited Influence of Unemployment on the Wage Bargain."

20. "Confidence, Crashes and Animal Spirits" (Farmer, 2012b). Dmitry Plotnikov, in his PhD dissertation "Three Essays in Economies with

Incomplete Factor Markets," (Plotnikov, 2010) and in the working paper, "Hysteresis in Unemployment and Jobless Recoveries," (Plotnikov, 2014) has extended this work to production economics.

21. *Models of Business Cycles* (Lucas Jr., 1987).

22. "Markups, Gaps, and Business Fluctuations" (Galí, Gertler and López-Salido, 2007).

23. "Harberger triangle" (Harberger, "Three Basic Postulates for Applied Welfare Economics: An Interpretive Essay," 1971) is a measure of the deadweight loss that arises from distortionary taxes in a classical model of demand and supply. An "Okun gap" (Okun, "Potential GNP: Its Measurement and Significance," 1962) is the difference between actual and potential GDP that arises in Keynesian models as a consequence of deficient aggregate demand.

24. "The Stock Market Crash of 2008 Caused the Great Recession: Theory and Evidence" (Farmer, 2012d), "The Stock Market Crash Really Did Cause the Great Recession" (Farmer, 2015b).

25. *Expectations, Employment and Prices* (Farmer, 2010a), "Animal Spirits, Persistent Unemployment and the Belief Function" (Farmer, 2012a), "Confidence, Crashes and Animal Spirits" (Farmer, 2012b), "Animal Spirits, Financial Crises and Persistent Unemployment" (Farmer, 2013a). Alternative models of bubbles include work by Lansing ("Rational and Near-Rational Bubbles Without Drift," 2010), Caballero and Krishnamurthy ("Bubbles and Capital Flow Volatility: Causes and Risk Management," 2006), and Martin and Ventura ("Economic Growth with Bubbles," 2012). For a historical account of bubbles, see the entertaining book *Extraordinary Popular Delusions and the Madness of Crowds* (Mackay, 1980 [1841]).

26. *Animal Spirits* (Akerlof and Shiller, 2009).

27. "Noise Trader Risk in Financial Markets" (DeLong, Shleifer, Summers, and Waldmann, 1990).

28. "The Rationality Debate, Simmering in Stockholm" (Shiller, 2014).

29. "Rational Fools: A Critique of the Behavioral Foundations of Economic Theory" (Sen, 1977), *Mathematical Psychics: An Essay on the Application of Mathematics to the Moral Sciences* (Edgeworth, 1881).

30. ""Rational Fools: A Critique of the Behavioral Foundations of Economic Theory" (Sen, 1977, p. 317).

31. "Rational Fools: A Critique of the Behavioral Foundations of Economic Theory" (Sen, 1977, p. 318).

32. *The Methodology of Scientific Research Programmes* (Lakatos, 1978).

33. *The Copernican Revolution* (Kuhn, 1957).

34. "Noise Trader Risk in Financial Markets" (DeLong, Shleifer, Summers, and Waldmann, 1990).
35. "Inflation Persistence" (Fuhrer and Moore, 1995).
36. "Unemployment Fluctuations with Staggered Nash Wage Bargaining" (Gertler and Trigari, 2009).
37. *Post-Keynesian Macroeconomic Theory* (Davidson, 2011).
38. "Auctions have emerged as the primary means of assigning spectrum licenses to companies wishing to provide wireless communication services. Since July 1994, the Federal Communications Commission (FCC) has conducted 33 spectrum auctions, assigning thousands of licenses to hundreds of firms" (Cramton, "Spectrum Auctions," 2002, p. 605). The 2012 Nobel Memorial Prize in Economics was awarded to Alvin Roth and Lloyd Shapley "for the theory of stable allocations and the practice of market design." Shapley worked on the theory; Roth put that theory into practice. "Roth has ... developed systems for matching doctors with hospitals, school pupils with schools, and organ donors with patients" (The Sveriges Riksbank Prize in Economic Sciences in Memory of Alfred Nobel 2012, "Alvin E. Roth Facts," 2012).

Chapter 6

1. "Unemployment and Labor Market Rigidities" (Nickell, 1997).
2. The book *Job Creation and Destruction*, by Stephen J. Davis, John C. Haltiwanger, and Scott Schuh (1996), provides an excellent introduction to the US data on job flows, interpreted through the lens of search theory.
3. Important contributions from each of these economists include, "Wage Determination and Efficiency in Search Equilibrium" (Diamond, 1982), "A Theory of Wage and Employment Dynamics" (Mortensen, 1970), and "Job Search and Participation" (Pissarides, 1976). The DMP model is a microeconomic model of a labor market. David Andolfatto ("Business Cycles and Labor-Market Search," 1996) and Monica Merz ("Search in the Labor Market and the Real Business Cycle," 1995) were the first to bring back the concept of unemployment to a modern DSGE model by integrating the DMP model with an otherwise standard DSGE model of business cycles.
4. "Chosen appropriately" means the bargaining weight must be related to a parameter of the search technology. The condition that guarantees that classical search equilibrium is socially optimal is called *the Hosios condition* (Hosios, "On the Efficiency of Matching and Related Models of Search and Unemployment," 1990).

5. In previously published work I have referred to what I call "the Keynesian search model" as "old-Keynesian economics."

6. "The Excess Demand for Labour: A Study of Conditions in Great Britain, 1946–56" (Dow and Dicks-Mireaux, 1958).

7. I used this same example in my book *How the Economy Works* (Farmer, 2010b).

8. When Friedman ("The Role of Monetary Policy," 1968) coined this term he defined it to be the equilibrium unemployment rate in a model where the equilibrium is unique and equal to the social planning optimum. I will construct a Keynesian search model where equilibrium is not unique. In this model, it is more appropriate to define the natural rate of unemployment to be the social planning optimum.

9. I normalized the labor force to one. To draw the graph, I assumed that 10% of the people in the labor force lose their jobs every month.

10. How would a general equilibrium theorist describe the markets and the price signals that cause the market to replicate the social planning optimum? Just as there are markets for labor and capital, so we would need markets for unemployment and vacancies; these are the factor inputs to the search technology. These markets would generate a relative price for the exclusive right to find a job for an unemployed worker and a relative price for the exclusive right to fill a vacancy for a corn producer. Three types of agents would populate these markets: households, production firms, and matchmaking firms.

Production firms and matchmaking firms would play different roles. Production firms would produce corn. Matchmaking firms would operate a search technology that finds a suitable job for every unemployed worker. Their role would be analogous to that of an Internet dating site that helps prospective marriage partners find their most suitable mate.

In an equilibrium that decentralizes the planning solution with markets, matchmaking firms would pay unemployed workers for the exclusive right to find them a job, and they would pay the firms that produce commodities for the exclusive right to fill their vacancies. After matching suitable workers with production firms, the matchmaking firm would sell the match back to the production firm.

In reality, we do not see matchmaking firms that operate in this way because the market would be difficult to police. It faces a *moral hazard problem.* There is an incentive for a dishonest unemployed worker to cheat and refuse to accept a job when it is offered. And as with Akerlof's ("The Market for 'Lemons': Quality Uncertainty and the Market Mechanism," 1970) description of the used car market, it only takes a few lemons to destroy the possibility that a competitive market can function at all. Because it would be difficult or impossible to force a matched worker to accept a job, the labor market is incomplete.

11. Farmer ("Aggregate Demand and Supply," 2008a; *Expectations, Employment and Prices,* 2010a; "Animal Spirits, Persistent Unemployment and the Belief Function," 2012a; "Confidence, Crashes and Animal Spirits," 2012b).

12. Friedman (*A Theory of the Consumption Function*, 1957), Ando and Modigliani ("The 'Life Cycle' Hypothesis of Saving: Aggregate Implications and Tests," 1963).

13. In an influential article "The Cyclical Behavior of Equilibrium Unemployment and Vacancies," Shimer (2005) showed that classical search models do a very poor job of explaining the cyclical volatility of the unemployment rate. In a related article, "Employment Fluctuations with Equilibrium Wage Stickiness," Robert Hall (2005) suggested a resolution to this issue. In a 1987 article titled "Costly Search and Recruiting," Peter Howitt and Preston McAfee (1987) showed there are many possible steady-state equilibria in search models. Following up on their idea, Hall proposed to select one equilibrium by fixing the wage. Although Hall's argument worked well empirically, he was criticized for not providing a proper microfoundation to the assumption of rigid wages. Subsequently, he refocused his research agenda on the microfoundations of wage bargaining. Unlike Hall, whose work is firmly rooted in the tradition of classical search theory, I developed a new approach—Keynesian search theory—in which I close my model with a new fundamental: the belief function.

14. For a fascinating alternative perspective, see the work by Roman Frydman and Michael Goldberg (*Imperfect Knowledge Economics: Exchange Rates and Risk*, 2007; "Opening Models of Asset Prices and Risk to Nonroutine Change," 2013). Frydman and Goldberg take the idea of nonstationarity seriously and they construct a theory to explain how people would behave in a nonstationary environment.

15. "Econometric Policy Evaluation: A Critique" (Lucas Jr., 1976).

16. I discussed this idea in "The Lucas Critique, Policy Invariance and Multiple Equilibria" (Farmer, 1990). I show there that the Lucas critique may not hold in models of multiple equilibria.
17. "A Theoretical Framework for Monetary Analysis" (Friedman, 1970a, p. 207, footnote 6).

Chapter 7

1. Representative works from these three authors include "Efficient Capital Markets: A Review of Theory and Empirical Work" by Eugene Fama (1970), "Large Sample Properties of Generalized Method of Moments Estimators" by Lars Hansen (1982), and "Do Stock Prices Move Too Much to Be Justified by Subsequent Changes in Dividends?" by Robert Shiller (1981).
2. I make these points in three single-author works (Farmer, "Qualitative Easing: How it Works and Why it Matters," 2012c; "Asset Prices in a Lifecycle Economy," 2014a; "Pricing Assets in an Economy with two Types of People", 2016) and in my coauthored paper (Farmer, Nourry, and Venditti, "The Inefficient Markets Hypothesis: Why Financial Markets Do Not Work Well in the Real World," 2012).
3. "Do Sunspots Matter?" (Cass and Shell, 1983). In a spoof on the work of Stanley Jevons, "Commercial Crises and Sun-spots" (Jevons, 1878), Cass and Shell refer to a nonfundamental shock as a *sunspot*. Jevons believed the sunspot cycle might affect economic activity through its influence on weather patterns. According to the Cass–Shell definition, a sunspot is a shock to the economy that causes the pattern of production and consumption to differ across states as a pure consequence of a change in beliefs.
4. The constant and the power may be fractions or negative numbers. In an important special case, the power is replaced by the logarithm of consumption. Conventional preferences are said to display the property of *constant relative risk aversion*. The "risk aversion" of a person is captured by the amount of money she would be willing to pay to avoid a gamble.
5. "Do Stock Prices Move Too Much to Be Justified by Subsequent Changes in Dividends?" (Shiller, 1981), "Stock Price Volatility: A Test Based on Implied Variance Bounds" (LeRoy and Porter, 1981). There has been a huge amount of research on excess volatility since the early work by Shiller and by LeRoy and Porter. John Cochrane wrote a survey ("Presidential Address: Discount Rates," 2011) in which he suggests asset prices do not display excess volatility if

one recognizes the market price of risk is time varying. Cochrane is forced to assume the rate at which the representative agent is willing to trade goods today for goods tomorrow is highly volatile and time varying, because he holds firmly to the classical paradigm in which all shocks are fundamental. Because the representative agent is a dubious construction at best, I am not personally convinced by explanations of volatile asset prices that invoke changes in his preferences.

6. "The Equity Premium: A Puzzle" (Mehra and Prescott, 1985).

7. For a comprehensive survey of exotic preferences, see "Exotic Preferences for Macroeconomists," by David Backus, Bryan Routledge, and Stanley Zin (2004). The first works to extend preferences beyond the class used normally by macroeconomists was by David Kreps and Evan Porteus ("Temporal Resolution of Uncertainty and Dynamic Choice Theory," 1978; "Temporal Von-Neumann Morgenstern and Induced Preferences," 1979). This work was extended by Larry Epstein and Stanley Zin ("Substitution, Risk Aversion and the Temporal Behavior of Consumption and Asset Returns: An Empirical Analysis," 1989; "Substitution, Risk Aversion and the Temporal Behavior of Consumption and Asset Returns: A Theoretical Framework," 1991). People with *Epstein–Zin preferences* care not just about expected future consumption, but also about when they acquire new knowledge about the future.

8. "The Equity Risk Premium: A Solution" (Rietz, 1988); "Rare Disasters, Asset Prices, and Welfare Costs" (Barro, 1999); *Rare Events and the Equity Premium Puzzle* (Barro, 2005).

9. For a survey of the literature on general equilibrium theory with incomplete markets, see *The Theory of Incomplete Markets* by Michael Magill and Martine Quinzii (2002).

10. *Nicholas Barbon* (Insurance Hall of Fame, 2008).

11. "The Short- and Long-Term Career Effects of Graduating in a Recession: Hysteresis and Heterogeneity in the Market for College Graduates" (Oreopoulos, Von-Wachter, and Heisz, 2012).

12. "Do Sunspots Matter? (Cass and Shell, 1983). Cass and Shell used the terms *intrinsic* and *extrinsic uncertainty* to refer to fundamental and nonfundamental shocks.

13. There is one subtlety here that is worth mentioning. Consider a simple world with two possible futures; I call them future A and future B. Roger Farmer might be born into future A or future

B. Should we consider Roger Farmer A to be a different person from Roger Farmer B? If we answer yes to that question, then asset market fluctuations, caused by nonfundamental shocks, are Pareto efficient and there is nothing we should try to do about them. If, conversely, we consider Roger Farmer A and Roger Farmer B to be the same person born into different futures, we should provide the insurance that Roger Farmer would have provided for himself, if he could have entered into a prenatal contract. I favor this latter interpretation, which is why I argue in favor of asset price stabilization. My argument is based on what the philosopher John Rawls calls the "veil of ignorance" (*A Theory of Justice*, 1971).

14. I have explored the idea that incomplete participation is important quantitatively in seven single-author and co-authored papers (Farmer, "Business Cycles with Heterogenous Agents," 2002a; "Fiscal Policy, Equity Premia, and Heterogenous Agents," 2002b; "Asset Prices in a Lifecycle Economy," 2014a; "Global Sunspots and Asset Prices in a Monetary Economy," 2015a; Farmer, Nourry, and Venditti, "Debt Deficits and Finite Horizons: The Stochastic Case," 2011; "The Inefficient Markets Hypothesis: Why Financial Markets Do Not Work Well in the Real World," 2012; Farmer, "Pricing Assets in an Economy with Two Types of People," 2016).

15. Farmer, "Pricing Assets in an Economy with Two Types of People," (2016).

16. "The Debt Deflation Theory of Great Depressions" (Fisher, 1933).

17. As Cochrane points out ("Presidential Address: Discount Rates," 2011), the assumption that people cannot make riskless profits in the asset markets implies movements in price-to-earnings ratios *must* be interpreted as fluctuations in the rate at which people are able to trade consumption goods today for state-dependent consumption goods tomorrow. Finance theorists call this object the *stochastic discount factor*. If one were to assume markets are complete, participation is complete, and there are no "frictions," one would be forced to conclude that large swings in the price-to-earnings ratio are Pareto efficient. I am unwilling to draw this conclusion because participation is not complete and because I find the contortions required to squeeze the facts into a complete markets model to be unpalatable.

18. "The Short- and Long-Term Career Effects of Graduating in a Recession: Hysteresis and Heterogeneity in the Market for College Graduates" (Oreopoulos, Von-Wachter, and Heisz, 2012).

19. In their widely cited study of financial crises *This Time Is Different* (Reinhart and Rogoff, 2011), Carmen Reinhart and Kenneth Rogoff distinguish financial crises from business cycle recessions. In 15 of 35 financial crises documented in their data, recovery after a crisis took 15 years or longer; in one case, India in 1929, the recovery took 31 years (Reinhart and Rogoff, "Recovery from Financial Crises: Evidence from 100 Episodes," 2014).

20. *Expectations, Employment and Prices* (Farmer, 2010a).

21. The money wage is constructed by dividing consumption to employees by full-time equivalent employees using the procedure described in *Expectations, Employment and Prices* (Farmer, 2010a). The real value of the stock market graphed in each of these two figures is constructed by dividing the S&P 500 by the money wage. These data are available on my website http://rogerfarmer. com.

22. "The Stock Market Crash of 2008 Caused the Great Recession: Theory and Evidence" (Farmer, 2012d), "The Stock Market Crash Really Did Cause the Great Recession" (Farmer, 2015b).

23. The stock market is the logarithm of the S&P 500 divided by a wage index. The unemployment variable is the logarithm of logistic transformation of the unemployment rate. Details are available on my website at http://rogerfarmer.com.

24. The equation that links two nonstationary but cointegrated variables is called a *cointegrating equation* (Hamilton, "Time Series Analysis," 1994).

25. "Investigating Causal Relations by Econometric Models and Cross-spectral Methods" (Granger, 1969).

26. I use the case of a court ruling as the fundamental event that triggers a crisis purely as an illustration. In the context of the 2008 crisis, it is difficult to find a plausible candidate for a fundamental event of any kind and, for that reason, I personally find the animal spirits explanation more plausible.

27. I am using the term *animal spirits* in the same way as in my 1994 paper, coauthored with Jang-Ting Guo (Farmer and Guo, "Real Business Cycles and the Animal Spirits Hypothesis," 1994) and as explained in my 2008 entry in the *New Palgrave Dictionary of Economics* (Farmer, *Animal Spirits*, 2008b). This is not the same as the usage by George Akerlof and Robert Shiller (*Animal Spirits*, 2009). For a discussion of the two concepts, see my review of Akerlof and Shiller (Farmer, "Review of: Animal Spirits: How

Human Psychology Drives the Economy and Why It Matters for Global Capitalism. By George A. Akerlof and Robert J. Shiller," 2009b).

Chapter 8

1. For a detailed exposition of the New Keynesian model, see the article by Jordi Galí and Mark Gertler ("The Science of Monetary Policy: A New Keynesian Perspective, 1999). An excellent source that explains New Keynesian economics at the level of an introductory graduate or advanced undergraduate class is the book *Monetary Policy, Inflation and the Business Cycle: An Introduction to the New Keynesian Framework and Its Applications* by Jordi Galí (2015). The book by Michael Woodford (2003), *Interest and Prices: Foundations of a Theory of Monetary Policy*, is more comprehensive but not as accessible as Galí's work for the beginning student.

2. For a fascinating discussion of the history of GDP accounting, see *GDP: A Brief But Affectionate History* (Coyle, 2014).

3. In 1962, Arthur Okun published an influential work, "Potential GNP: Its Measurement and Significance," on the statistical relationship between the unemployment rate and the output gap in the United States. Okun estimated a relationship on data from 1947 through 1960 and found that, for every one-percentage point increase in the output gap, the unemployment rate falls by 0.3 percentage points. That relationship changed somewhat after 1970 and, since 1970, the coefficient that connects the unemployment rate with the output gap is closer to one half than one third. The statistical connection in data between the unemployment rate and the output gap is known as *Okun's Law*.

4. Andy Haldane (2012), a chief economist for the Bank of England, makes the case in a piece for VoxEU titled "What Have Economists Ever Done for Us?" that the emergence of DSGE models was partly to blame for a collective loss of memory by economists about the relationship between money and credit.

5. *The Black Swan: The Impact of the Highly Improbable* (Taleb, 2010). A seven-standard deviation event refers to the probability that a random variable is more than seven deviations away from its mean. If shocks to the economy were normally distributed, a seven-standard deviation event would be expected to occur only once every 1,300,000,000,000 years. To put that number in perspective, the solar system is estimated to be roughly 4,600,000,000 years old.

6. The name *Farmer Monetary Model* was suggested by the editors of a volume in which "Animal Spirits, Persistent Unemployment and the Belief Function" (Farmer, 2012a) first appeared.

7. *Monetary Policy Rules* (Taylor, 1999).

8. "Staggered Prices in a Utility Maximizing Model" (Calvo, 1983) (see footnote 11 in Chapter 5 above).

9. A well-designed policy is one that satisfies what Michael Woodford has called *the Taylor Principle* (Woodford, *Interest and Prices: Foundations of a Theory of Monetary Policy*, 2003, p. 90). The Taylor Principle asserts that the central bank should raise or lower the interest rate by more than one for one in response to an increase or a decrease in the inflation rate.

10. For an application that adds all three sources of additional persistence, see "Factor Analysis in a New Keynesian Model" (Beyer, Farmer, Henry, and Marcellino, 2008).

11. "Natural Rate Doubts" (Beyer and Farmer, 2007).

12. "Natural Rate Doubts" (Beyer and Farmer, 2007).

13. "Natural Rate Doubts" (Beyer and Farmer, 2007). To be more precise, we cannot reject the hypothesis, using 240 quarters of data, that each of these variables has a unit root. That is a weaker statement than saying they are nonstationary. Nonstationary series and a highly persistent series are hard to tell apart in finite data samples. For example, Bradley Ewing and Phanindra Wunnava ("Unit Roots and Structural Breaks in North American Unemployment Rates," 2001) prefer a model in which the unemployment rate is stationary around a trend that changes occasionally. The important issue for the argument I make in this book is that a transformation of the unemployment rate has unit root; it is, are changes in the number to which the unemployment rate is converging caused by changes in the natural rate or by changes in aggregate demand? The unit root model is, after all, just a limiting case of the structural breaks model, in which the break occurs every period.

14. A linear combination of two variables, x and y, is a new variable $z = \lambda x + (1 - \lambda)y$, where the weight, λ, is a number between zero and one.

15. "Some Properties of Time Series Data and Their Use in Econometric Model Specification" (Granger, 1981).

16. Difference equations describe how a variable depends on its own past values. They are widely used by economists to describe the

motion of economic time series. In the natural sciences, it is more common to model change using differential equations. Differential equations assume time is a continuous variable. Difference equations assume, instead, that time proceeds in a sequence of discrete periods.

17. Following the influential article "Trends and Random Walks in Macroeconomic Time Series" by Charles Nelson and Charles Plosser (1982), a large body of literature developed that studied the question: Does the GDP have a unit root? In my work, I have argued economic data are well described by variables that have a unit root. Others claim (Ewing and Wunnava, "Unit Roots and Structural Breaks in North American Unemployment Rates," 2001), for example, that there are occasional breaks in an otherwise stable process and that the unemployment rate returns to a different level after every break. Differences with regard to the best way to model breaks are not important; what causes them is. The survey paper "Permanent and Transitory Components of GNP and Stock Prices" by John Cochrane (1994) contains an excellent discussion of these issues.

18. I show in "Animal Spirits, Persistent Unemployment and the Belief Function" (Farmer, 2012a) that it is not enough to assume that demand shocks are persistent. To explain the data, the New Keynesian model must also be hit by persistent supply shocks. That implication is not usually explicit. A rare example of a Keynesian model that does make it explicit is the work by Robert Gordon (Gordon, *The Phillips Curve Is Alive and Well: Inflation and the NAIRU during the Slow Recovery*, 2013). Gordon distances himself from New Keynesian economics and he includes explicitly a backward-looking Phillips Curve in which the non-accelerating inflation rate of unemployment (NAIRU) is nonstationary.

19. "Trends and Random Walks in Macroeconomic Time Series" (Nelson and Plosser, 1982).

20. I showed in Chapter 4 that labor force participation does not move much over the business cycle. Most movements in participation are caused by demographics as the Baby Boom generation moves through the population or by sociological factors that have changed the role of women in the labor market. For that reason, when I present data in this chapter, I divide real GDP by the labor force as my measure of GDP per person. Sociological factors can also be related to economics. See, for example, "Technology and the Changing

Family: A Unified Model of Marriage, Divorce, Educational Attainment and Married Female Labor-Force Participation" by Jeremy Greenwood, Nezih Guner, Georgi Kocharkov, and Cezar Santos (2016).

Chapter 9

1. John Taylor makes the case in "A Monetary Policy for the Future (Taylor 2015). Ben Bernanke responds in "The Taylor Rule: A Benchmark for Monetary Policy?" (Bernanke, 2015).

2. "Of Money" (Hume, 1987 [1777]).

3. *Rethinking Expectations: The Way Forward for Macroeconomics* (Frydman and Phelps, 2013).

4. "Mr. Keynes on Underemployment Equilibrium" (Hansen, 1936), "Mr. Keynes and the Classics: A Suggested Interpretation" (Hicks, 1937).

5. "Macroeconomics and the Financial Cycle: Hamlet without the Prince?" (Borio, 2013).

6. "Inflation in the Great Recession and New Keynesian Models" (Del Negro, Schorfheide, and Giannoni, 2015, p. 168).

7. *The Holy Grail of Macroeconomics: Lessons from Japan's Great Recession* (Koo, 2008) develops a theory of "balance sheet recessions."

8. "Pricing Assets in an Economy with Two Types of People" (Farmer, 2016). I am not the only economist, nor am I the first, to seek an explanation for financial cycles and the associated persistence of discount rates. There is a tremendous amount of ongoing research by economists, some of whom identify themselves as New Keynesians and some of whom do not. Two influential examples include the work of Kiyotaki and Moore ("Credit Cycles," 1997), who talk of "credit cycles"; and Geanakoplos ("The Leverage Cycle," 2010), who refers to the "leverage cycle."

9. I first used a function like this to select an equilibrium in "The Lucas Critique, Policy Invariance and Multiple Equilibria" (Farmer, 1990) and I referred to it as a belief function in the first edition of my book *The Macroeconomics of Self-fulfilling Prophecies* (1993). In his PhD dissertation, "Three Essays in Incomplete Factor Markets," (Plotnikov, 2010), Dmitry Plotnikov used this idea in a more sophisticated model than I present here. Plotnikov's model includes capital formation. In the IMF working paper, "Hysteresis in Unemployment and Jobless Recoveries" (Plotnikov, 2014) he finds

that a model, driven by shocks to a belief function, explains hysteresis in US data.

10. "Animal Spirits, Persistent Unemployment and the Belief Function" (Farmer, 2012a), A *Theory of the Consumption Function* (Friedman, 1957).

11. "Animal Spirits, Persistent Unemployment and the Belief Function" (Farmer, 2012a).

12. I discussed this idea in "Why Does Data Reject the Lucas Critique?" (Farmer, 2002c), in which I introduced a concept that I called *generalized adaptive expectations*. This concept is related to the work of George Evans and Seppo Honkapohja (*Learning and Expectations in Macroeconomics*, 2001). They propose we restrict attention to rational expectations equilibria that can be learned using some plausible mechanism. One such mechanism is the application of least-squares regressions to learn about the connection between future prices and current economic variables. I agree with the Evans and Honkapohja proposal; but rather than use their criterion to select one of the many rational expectations equilibria, I propose the learning rule itself should become part of the economic model. One might envisage a range of plausible rules that people might use to learn about the world in which they live. I take it as axiomatic that the rule should coincide with a rational expectations equilibrium if it is applied repeatedly in a stationary environment.

13. A person's belief is rational if her subjective probability distribution about a future variable coincides with its actual probability distribution. The rational expectations assumption is not a property of the world; it is a consistency requirement for an economic model.

14. "Expectations and the Neutrality of Money" (Lucas Jr., 1972).

15. "Existence of a Competitive Equilibrium for a Competitive Economy" (Arrow and Debreu, 1954).

16. Timothy Kehoe and David Levine have shown that, in models of overlapping generations, there is, generically, a continuum of equilibria ("Comparative Statics and Perfect Foresight in Infinite Horizon Economies," 1985). *Generically* means that multiplicity is not, in any sense, unusual. If you were to consider a large class of possible models, distinguished by their assumptions about preferences and technology, in a nontrivial fraction of those models there would be a continuum of equilibria. The fact that there may be a continuum of equilibria was known to be true in overlapping generations of money. Kehoe and Levine showed it is also true in

models of exchange with no money when there are multiple goods and multiple types of people.

17. The real interest rate would equal the difference between the representative agent's time preference rate and the growth rate of potential output. And the inflation rate and the interest rate would be solved uniquely by combining these identities with the Taylor Rule. The steady-state equilibrium of this model is unique.

18. When a system obeys that property, we say that it displays *hysteresis*. The work of Blanchard and Summers ("Hysteresis and the European Unemployment Problem," 1986; "Hysteresis in Unemployment," 1987) drew the attention of the profession to this possibility. For recent examples of economic models that display hysteresis in a fully developed DSGE model see Farmer ("Confidence, Crashes and Animal Spirits," 2012b) and Plotnikov ("Hysteresis in Unemployment and Jobless Recoveries," 2014).

19. "Animal Spirits, Persistent Unemployment and the Belief Function" (Farmer, 2012a).

20. "The Phillips Curve Is Alive and Well: Inflation and the NAIRU During the Slow Recovery" (Gordon, 2013). Alternatively, a researcher might assume the natural rate of unemployment is described by a persistent mean-reverting process subject to occasional structural breaks.

21. *A Theory of the Consumption Function*, (Friedman, 1957).

22. A more realistic assumption is that the *growth rate* of permanent income, defined in dollars, is equal to the last period's nominal income growth. That is the assumption I made in my empirical work (Farmer, "Animal Spirits, Persistent Unemployment and the Belief Function," 2012a). I maintain the simpler example in this parable to ease my exposition.

23. "The Debt Deflation Theory of Great Depressions" (Fisher, 1933).

Chapter 10

1. CEPREMAP stands for Centre Pour la Recherche Économique et ses Applications, and it is one of the leading economic research institutions in France. The École Polytechnique is one of a handful of Grandes Écoles, a group of elite French institutions of higher learning, that have historically trained France's intellectuals, scientists, engineers, and statesmen. Leading figures at Penn included Costas Azariadis, Dave Cass, and Karl Shell. I was an assistant professor at Penn and Michael Woodford was a visiting graduate student. In France, Jean Michel Grandmont and Roger Guesnerie promoted the

multiple-equilibria agenda. This was an exciting time to be starting a career in economics!

2. My PhD dissertation, "Macroeconomics and Equilibrium" (Farmer, 1982), dropped that assumption in a model in which the frequency of bankruptcies varies with different fiscal policies. The central part of that dissertation was published as, "A New Theory of Aggregate Supply" (Farmer, 1984).

3. That work appeared in an unpublished paper joint with Andrew Hollenhorst (Farmer and Hollenhorst, "Shooting the Auctioneer," 2006) and in the paper I presented at a conference in honor of Axel Leijonhufvud held at the University of California Los Angeles in August 2006 that was published in a Festschrift for Axel Leijonhufvud (Farmer, "Old Keynesian Economics," 2008c).

4. I discuss this distinction in detail in my survey (Farmer, "The Evolution of Endogenous Business Cycles," 2014c). First-generation models include the papers of Azariadis ("Self-fulfilling Prophecies," 1981), Cass and Shell ("Do Sunspots Matter?," 1983), Farmer and Woodford ("Self-fulfilling Prophecies and the Business Cycle," 1984; "Self-fulfilling Prophecies and the Business Cycle," 1997), Benhabib and Farmer ("The Monetary Transmission Mechanism," 2000), and Farmer and Guo ("The Econometrics of Indeterminacy," 1995). Second-generation models for which there is potentially steady-state indeterminacy include those by Farmer (*Expectations, Employment and Prices*, 2010a; "Confidence, Crashes and Animal Spirits," 2012b). For methods of estimating models with indeterminacy using standard software packages see Farmer, Khramov, and Nicolò ("Solving and Estimating Indeterminate DSGE Models," 2015). Recent work on business cycles driven by "sentiment," for example, Angeletos and La'O ("Sentiments," 2013), and Benhabib, Wang, and Wen ("Sentiments and Aggregate Demand Fluctuations," 2015) do not fall into this category. In the Angeletos and La'O model, there is a unique equilibrium that is socially efficient. That does not, to me, seem to be a very fruitful way of modeling the apparent large welfare losses that characterize major recessions.

5. "Aggregate Demand and Supply" (Farmer, 2008a).

6. I am ignoring complications introduced by depreciation, indirect taxation, and foreign trade.

7. In Keynesian economics, the line labeled $X = (A + I + G) + bY$ is the aggregate demand curve. It slopes up with a slope b, less than one.

I and *G* represent investment expenditure and government purchases of goods and services, respectively; *A* is a constant.

8. The Marginal Propensity to Consume (MPC) is a number between zero and one. If the MPC is zero, an extra $100,000 of investment expenditure will cause a $100,000 increase in equilibrium income. In that case, the multiplier is one. If the MPC were equal to one, the multiplier would be very large—approaching a theoretical limit of infinity. Theoretically, the multiplier is the sum of a geometric progression:

$$\text{Multiplier} = 1 + b + b^2 + b^3 + \cdots = \frac{1}{1-b}.$$

Here's how it works. Toyota executives decide to build a new plant in Kentucky. That plant involves a $50 million investment, takes two years to build, and creates 500 construction jobs. Each of the newly hired workers earns $30,000 and, in total, they earn a wage income of $15 million during the construction phase of the plant. Each worker spends 90% of his income and saves the remaining 10%. The increased consumption spending causes aggregate demand to go up by a further $13.5 million (90% of $15 million).

Of the $13.5 million, 20% is spent on home furnishings and electronics, 60% is spent on food and entertainment, and the other 20% is spent on clothes. Walmart in Kentucky experiences an increase in demand for Sub-Zero refrigerators as the newly employed construction workers begin to spend their earnings.

Walmart places an order for Sub-Zero fridges in Wisconsin, which employs thirty more employees to meet the increased demand. All in all, the additional consumption spending of $13.5 million by construction workers at the Toyota plant creates $13.5 million in new jobs. Some of that is spent on appliances, manufactured in Wisconsin. Some of it is spent on oranges, grown in Haines City, Florida. Some of it is spent on garments, manufactured in East Los Angeles, and some of it is spent on restaurant food back home in Georgetown, Kentucky.

The newly employed workers at the Sub-Zero plant in Wisconsin, newly employed agricultural workers in Florida, garment workers in East Los Angeles, waiters at restaurants in Georgetown, Kentucky, and in Haines City, Florida all spend 90% of their income, leading to a further $12.15 million increase in consumption. A piece of relatively simple algebra establishes that the end result of this process is that aggregate demand goes up by 10 times the initial increase in aggregate demand.

9. GDP, investment, government purchases, and consumption change from one year to the next for two reasons. The first is because of changes in the value of money; we call that *inflation*. The second is because of changes in productivity; we call that *growth*. I developed the technique of measuring data in wage units in my book, *Expectations, Employment and Prices* (Farmer, 2010a).

10. *A Theory of the Consumption Function* (Friedman, 1957), "The 'Life Cycle' Hypothesis of Saving: Aggregate Implications and Tests" (Ando and Modigliani, 1963).

11. Ralph Hawtrey, a senior Treasury official during the 1920s, presents the case in an article in the journal *Economica* (Hawtrey, "Public Expenditure and the Demand for Labour," 1925).

12. Hansard: House of Commons Debate, "Disposal of Surplus," 1929.

13. See "The 'Treasury View' on Public Works and and Employment in the Interwar Period" (Peden, 1984). The Treasury view is sometimes confounded with the classical economic proposition known as Say's Law. Jean-Baptiste Say, a French economist writing during the early nineteenth century, argued there can never be deficient demand because, in Say's words,

> a product is no sooner created than it, from that instant, affords a market for other products to the full extent of its own value. When the producer has put the finishing hand to his product, he is most anxious to sell it immediately…. But the only way of getting rid of money is in the purchase of some product or other. Thus the mere circumstance of creation of one product immediately opens a vent for other products. (Say, *A Treatise on Political Economy*, 1834, p. 138–139).

It is useful to distinguish these two propositions. I will associate Say's Law with the proposition that there is a unique equilibrium level of employment determined solely by fundamentals. The Treasury view asserts increased government expenditure will not reduce the unemployment rate. That is a distinct claim independent of Say's Law.

14. "Don't Know Much about History" (Krugman, 2008).

15. The important point is that the central bank fixes the interest rate at a constant number that does not respond to market conditions. It does not have to be zero. For example, following the Great Recession, the Federal Open Market Committee in the US set the interest rate in a band between 0% to 0.25%. Bank Rate, in the UK, was set at 0.5%.

16. The return you will receive from buying a thirty-year bond and selling it one year later is, normally, higher than the return you will earn by buying and holding a one-year Treasury bond. This return, called the *yield* on the bond, is equal to the fixed interest rate on the bond, plus the change in the price of the bond between the date it is bought and the date at which is sold. The central bank can set the overnight rate. In a capitalist economy, the financial markets set the yields on bonds of all other maturities.

17. "The Stimulus Plan, Unemployment and Economic Theory: Why I Don't Believe in Fairies" (Farmer, 2010e).

18. "Is Joe Biden Disingenuous or Misinformed?" (Mankiw, 2009).

19. *New Keynesian Economics: Vol. 2: Coordination Failures and Real Rigidities* (Mankiw and Romer, 1991).

20. "An Empirical Characterization of the Dynamic Effects of Changes in Government Spending and Taxes on Output" (Blanchard and Perotti, 2002).

21. "The Evolution of Economic Understanding and Postwar Stabilization Policy" (Romer and Romer, 2002).

22. "Government Spending and Private Activity," (Ramey, 2013).

23. For an excellent summary of recent evidence, see the post "How Big Is the Multiplier? by James Hamley (2012). In my view, the best econometric work on this topic is by Valerie Ramey and her coauthors Sarah Zubairy and Michael Owyang. See, for example, "Government Spending and Private Activity" (Ramey, 2013), "Macroeconomic Shocks and their Propagation" (Ramey, 2016), "Government Spending Multipliers in Good Times and in Bad: Evidence from U.S. Historical Data" (Ramey and Zubairy, 2014), and "Are Government Spending Multipliers Greater during Periods of Slack? Evidence from Twentieth-Century Historical Data, (Owyang, Ramey, and Zubairy, 2013).

24. "Does Fiscal Policy Matter? Blinder and Solow Revisited" (Farmer and Plotnikov, 2012).

25. "The Golden Rule of Capital Accumulation: A Fable For Growthmen" (Phelps, 1961).

26. In an article titled "Financial Stability and the Role of the Financial Policy Committee" (Farmer, 2014b), I made the case that the maturity structure of debt in the hands of the public matters because our children and our grandchildren cannot participate in financial markets that open before they are born.

27. I discuss policies to restore full employment, as alternatives to traditional fiscal policy, in the following three works: "Does Fiscal Policy Matter? Blinder and Solow Revisited" (Farmer and Plotnikov, 2012), "Macroeconomics for the 21st Century: Full Employment as a Policy Goal" (Farmer, 2010d), and "How to Reduce Unemployment: A New Policy Proposal" (Farmer, 2010c).

28. "Animal Spirits in a Monetary Model" (Farmer and Platonov, 2016). See also my coauthored work with Dmitry Plotnikov, "Does Fiscal Policy Matter? Blinder and Solow Revisited" (Farmer and Plotnikov, 2012).

Chapter 11

1. *Lombard Street* (Bagehot, 1873) has been reprinted many times and is available on the Internet from the Library of Economics and Liberty (Bagehot, *Lombard Street: A Description of the Money Market*, 2002).

2. That, at least, is the official line. The Fed cites legal and operational difficulties in lowering the Federal Funds rate below 0.1% ("Negative Nominal Central Bank Policy Rates: Where Is the Lower Bound?", McAndrews, 2015). The Swiss National Bank, the European Central Bank, the Danmarks Nationalbank, and the Swedish Riksbank have recently experimented with negative money interest rates. Most economists see a limit to this policy because private agents have an incentive to hoard cash, which pays a zero rate of interest, when deposits at the central bank are effectively taxed. This argument has been contested by Willem Buiter ("Negative Nominal Interest Rates: Three Ways to Overcome the Zero Lower Bound," 2009), who provides several ways in which a central bank might circumvent the zero lower bound.

3. *A Monetary History of the United States, 1867–1960* (Friedman & Schwartz, 1963).

4. "We Need More Quantitative Easing to Create Jobs" (Farmer, 2010f). Willem Buiter, former member of the Monetary Policy Committee of the Bank of England suggested this terminology (Buiter,

"Quantitative Easing and Qualitative Easing: A Terminological and Taxonomic Proposal," 2008).

5. My view is supported by substantial evidence. See for example, the work of Joseph E. Gagnon, Matthew Raskin, Julie Remache, and Brian P. Sack ("Large-Scale Asset Purchases by the Federal Reserve: Did They Work?, 2011a); Gagnon, Raskin, Remache, and Sack ("The Financial Market Effects of the Federal Reserve's Large-Scale Asset Purchases," 2011b); or the paper by James D. Hamilton and Jing Cynthia Wu ("The Effectiveness of Alternative Monetary Policy Tools in a Zero Lower Bound Environment," 2012).

6. "The Monetarist Counter Revolution in Economics" (Friedman, 1970b, page 11.)

7. "Remit for the Bank of England Monetary Policy Committee," (Osborne, 2015, no page numbers).

8. A more recent episode occurred on June 19, 2013, when Chairman Bernanke made a rather mild statement that the policy of quantitative easing the Federal Reserve had been following might slow down later in the year. The Federal Reserve had been pumping $85 billion a month into the US economy, and merely the mention that this policy might soon be reduced caused markets all over the world to tumble by four percentage points in two days.

9. "Qualitative Easing, a New Tool for the Stabilization of Financial Markets" (Farmer, 2013c), "Qualitative Easing: How It Works and Why It Matters" (Farmer, 2012c).

10. "What Keynes Should Have Said" (Farmer, 2009c). My VOX piece was written to publicize my books *How the Economy Works: Confidence, Crashes and Self-fulfilling Prophecies* (Farmer, 2010b), and *Expectations Employment and Prices* (Farmer, 2010a).

11. "What Keynes Should Have Said" (Farmer, 2009c).

12. "A New Monetary Policy for the Twenty-First Century" (Farmer, 2009a).

13. "A New Monetary Policy for the Twenty-First Century" (Farmer, 2009a).

14. "A New Monetary Policy for the Twenty-First Century" (Farmer, 2009a).

15. "Quartz" (Kimball, 2013b).

16. Parliament TV (Farmer, 2013b).

17. "Treasury News" (Summers, 1998).

18. "Billionaire Who Broke the Bank of England" (Litterick, 2002).

19. "Financial Stability and the Role of the Financial Policy Committee" (Farmer, 2014b).

20. On average, the real interest rate available by purchasing and holding stocks has been 6% in a century of data. If the real interest rate were to remain constant forever at 6%, the price-to-earnings ratio would equal 16.7, which is the reciprocal of the interest rate. The return to the stock equals $(P + E)/P = E/P + 1$, which must equal $1 + r$, where r is the interest rate on a bond. If the stock and the bond pay the same return, the price-to-earnings ratio is related to the interest rate by the expression $1/r = P/E$. When $r = 0.06$, this implies $P/E = 16.7$.

21. The policy I am describing is not without precedent. A number of central banks have bought equity. The Hong Kong monetary authority bought shares during the Asian financial crisis and came out ahead (Goodhart and Dai, *Intervention to Save Hong Kong*, 2003). Taiwan has bought shares of individual companies in the past, but on a small scale and without any coherent guiding philosophy. But a policy of actively maintaining the price of a stock market index has never been tried.

22. The theory of economic growth implies that output per person will be maximized in the steady state if the real interest rate equals the growth rate of the economy, a result that is called the *golden rule* (Phelps, "The Golden Rule of Capital Accumulation: A Fable for Growthmen," 1961).

23. "Quarterly Update: Foreign Ownership of U.S. Assets" (Greenberg, 2014).

24. "The UK's External Balance Sheet: The International Investment Position (IIP)" (Whitard, 2012).

25. That system, called the *Bretton Woods system*, was dismantled in 1971, when most countries in the world moved to a system of floating exchange rates (Stephey, "A Brief History of Bretton Woods System," 2008).

26. Scott Sumner's views are summarized in a recent piece from the *Cato Journal* (Sumner, "Nominal GDP Targeting: A Simple Rule to Improve Fed Performance," 2014) and in a series of articles on his blog (Sumner, "The Money Illusion," 2009). Willem Buiter's (2009) views are contained in the working paper "Negative Nominal Interest Rates: Three Ways to Overcome the Zero Lower Bound." Michael Woodford discusses forward guidance in a paper presented at a conference held at the annual 2012 Jackson Hole Conference

("Methods of Policy Accommodation at the Interest-Rate Lower Bound," 2012).

27. "A New Monetary Policy for the 21st Century," (Farmer, 2008d).
28. For an elaboration of that view, see, for example, the article by Evan Koenig, Vice President of the Dallas Fed ("All in the Family: The Close Connection between Nominal-GDP Targeting and the Taylor Rule," 2012).
29. "Robert Shiller's Favorite Financial Innovation: An IPO for the USA" (Shiller, 2012).
30. "Negative Nominal Interest Rates: Three Ways to Overcome the Zero Lower Bound" (Buiter, 2009). Miles Kimball has supported a move to negative interest rates on his blog ("How and Why to Eliminate the Zero Lower Bound," 2013a).
31. "Methods of Policy Accommodation at the Interest-Rate Lower Bound" (Woodford, 2012).
32. "Qualitative Easing: How It Works and Why It Matters" (Farmer, 2012c, page 3). I have since updated this paper under a new title, "The Theory of Unconventional Monetary Policy" (Farmer and Zabczyk, 2016). The new version is coauthored with Pawel Zabczyk of the Bank of England.
33. The recent financial legislation in the United Kingdom and the United States was designed to address a problem that economists call *moral hazard*. This problem has been dealt with extensively in a spate of books that followed the 2007 financial crisis. Gary Gorton explains how the financial crisis was similar in nature to nineteenth-century panics. In his view, a new shadow banking system, largely unregulated, replaced the traditional banking system as the cause of instability (*Slapped by the Invisible Hand*, 2010). To correct a future financial crisis, Larry Kotlikoff proposes that banks should hold 100% reserves (*Jimmy Stewart Is Dead: Ending the World's Ongoing Financial Plague with Limited Purpose Banking*, 2011), Anat Admati and Martin Hellwig propose to force banks to hold large equity buffers to help reduce the risk to taxpayers in the event of a systemic crisis (*The Banker's New Clothes*, 2013), and Simon Johnson and James Kwak point to the political influence of Wall Street as a potential obstacle to reform (*13 Bankers: The Wall Street Takeover and the Next Financial Meltdown*, 2010). I agree with these authors and I lend my voice to their call for tighter financial regulation. But, in my view, the regulations that have been proposed do not go far enough.

REFERENCES

Abel, A. B. (1990). Asset prices under habit formation and catching up with the Joneses. *The American Economic Review Papers and Proceedings* 80(2):38–42.

Admati, A., and Hellwig, M. (2013). *The banker's new clothes.* Princeton, NJ: Princeton University Press.

Akerlof, G. A. (1970). The market for "lemons": Quality uncertainty and the market mechanism. *Quarterly Journal of Economics* 84(3):488–500.

Akerlof, G. A., and Shiller, R. J. (2009). *Animal spirits.* Princeton, NJ: Princeton University Press.

Alchian, A., and Klein, B. (1973). On a correct measure of inflation. *Journal of Money Credit and Banking* 5(1):173–191.

Ando, A., and Modigliani, F. (1963). The "life cycle" hypothesis of saving: Aggregate implications and tests. *American Economic Review* 53(1):55–84.

Andolfatto, D. (1996). Business cycles and labor-market search. *American Economic Review* 86(1):112–132.

Angeletos, G.-M., and La'O, J. (2013). Sentiments. *Econometrica* 81(2):739–779.

Arrow, K. J., and Debreu, G. (1954). Existence of a competitive equilibrium for a competitive economy. *Econometrica* 22(3):265–290.

Azariadis, C. (1981). Self-fulfilling prophecies. *Journal of Economic Theory* 25(3):380–396.

Backus, D. K., Routledge, B. R., and Zin, S. E. (2004). Exotic preferences for macroeconomists. *NBER Macroeconomics Annual 2004* 19:319–413.

Bagehot, W. (1873). *Lombard street*. London: Henry S. King.

Bagehot, W. (2002, February 1). Lombard street: A description of the money market. Retrieved June 30, 2015, from http://www.econlib.org/library/Bagehot/bagLom8.html.

Balke, N. S., and Gordon, R. J. (1989). The estimation of prewar gross national product: Methodology and new evidence. *Journal of Political Economy* 97(1):38–92.

Barro, R. J. (1974). Are government bonds net wealth? *Journal of Political Economy* 82(6):1095–1117.

Barro, R. J. (1977). Long-term contracting, sticky prices and monetary policy. *Journal of Monetary Economics* 3:5–31.

Barro, R. J. (1999). Rare disasters, asset prices, and welfare costs. *American Economic Review* 99(1):243–264.

Barro, R. J. (2005). Rare events and the equity premium puzzle. NBER working paper no. 11310. Cambridge MA; National Bureau of Economic Research.

Benhabib, J., and Farmer, R. E. (1994). Indeterminacy and increasing returns. *Journal of Economic Theory* 63:19–46.

Benhabib, J., and Farmer, R. E. (2000). The monetary transmission mechanism. *Review of Economic Dynamics* 3(3):523–550.

Benhabib, J., Wang, P., and Wen, Y. (2015). Sentiments and aggregate demand fluctuations. *Econometrica* 83(2):549–585.

Bentham, J. (2002). An introduction to the principles of morals and legislation. Retrieved January 7, 2016, from http://www.econlib.org/library/Bentham/bnthPML.html.

Berensten, A., Menzio, G., and Wright, R. (2011). Inflation and unemployment in the long run. *American Economic Review* 1:371–398.

Bernanke, B. S. (2002, November 8). Remarks by Governor Ben S. Bernanke at the Conference to Honor Milton Friedman. Retrieved June 28, 2015, from http://www.federalreserve.gov/boarddocs/Speeches/2002/20021108/default.htm.

Bernanke, B. S. (2015, April 28). The Taylor Rule: A benchmark for monetary policy? Retrieved April 9, 2016, from http://www.brookings.edu/blogs/ben-bernanke/posts/2015/04/28-taylor-rule-monetary-policy.

Bernanke, B. S., Laubach, T., Mishkin, F. S., and Posen, A. S. (1999). *Inflation targeting: Lessons from the international experience*. Princeton, NJ: Princeton University Press.

Beyer, A., and Farmer, R. E. (2007). Natural rate doubts. *Journal of Economic Dynamics and Control* 31(121):797–825.

Beyer, A., Farmer, R. E., Henry, J., and Marcellino, M. (2008). Factor analysis in a new Keynesian model. *Econometrics Journal* 11:271–286.

Blanchard, O. J., and Perotti, R. (2002). An empirical characterization of the dynamic effects of changes in government spending and taxes on output. *Quarterly Journal of Economics* 117(4):1229–1368.

Blanchard, O. J., and Summers, L. H. (1986). Hysteresis and the European unemployment problem. In *NBER macroeconomics annual*, ed. S. Fischer, vol. 1, pp. 15–90. Boston, MA: National Bureau of Economic Research.

Blanchard, O. J., and Summers, L. H. (1987). Hysteresis in unemployment. *European Economic Review* 31:288–295.

Borio, C. (2013, February 2). Macroeconomics and the financial cycle: Hamlet without the Prince? Retrieved August 8, 2015, from http://www.voxeu.org/article/macroeconomics-and-financial-cycle-hamlet-without-prince.

Brown, A. (2010, July). Essays in macroeconomics and international trade. PhD diss., University of California Los Angeles.

Buiter, W. H. (2008, December 9). Quantitative easing and qualitative easing: A terminological and taxonomic proposal. Retrieved June 30, 2015, from http://blogs.ft.com/maverecon/2008/12/quantitative-easing-and-qualitative-easing-a-terminological-and-taxonomic-proposal/#axzz3eaQ8lflM.

Buiter, W. H. (2009, June). Negative nominal interest rates: Three ways to overcome the zero lower bound. NBER working paper no. 15118. Cambridge MA; National Bureau of Economic Research.

Burgen, S. (2013, August 30). Spain youth unemployment reaches record 56.1%. *The Guardian*. Retrieved June 28, 2015, from http://www.theguardian.com/business/2013/aug/30/spain-youth-unemployment-record-high.

Caballero, R. J., and Krishnamurthy, A. (2006). Bubbles and capital flow volatility: Causes and risk management. *Journal of Monetary Economics* 53(1):35–53.

Calvo, G. A. (1983). Staggered prices in a utility maximizing model. *Journal of Monetary Economics* 12:383–398.

Cass, D., and Shell, K. (1983). Do sunspots matter? *Journal of Political Economy* 91:193–227.

Central Intelligence Agency. (2015, June 24). The world factbook. Retrieved June 28, 2015, from https://www.cia.gov/library/publications/the-world-factbook/geos/us.html.

Cherrier, B., and Saïdi, A. (2015, November). The indeterminate fate of sunspots in economics. Retrieved January 7, 2016, from http://poseidon01.ssrn.com/delivery.php?ID=013084113099074067 091096121111080007125015095067062090018070008096126064064 108011010110601601508127058125126016021097076029047047048 043099077083127123117099028032021062025124105116105105064 0750612712111808909406401609509608712308108607102101711 7&EXT=pdf.

Christiano, L. J., Eichenbaum, M., and Evans, C. (2005). Nominal rigidities and the dynamics effects of a shock to monetary policy. *Journal of Political Economy* 113:1–45.

Cochrane, J. H. (1994). Permanent and transitory components of GNP and stock prices. *Quarterly Journal of Economics* 109(1):241–265.

Cochrane, J. H. (2011). Presidential address: Discount rates. *Journal of Finance* 66(4):1047–1108.

Coibion, O., and Gorodnichenko, Y. (2012). Why are target interest rate changes so persistent? *American Economic Journal: Macroeconomics* 4(4):126–162.

Constantinides, G. M. (1990). Habit formation: A resolution of the equity premium puzzle. *Journal of Political Economy* 98(3):519–543.

Corpe, K. (2014). Forecasting UK unemployment using stock market prices. Unpublished report. Research conducted at the Bank of England.

Coyle, D. (2014). *GDP: A brief but affectionate history*. Princeton, NJ: Princeton University Press.

Cramton, P. (2002). Spectrum Auctions. In *Handbook of telecommunications economics*, ed. M. Cave, S. Majumdar, and I. Vogelsang (pp. 605–639). Amsterdam: Elsevier Science B.V.

Davidson, P. (2011). *Post-Keynesian macroeconomic theory*. 2nd ed. Cheltenham: Edward Elgar.

Davis, S. J., Haltiwanger, J. C., and Schuh, S. (1996). *Job creation and destruction*. Cambridge, MA: MIT Press.

Del Negro, M., Schorfheide, F., and Giannoni, M. (2015). Inflation in the Great Recession and New Keynesian models. *American Economic Journal: Macroeconomics* 7(1):168–196.

DeLong, J. B., Shleifer, A., Summers, L. H., and Waldmann, R. J. (1990). Noise trader risk in financial markets. *Journal of Political Economy* 98(4):703–738.

De Vroey, M. (2006). The temporary equilibrium method: Hicks against Hicks. *European Journal of the History of Economic Thought* 13(2):259–278.

De Vroey, M. (2016). *A history of macroeconomics: from Keynes to Lucas and beyond.* New York: Cambridge University Press.

Diamond, P. A. (1982). Wage determination and efficiency in search equilibrium. *Review of Economic Studies* 49:217–227.

DiCecio, R. D., Engemann, K. M., Owyang, M. T., and Wheeler, C. H. (2008). Changing trends in the labor force: A survey. *Federal Reserve Bank of St. Louis Review* January/February:47–62.

Dow, J. C., and Dicks-Mireaux, L. A. (1958). The excess demand for labour: A study of conditions in Great Britain, 1946–56. *Oxford Economic Papers* 10(1):–33.

Drehmann, M., Borio, C., and Tsatsaronis, K. (2011). Anchoring countercyclical capital buffers: The role of credit aggregates. *International Journal of Central Banking* 7(4):189–240.

Edgeworth, F. Y. (1881). *Mathematical psychics: An essay on the application of mathematics to the moral sciences.* London: C. Kegan Paul.

Epstein, L., and Zin, S. (1989). Substitution, risk aversion and the temporal behavior of consumption and asset returns: An empirical analysis. *Journal of Political Economy* 99:263–286.

Epstein, L., and Zin, S. (1991). Substitution, risk aversion and the temporal behavior of consumption and asset returns: A theoretical framework. *Econometrica* 57:937–969.

Evans, G. W., and Honkapohja, S. (2001). *Learning and expectations in macroeconomics.* Princeton, NJ: Princeton University Press.

Ewing, B. T., and Wunnava, P. V. (2001). Unit roots and structural breaks in North American unemployment rates. *North American Journal of Economics and Finance* 12:273–282.

Fama, E. F. (1970). Efficient capital markets: A review of theory and empirical work. *Journal of Finance* 25(2):383–417.

Farmer, R. E. (1982). Macroeconomics and equilibrium. PhD diss., University of Western Ontario.

Farmer, R. E. (1984). A new theory of aggregate supply. *American Economic Review* 74(5):920–929.

Farmer, R. E. (1990). The Lucas critique, policy invariance and multiple equilibria. *Review of Economic Studies* 105(1):43–60.

Farmer, R. E. (1993). *The macroeconomics of self-fulfilling prophecies.* 1st ed. Cambridge, MA: MIT Press.

Farmer, R. E. (2002a). Business cycles with heterogeneous agents. University of California Los Angeles [mimeo].

Farmer, R. E. (2002b). Fiscal policy, equity premia, and heterogeneous agents. University of California Los Angeles [mimeo].

Farmer, R. E. (2002c). Why does data reject the Lucas critique? *Annales d'Économie et de Statistique* 67/68:111–129.

Farmer, R. E. (2006). Old Keynesian economics. Paper presented at a conference in honor of Axel Leijonhufvud, University of California Los Angeles, August 30, 2006.

Farmer, R. E. (2008a). Aggregate demand and supply. *International Journal of Economic Theory* 4(1):77–94.

Farmer, R. E. (2008b). Animal spirits. Retrieved January 30, 2016, from http://www.dictionaryofeconomics.com/ article?id=pde2008_A000105.

Farmer, R. E. (2008c). Old Keynesian economics. In *Macroeconomics in the small and the large*, ed. R. E. Farmer (pp. 23–43). Cheltenham, UK: Edward Elgar.

Farmer, R. E. (2008d December 30). A new monetary policy for the twenty first century. Retrieved April 12, 2016 from http://blogs. ft.com/ economistsforum/2008/12/how-to-prevent-the-great-depression-of-2009/.

Farmer, R. E. (2009a January 12). A new monetary policy for the twenty first century. Retrieved July 1, 2015, from http://blogs.ft.com/ economistsforum/2009/01/a-new-monetary-policy-for-the-21st-century/.

Farmer, R. E. (2009b). Review of: Animal spirits: How human psychology drives the economy and why it matters for global capitalism. By George A. Akerlof and Robert J. Shiller. *The Economic Record* 85(270):357–369.

Farmer, R. E. (2009c February 4). What Keynes should have said. Retrieved April 11, 2015, from http://www.voxeu.org/article/ government-should-target-stock-market.

Farmer, R. E. (2010a). *Expectations, employment and prices.* New York, NY: Oxford University Press.

Farmer, R. E. (2010b). *How the economy works: Confidence, crashes and self-fulfilling prophecies.* New York, NY: Oxford University Press.

Farmer, R. E. (2010c). How to reduce unemployment: A new policy proposal. *Journal of Monetary Economics: Carnegie Rochester Conference Issue* 57(5):557–572.

Farmer, R. E. (2010d). Macroeconomics for the 21st century: Full employment as a policy goal. *National Institute Economic Review* 211(109):45–50.

Farmer, R. E. (2010e). The stimulus plan, unemployment and economic theory: Why I don't believe in fairies. Retrieved August 21, 2015, from http://blogs.ft.com/economistsforum/2010/01/the-stimulus-plan-unemployment-and-economic-theory-why-i-dont-believe-in-fairies/.

Farmer, R. E. (2010f). We need more quantitative easing to create jobs. Retrieved July 1, 2015, from http://blogs.ft.com/economistsforum/2010/08/we-need-more-quantitative-easing-to-create-jobs/#more-11311.

Farmer, R. E. (2012a). Animal spirits, persistent unemployment and the belief function. In *Rethinking expectations: The way forward for macroeconomics,* ed. R. Frydman and E. S. Phelps, pp. 251–276. Princeton, NJ: Princeton University Press.

Farmer, R. E. (2012b). Confidence, crashes and animal spirits. *Economic Journal* 122(559):155–172.

Farmer, R. E. (2012c). Qualitative easing: How it works and why it matters. NBER working paper no. 18421. Cambridge MA; National Bureau of Economic Research.

Farmer, R. E. (2012d). The stock market crash of 2008 caused the Great Recession: Theory and evidence. *Journal of Economic Dynamics and Control* 36:697–707.

Farmer, R. E. (2013a). Animal spirits, financial crises and persistent unemployment. *Economic Journal* 123(568):317–340.

Farmer, R. E. (2013b, June). Parliament TV. Retrieved April 12, 2016, from http://www.publications.parliament.uk/pa/cm201213/cmselect/cmtreasy/writev/qe/m20.htm.

Farmer, R. E. (2013c). Qualitative easing, a new tool for the stabilization of financial markets. *Bank of England Quarterly Bulletin* Q4:405–413.

Farmer, R. E. (2013d). The natural rate hypothesis: An idea past its sell-by-date. *Bank of England Quarterly Bulletin* Q3:244–256.

Farmer, R. E. (2014a). Asset prices in a lifecycle economy. NBER working paper no. 19457. Cambridge MA; National Bureau of Economic Research.

Farmer, R. E. (2014b). Financial stability and the role of the financial policy committee. *The Manchester School* 82(S1):35–43.

Farmer, R. E. (2014c). The evolution of endogenous business cycles. *Macroeconomic Dynamics* 20:554–557.

Farmer, R. E. (2015a, January). Global sunspots and asset prices in a monetary economy. NBER working paper no. 20831. Cambridge MA; National Bureau of Economic Research.

Farmer, R. E. (2015b). The stock market crash really did cause the Great Recession. *Oxford Bulletin of Economics and Statistics* 77(5):617–633.

Farmer, R. E. (2016). Pricing assets in an economy with two types of people. NBER working paper no. 22228. Cambridge MA; National Bureau of Economic Research.

Farmer, R. E., and Guo, J. T. (1994). Real business cycles and the animal spirits hypothesis. *Journal of Economic Theory* 63:42–73.

Farmer, R. E., and Guo, J.-T. (1995). The econometrics of indeterminacy. *Carnegie Rochester Series on Public Policy* 43:225–273.

Farmer, R. E., and Hollenhorst, A. (2006). Shooting the auctioneer. University of California Los Angeles [mimeo].

Farmer, R. E., Khramov, V., and Nicolò, G. (2015). Solving and estimating indeterminate DSGE models. *Journal of Economic Dynamics and Control* 54:17–36.

Farmer, R. E., Nourry, C., and Venditti, A. (2011). Debt deficits and finite horizons: The stochastic case. *Economics Letters* 111:47–49.

Farmer, R. E., Nourry, C., and Venditti, A. (2012). The inefficient markets hypothesis: Why financial markets do not work well in the real world. NBER working paper no. 18647. Cambridge MA; National Bureau of Economic Research.

Farmer, R. E., and Platonov, K. (2016). Animal spirits in a monetary model. NBER working paper no. 22136. Cambridge MA; National Bureau of Economic Research.

Farmer, R. E., and Plotnikov, D. (2012). Does fiscal policy matter? Blinder and Solow revisited. *Macroeconomic Dynamics* 16(Suppl. 1):149–166.

Farmer, R. E., and Woodford, M. (1984). Self-fulfilling prophecies and the business cycle. Caress working paper no. 84–12. Philadelphia PA: University of Pennsylvania.

Farmer, R. E., and Woodford, M. (1997). Self-fulfilling prophecies and the business cycle. *Macroeconomic Dynamics* 1(4):740–769.

Farmer, R. E., and Zabczyk, P. (2016). The theory of unconventional policy. NBER working paper no. 22135. Cambridge MA; National Bureau of Economic Research.

Fischer, S. (1977). Long-term contracts, rational expectations and the optimal money supply rule. *Journal of Political Economy* 85:191–205.

Fisher, I. (1933). The debt deflation theory of great depressions. *Econometrica* 1(4):337–357.

Fitoussi, J.-P., Jestaz, D., Phelps, E. S., and Zoega, G. (2000). Roots of the recent recoveries: Labor reforms or private sector forces. *Brookings Papers on Economic Activity* 1:237–312.

Friedman, M. (1953). *Essays in positive economics.* Chicago, IL: University of Chicago Press.

Friedman, M. (1957). *A theory of the consumption function*. Princeton, NJ: Princeton University Press.

Friedman, M. (1960). *A program for monetary stability*. New York, NY: Fordham University Press.

Friedman, M. (1968). The role of monetary policy. *American Economic Review* 58(March):1–17.

Friedman, M. (1970a). A theoretical framework for monetary analysis. *Journal of Political Economy* 78(2):193–238.

Friedman, M. (1970b). "The Monetarist Counter Revolution in Economics," IEA Occasional Paper no. 33, Institute of Economic Affairs, first published by the Institute of Economics Affairs. Retrieved online, April 11 2016 from http://0055d26.netsolhost.com/friedman/pdfs/other_academia/IEA.1970.pdf.

Friedman, M., and Schwartz, A. J. (1963). *A monetary history of the United States, 1867–1960*. Princeton, NJ: Princeton University Press.

Frisch, R. (1933). Propagation problems and impulse problems in dynamic economics. In *Economic essays in honor of Gustav Cassel: Reprinted in readings in business cycles, 1966*, ed. R. Gordon and L. Klein, vol. X, pp. 1–35. London: Allen and Unwin.

Fritsche, U., and Pierdzioch, C. (2016). Animal spirits, the stock market, and the unemployment rate: Some evidence for German data. *DEP (Socioeconomics) Discussion Papers Macroeconomics and Finance Series*.

Frydman, R., and Goldberg, M. D. (2007). *Imperfect knowledge economics: Exchange rates and risk*. Princeton, NJ: Princeton University Press.

Frydman, R., and Goldberg, M. D. (2013). Opening models of asset prices and risk to nonroutine change. In *Rethinking expectations: The way forward for macroeconomics*, ed. R. Frydman and E. E. Phelps, pp. 207–250. Princeton, NJ: Princeton University Press.

Frydman, R., and Phelps, E. S., eds. (2013). *Rethinking expectations: The way forward for macroeconomics*. Princeton, NJ: Princeton University Press.

Fuhrer, J. C., and Moore, G. R. (1995). Inflation persistence. *Quarterly Journal of Economics* 440:127–159.

Gagnon, J. E., Raskin, M., Remache, J., and Sack, B. P. (2011a). Large-scale asset purchases by the Federal Reserve: Did they work? *Economic Policy Review: Federal Reserve Bank of New York* May:41–59.

Gagnon, J. E., Raskin, M., Remache, J., and Sack, B. P. (2011b). The financial market effects of the Federal Reserve's large-scale asset purchases. *International Journal of Central Banking* 7(1):3–43.

Galí, J. (2015). *Monetary policy, inflation and the business cycle: An introduction to the New Keynesian framework and its applications.* 2nd ed. Princeton, NJ: Princeton University Press.

Galí, J., and Gertler, M. (1999). The science of monetary policy: A New Keynesian perspective. *Journal of Economic Literature* XXXVII:1661–1707.

Galí, J., Gertler, M., and López-Salido, J. D. (2007). Markups, gaps, and the welfare costs of business fluctuations. *Review of Economics and Statistics*, 89(1):44–59.

Geanakoplos, J. (2010). The leverage cycle. In *NBER macroeconomics annual 2009*, ed. D. Acemoglu, K. Rogoff, and M. Woodford, vol. 24, pp. 1–65. Chicago, IL: University of Chicago Press.

Gelain, P., and Guerrazzi, M. (2010). A DSGE model from the Old Keynesian economics: An empirical investigation. University of St. Andrews, Centre for Dynamic Macroeconomic Analysis Working Paper Series, no. CDMA10/14. St. Andrews Scotland; University of St. Andrews.

Gertler, M., Sala, L., and Trigari, A. (2008). An estimated DSGE model with unemployment and staggered wage bargaining. *Journal of Money Credit and Banking* 40(8):1713–1764.

Gertler, M., and Trigari, A. (2009). Unemployment fluctuations with staggered Nash wage bargaining. *Journal of Political Economy* 117(1):38–86.

Goodhart, C., and Dai, L. (2003). *Intervention to save Hong Kong.* Oxford: Oxford University Press.

Gordon, R. J. (2013). The Phillips Curve is alive and well: Inflation and the NAIRU during the slow recovery. NBER working paper no. 19390. Cambridge MA; National Bureau of Economic Research.

Gorton, G. (2010). *Slapped by the invisible hand.* Oxford: Oxford University Press.

Granger, C. W. (1969). Investigating causal relations by econometric models and cross-spectral methods. *Econometrica* 37(3):424–438.

Granger, C. W. (1981). Some properties of time series data and their use in econometric model specification. *Econometrica* 16:121–130.

Gray, J. A. (1976). Wage indexation: A macroeconomic approach. *Journal of Monetary Economics* 2(2):221–235.

Greenberg, M. R. (2014, November 6). Quarterly update: Foreign ownership of U.S. assets. Retrieved February 8, 2016, from http://www.cfr.org/united-states/quarterly-update-foreign-ownership-us-assets/p25685.

Greenwood, J., Guner, N., Kocharkov, G., and Santos, C. (2016). Technology and the changing family: A unified model of marriage, divorce, educational attainment and married female labor-force participation. *American Economic Journal: Macroeconomics* 8(1):1–41.

Guerrazzi, M. (2010). Expectations employment and prices: A suggested interpretation of the new "Farmerian economics." Munich Personal RePec Archive, working paper no. 30832. Munich, Germany: Munich University Library.

Guerrazzi, M. (2011). Search and stochastic dynamics in the Old Keynesian economics: A rationale for the Shimer puzzle. *Metroeconomica* 62(4):561–586.

Guerrazzi, M. (2012). The "Farmerian" approach to ending finance-induced recession: Notes on stability and dynamics. *Economic Notes by Banca Monte dei Paschi di Siena SpA* 41(1/2):81–99.

Haldane, A. G. (2012, October 01). What have economists ever done for us? Retrieved January 12, 2016, from http://www.voxeu.org/article/what-have-economists-ever-done-us.

Hall, R. E. (2005). Employment fluctuations with equilibrium wage stickiness. *American Economic Review* 95(1):50–65.

Hall, R. E., and Milgrom, P. R. (2008). The limited influence of unemployment on the wage bargain. *American Economic Review* 98(4):1653–1674.

Hamilton, J. D. (1994). *Time series analysis.* Princeton, NJ: Princeton University Press.

Hamilton, J. D., and Wu, J. C. (2012). The effectiveness of alternative monetary policy tools in a zero lower bound environment. *Journal of Money Credit and Banking* 44(1):3–36.

Hamley, J. (2012, October 24). How big is the multiplier? Retrieved August 31, 2015, from http://ordinary-gentlemen.com/blog/2012/10/24/how-big-is-the-multiplier.

Hansard: House of Commons Debate. (1929, April). Disposal of surplus. Retrieved April 12, 2016, from http://hansard.millbanksystems.com/commons/1929/apr/15/disposal-of-surplus.

Hansen, A. (1936). Mr. Keynes on underemployment equilibrium. *Journal of Political Economy* 44(5):667–686.

Hansen, L. P. (1982). Large sample properties of generalized method of moments estimators. *Econometrica* 50:1029–1054.

Harberger, A. (1971). Three basic postulates for applied welfare economics: An interpretive essay. *Journal of Economic Literature* 9:785–797.

Hawtrey, R. G. (1925). Public expenditure and the demand for labour. *Economica* 5:38–48.

Hayek, F. A. (1944). *The road to serfdom.* Chicago, IL: University of Chicago Press.

Hayek, F. A. (1988). *The fatal conceit: The errors of socialism.* Chicago, IL: University of Chicago Press.

Heathcote, J., and Perri, F. (2012). Wealth and volatility. Federal Reserve Bank of Minneapolis [mimeo].

Hicks, J. R. (1937). Mr. Keynes and the classics: A suggested interpretation. *Econometrica* 5(2):147–159.

Hicks, J. R. (1946 [1939]). *Value and capital.* 2nd ed. Oxford: Clarendon Press.

Hodrick, R. J., and Prescott, E. C. (1997). Post-war U.S. business cycles: A descriptive empirical investigation. *Journal of Money Credit and Banking* 29:1–16.

Hosios, A. (1990). On the efficiency of matching and related models of search and unemployment. *Review of Economic Studies* 57:279–298.

Howitt, P., and McAfee, R. P. (1987). Costly search and recruiting. *International Economic Review* 28(1):89–107.

Hume, D. (1987 [1777]). "Of money." In *Essays, Moral, Political and Literary,* ed. E. Miller, pp. 281–294. Indianapolis, IN: Liberty Fund. Based on the 1777 edition originally published as vol 1. of *Essays and treatises on several subjects.*

Insurance Hall of Fame. (2008, August 17). Nicholas Barbon. Retrieved June 28, 2015, from http://www.insurancehalloffame.org/laureateprofile.php?laureate=117.

Jevons, W. S. (1878). Commercial crises and sun-spots. *Nature* xix:33–37.

Johnson, S., and Kwak, J. (2010). *13 Bankers: The Wall Street takeover and the next financial meltdown.* New York, NY: Random House.

Kahn, R. (1931). The relationship of home investment to unemployment. *Economic Journal* 41(162):173–198.

Kashiwagi, M. (2010). Search theory and the housing market. PhD diss., University of California Los Angeles.

Kashiwagi, M. (2014) Sunspots and self-fulfilling beliefs in the U.S. housing market. *Review of Economic Dynamics* 17:654–676.

Kehoe, T. J., and Levine, D. K. (1985). Comparative statics and perfect foresight in Infinite horizon economies. *Econometrica* 53:433–453.

Keynes, J. M. (1936). *The general theory of employment, interest and money.* London: MacMillan.

Keynes, J. M. (1937). The General Theory of Employment. *The Quarterly Journal of Economics*, 51(2):209–223.

Kimball, M. (2013a, September 30). How and why to eliminate the zero lower bound. Retrieved September 2, 2015, from http://blog.supplysideliberal.com.

Kimball, M. (2013b, January 3). Quartz. Retrieved August 21, 2015, from http://qz.com/40235/why-the-us-needs-its-own-sovereign-wealth-fund/.

King, R. G., and Watson, M. (1997). Testing long-run neutrality. *Federal Reserve Bank of Richmond Economic Quarterly* 83(3):69–101.

Kiyotaki, N., and Moore, J. (1997). Credit cycles. *Journal of Political Economy* 105(2):211–248.

Klenow, P. J., and Malin, B. A. (2011). "Microeconomic evidence on price setting." In the *Handbook of monetary economics 3A*, ed B. Friedman and M. Woodford, pp. 231–284. Amsterdam, Elsevier.

Kocherlakota, N. (2012). Incomplete labor markets. Federal Reserve Bank of Minneapolis [mimeo].

Koenig, E. (2012). All in the family: The close connection between nominal-GDP targeting and the Taylor Rule. *Federal Reserve Bank of Dallas Staff Papers 17*.

Koo, R. (2008). *The Holy Grail of macroeconomics: Lessons from Japan's Great Recession*. New York, NY: Wiley.

Kotlikoff, L. (2011). *Jimmy Stewart is dead: Ending the world's ongoing financial plague with limited purpose banking*. Hoboken, NJ: Wiley.

Kreps, D., and Porteus, E. (1978). Temporal resolution of uncertainty and dynamic choice theory. *Econometrica* 46:185–200.

Kreps, D., and Porteus, E. (1979). Temporal Von-Neumann Morgenstern and induced preferences. *Journal of Economic Theory* 20:81–109.

Krugman, P. (2008, December 11). Don't know much about history. Retrieved August 31, 2015, from http://krugman.blogs.nytimes.com/2008/12/11/dont-know-much-about-history/.

Krugman, P. (2015, April 29). The austerity delusion. Retrieved June 28, 2015, from http://www.theguardian.com/business/ng-interactive/2015/apr/29/the-austerity-delusion.

Kuhn, T. S. (1957). *The Copernican revolution*. Harvard, MA: Harvard University Press.

Kuhn, T. S. (1962). *The structure of scientific revolutions*. Chicago, IL: University of Chicago Press.

Kydland, F. E., and Prescott, E. C. (1982). Time to build and aggregate fluctuations. *Econometrica* 50:1345–1370.

Lakatos, I. (1978). *The methodology of scientific research programmes.* Cambridge: Cambridge University Press.

Lakatos, I., and Musgrave, A., eds. (1970). *Criticism and the growth of knowledge.* Cambridge, UK: Cambridge University Press.

Lansing, K. J. (2010). Rational and near-rational bubbles without drift. *Economic Journal* 549:1149–1174.

Leijonhufvud, A. (1981). *Information and coordination: Essays in macroeconomic theory.* Oxford: Oxford University Press.

Leroy, S., and Porter, R. (1981). Stock price volatility: A test based on implied variance bounds. *Econometrica* 49:97–113.

Levenson, T. (2015). *The hunt for Vulcan: … And how Albert Einstein destroyed a planet, discovered relativity, and deciphered the universe.* New York, NY: Random House.

Lipsey, R. G. (1960). The relation between unemployment and the rate of change of money wage rates in the United Kingdom, 1861–1957: A further analysis. *Economica* 27(105):1–31.

Lipsey, R. G., and Scarth, W. (2011). *Inflation and unemployment: The evolution of the Phillips Curve.* London: Edward Elgar.

Litterick, D. (2002, September 13). Billionaire who broke the Bank of England. Retrieved August 21, 2015, from http://www.telegraph.co.uk/finance/2773265/Billionaire-who-broke-the-Bank-of-England.html.

Long, J. B., and Plosser, C. I. (1983). Real business cycles. *Journal of Political Economy* 91(1):39–69.

LucasJr., R. E. (1972). Expectations and the neutrality of money. *Journal of Economic Theory* 4:103–124.

Lucas Jr., R. E. (1976). Econometric policy evaluation: A critique. *Carnegie-Rochester Conference Series on Public Policy* 1:19–46.

Lucas Jr., R. E. (1987). *Models of business cycles.* New York, NY: Blackwell.

Lucas Jr., R. E., and Rapping, L. A. (1969). Real wages employment and inflation. *Journal of Political Economy* 77:721–54.

Mackay, C. (1980 [1841]). *Extraordinary popular delusions and the madness of crowds.* New York, NY: Harmony Books.

Magill, M., and Quinzii, M. (2002). *The theory of incomplete markets.* Cambridge, MA: MIT Press.

Mankiw, G. (2009, January 23). Is Joe Biden disingenuous or misinformed? Retrieved September 2, 2015, from http://

gregmankiw.blogspot.com/2009/01/is-joe-biden-disingenuous-or. html.

Mankiw, N. G., and Reis, R. (2007). Sticky information in general equilibrium. *Journal of the European Economic Association* 5(2–3):603–613.

Mankiw, N. G., and Romer, D., eds. (1991). *New Keynesian economics. Vol. 2: Coordination failures and real rigidities.* Cambridge, MA: MIT Press.

Martin, A., and Ventura, J. (2012). Economic growth with bubbles. *American Economic Review* 102(6):3033–3058.

McAndrews, J. (2015, May 08). Negative nominal central bank policy rates: Where is the lower bound? Retrieved April 11, 2016, from https://www.newyorkfed.org/newsevents/speeches/2015/ mca150508.html.

Mehra, R., and Prescott, E. C. (1985). The equity premium: A puzzle. *Journal of Monetary Economics* 15:145–161.

Merz, M. (1995). Search in the labor market and the real business cycle. *Journal of Monetary Economics* 36:269–300.

Miao, J., Wang, P., and Xu, Z. (2012). Stock market bubbles and unemployment. Boston University [mimeo].

Michaillat, P., and Saez, E. (2013, July). A model of aggregate demand and unemployment. NBER working paper no. 18826. Cambridge MA; National Bureau of Economic Research.

Michaillat, P., and Saez, E. (2014, January). An economical business cycle model. NBER working paper no. 119777. Cambridge MA; National Bureau of Economic Research.

Modigliani, F. (1977). The monetarist controversy, or should we forsake stabilization policies. *American Economic Review* 67:1–19.

Mortensen, D. T. (1970). A theory of wage and employment dynamics. In *Microeconomic foundations of employment and inflation theory,* ed. E. S. Phelps, G. C. Archibald, and A. A. Alchian, pp: 167–211. New York, NY: W. W. Norton.

Muth, J. F. (1961). Rational expectations and the theory of price movements. *Econometrica* 29(3):315–335.

Nelson, C. R., and Plosser, C. I. (1982). Trends and random walks in macroeconomic time series. *Journal of Monetary Economics* 10:139–162.

Nickell, S. (1997). Unemployment and labor market rigidities. *Journal of Economic Perspectives* 11(3):55–74.

Okun, A. (1962). Potential GNP: Its measurement and significance. *Proceedings of Business and Economic Statistics Section of the American Statistical Association* 98–104.

Oreopoulos, P., Von-Wachter, T., and Heisz, A. (2012). The short- and long-term career effects of graduating in a recession: Hysteresis and heterogeneity in the market for college graduates. *American Economic Journal: Applied Economics* 4(1):1–29.

Osborne, G. (2015, March 18). Remit for the Bank of England Monetary Policy Committee. Retrieved January 31, 2016, http://www.bankofengland.co.uk/monetarypolicy/Documents/pdf/chancellorletter180315.pdf.

Owyang, M. T., Ramey, V. A., and Zubairy, S. (2013). Are government spending multipliers greater during periods of slack? Evidence from twentieth-century historical data. *American Economic Review: Papers and Proceedings* 103(3):129–134.

Paul, R. (2009). *End the Fed.* New York, NY: Grand Central Publishing.

Pearce, K. A., and Hoover, K. D. (1995). After the revolution: Paul Samuelson and the textbook Keynesian model. *History of Political Economy* 27(5):183–216.

Peden, G. C. (1984). The "Treasury view" on public works and employment in the interwar period. *Economic History Review* 37(2):167–181.

Phelps, E. S. (1961). The golden rule of capital accumulation: A fable for growthmen. *American Economic Review* 51:638–643.

Phelps, E. S. (1968). Money wage dynamics and labor market equilibrium. *Journal of Political Economy* 76:678–711.

Phelps, E. S. (1994). *Structural slumps.* Cambridge, MA: Harvard University Press.

Phillips, A. W. (1958). The relationship between unemployment and the rate of change of money wages in the United Kingdom 1861–1957. *Economica* 25(100):283–299.

Pigou, A. C. (1927). *Industrial fluctuations.* London: McMillan.

Pissarides, C. A. (1976). Job search and participation. *Economica* 43:333–349.

Plotnikov, M. (2010). Three essays on macroeconomics with incomplete factor markets. PhD diss., University of California Los Angeles.

Plotnikov, D. (2014, May). Hysteresis in unemployment and jobless recoveries. IMF working paper no. 14/77, Washinton DC, International Monetary Fund.

Popper, K. (1963). *Conjectures and refutations: The growth of scientific knowledge.* London: Routledge.

Ramey, V., and Zubairy, S. (2014, November). Government spending multipliers in good times and in bad: Evidence from U.S. historical data. NBER working paper no. 20719. Cambridge MA; National Bureau of Economic Research.

Ramey, V. (2013). Government spending and private activity. In *Fiscal policy after the crisis*, ed. A. Alesina and F. Giavazzi, pp. 19–55. Chicago, IL: University of Chicago Press.

Ramey, V. (2016, February). Macroeconomic shocks and their propagation. NBER working paper no. 21978. Cambridge, MA: National Bureau of Economic Research.

Ramsey, F. P. (1928). A mathematical theory of saving. *Economic Journal* 38(152):543–559.

Rawls, J. (1971). *A theory of justice.* Cambridge, MA: Harvard University Press.

Reinhart, C. M., and Rogoff, K. S. (2011). *This time is different.* Princeton, NJ: Princeton University Press.

Reinhart, C. M., and Rogoff, K. S. (2014). Recovery from financial crises: Evidence from 100 episodes. *American Economic Review: Papers and Proceedings* 104(5):50–55.

Rietz, T. A. (1988). The equity risk premium: A solution. *Journal of Monetary Economics* 22(1):117–131.

Robinson, J. (1978). *Contributions to modern economics.* Oxford: Academic Press.

Romer, C. (1986). Spurious volatility in historical unemployment data. *Journal of Political Economy* 94(1):1–37.

Romer, C. (1989). The prewar business cycle reconsidered: New estimates of gross national product, 1869–1908. *Journal of Political Economy* 97(1):1–37.

Romer, C., and Romer, D. (2002). The evolution of economic understanding and postwar stabilization policy. In *Rethinking stabilization policy*, A symposium sponsored by the Federal Reserve Bank of Kansas City Jackson Hole, Wyoming August 29–31, pp. 11–78. Kansas City: Federal Reserve Bank of Kansas City.

Rotemberg, J. J. (1982). Sticky prices in the United States. *Journal of Political Economy* 90:1187–1211.

Samuelson, P. A. (1955). *Economics: An introductory analysis.* 3rd ed. New York, NY: McGraw Hill.

Samuelson, P. A., and Solow, R. M. (1960). Analytical aspects of anti-inflation policy. *American Economic Review* 50:177–194.

Say, J.-B. (1834). *A treatise on political economy*. 6th American ed. Philadelphia, PA: Grig and Elliott.

Schmitt-Grohé, S., and Uribe, M. (2011). Pegs and pain. NBER working paper no. 16847. Cambridge MA; National Bureau of Economic Research.

Schmitt-Grohé, S., and Uribe, M. (2014). Pegs, downward wage rigidity, and unemployment: The role of financial structure. In *Capital Mobility and Monetary Policy*, eds. Fuentes, M. D., Raddatz, C. E., and Reinhart, C. M., pp: 69–95. Santiago, Chile, Central Bank of Chile.

Sen, A. (1977). Rational fools: A critique of the behavioral foundations of economic theory. *Philosophy and Public Affairs* 6(4):317–344.

Shell, K. (1971). Notes on the economics of infinity. *Journal of Political Economy* 79:1002–1011.

Shell, K. (1977). Monnaie et allocation intertemporelle. Malinvaud Seminar, CNRS Paris [mimeo].

Shiller, R. J. (1981). Do stock prices move too much to be justified by subsequent changes in dividends? *American Economic Review* 71:421–436.

Shiller, R. J. (2012, July 10). Robert Shiller's favorite financial innovation: An IPO for the USA. Retrieved January 31, 2016, http://www.forbes.com/sites/nathanvardi/2012/07/10/robert-shillers-favorite-financial-innovation-an-ipo-for-the-usa/#1721713e1d0f.

Shiller, R. (2014, January 18). The rationality debate, simmering in Stockholm, New York Times Business Day. Retrieved August 13, 2015, from http://www.nytimes.com/2014/01/19/business/the-rationality-debate-simmering-in-stockholm.html?_r=0.

Shiller, R. (2015, June 26). Online data source for irrational exuberance. Retrieved June 26, 2015, from http://www.econ.yale.edu/~shiller/data.htm.

Shimer, R. (2005). The cyclical behavior of equilibrium unemployment and vacancies. *American Economic Review* 95(1):25–49.

Sims, C. A. (1989). Models and their uses. *American Journal of Agricultural Economics* 71:489–494.

Sims, C. A. (2003). Implications of rational inattention. *Journal of Monetary Economics* 50(3):665–690.

Sims, C. A., and Zha, T. (2006). Were there regime switches in US monetary policy? *American Economic Review* 96(1): 54–81.

Smets, F., and Wouters, R. (2003). An estimated dynamic stochastic general equilibrium model of the Euro area. *Journal of the European Economic Association* 1(5):1123–1175.

Smith, A. (1776). *An inquiry into the nature and causes of the wealth of nations.* Chicago, IL: University of Chicago.

Stephey, M. J. (2008, October 21). A brief history of Bretton Woods system. Retrieved February 8, 2016, from http://content.time.com/time/business/article/0,8599,1852254,00.html.

Summers, L. (1998, July 22). Treasury news. Retrieved August 21, 2015, from http://clinton2.nara.gov/WH/New/socsec/frames/treas2.html.

Sumner, S. B. (2009, February 28). The money illusion. Retrieved September 2, 2015, from http://www.themoneyillusion.com/?page_id=3443.

Sumner, S. B. (2014). Nominal GDP targeting: A simple rule to improve Fed performance. *Cato Journal* 34(2):315–337.

Taleb, N. (2010). *The black swan: The impact of the highly improbable.* New York, NY: Random House.

Taylor, J. B. (1999). *Monetary policy rules.* Chicago, IL: University of Chicago Press.

Taylor, J. B. (2015, April 15). A monetary policy for the future. Retrieved April 9, 2016, from http://web.stanford.edu/~johntayl/2015_pdfs/A_Monetary_Policy_For_the_Future-4-15-15.pdf.

The Sveriges Riksbank Prize in Economic Sciences in Memory of Alfred Nobel 2012. (2012, September). Alvin E. Roth facts. Retrieved February 5, 2016, from http://www.nobelprize.org/nobel_prizes/economic-sciences/laureates/2012/roth-facts.html.

Thomas, E. (1979). *The collected poems of Edward Thomas.* London: Faber and Faber.

Whitard, D. (2012, March 12). The UK's external balance sheet: The international investment position (IIP). Retrieved February 8, 2016, from http://www.ons.gov.uk/ons/dcp171766_259471.pdf.

Wicksell, K. (1965 [1898]). *Interest and prices,* trans. R. F. Kahn. New York, NY: Augustus Kelley.

Wiederholt, M. (2010). Rational inattention. Retrieved January 11, 2016, from http://www.dictionaryofeconomics.com/article?id=pde2010_R000281.

Woodford, M. (2003). *Interest and prices: Foundations of a theory of monetary policy.* Princeton, NJ: Princeton University Press.

Woodford, M. (2012). Methods of policy accommodation at the interest-rate lower bound. Columbia University [mimeo].

Yun, T. (1996). Nominal price rigidity, money supply endogeneity, and business cycles. *Journal of Monetary Economics* 37:345–370.

INDEX OF NAMES

Prescott, Edward C., 28, 48–50, 52, 92, 200, 214n15, 217nn4–5, 218n9, 226n6, 237n9

Quinzii, Martine, 226n9

Ramey, Valerie, 174–175, 238nn22–23
Ramsey, Frank P., 48, 217n4
Rapping, Leonard, 47–48, 64, 217n3, 220n18
Raskin, Matthew, 239n5
Rawls, John, 226n13
Reinhart, Carmen M., 228n19
Reis, Ricardo, 219n13
Remache, Julie, 239n5
Rietz, Thomas, 93, 226n8
Robinson, Joan, 26, 29, 214n6
Rogoff, Kenneth S., 13, 228n19
Romer, Christina, 174–175, 209n7, 238n21
Romer, David, 51, 174–175, 217n7, 238n19, 238n21
Roosevelt, Franklin Delano, 161
Rotemberg, Julio J., 62–63, 219n9
Roth, Alvin, 222n38
Routledge, Bryan R., 92, 226n7

Sack, Brian P., 239n5
Saez, Emmanuel, 215n19
Saïdi, Aurélian, 214n7, 214n12, 214n17
Sala, Luca, 65, 220n19
Samuelson, Paul, 13, 25–26, 34–38, 44–45, 51, 58–59, 66, 108, 201, 212n21, 213n5, 215n5, 216n9, 218n1
Santos, Cezar, 231n20
Sargent, Thomas, 173
Say, Jean-Baptiste, 31–32, 215n2, 237n13
Scarth, William, 216n7
Schmitt-Grohé, Stephanie, 215n19
Schorfheide, Frank, 135, 232n6

Schuh, Scott, 222n2
Schwartz, Anna J., 7, 210n12, 239n3
Sen, Amartya, 68–69, 229nn29–31
Shapley, Lloyd, 222n38
Shell, Karl, 26–28, 91, 95, 213n27, 214n8, 214nn10–11, 225n3, 226n12, 234n1, 235n4
Shiller, Robert J., 68–69, 90–92, 95, 97, 200–201, 211n16, 221n16, 221n26, 221n28, 225n1, 225n5, 228n27, 242n29
Shimer, Robert, 224n13
Shleifer, Andrei, 221n27, 222n34
Sims, Christopher A., 210n10, 219n13, 219n14
Smets, Frank, 217n8
Smith, Adam, 31, 215n1
Solow, Robert M., 13, 36–38, 45, 215n19, 216n9
Soros, George, 192, 196
Stephey, M. J., 241n25
Stiglitz, Joseph, 13
Summers, Lawrence, 181, 191, 212n22, 221n27, 222n34, 234n18, 240n17
Sumner, Scott, 199–202, 241n26

Taleb, Nassim, 112, 229n5
Taylor, John B., 114, 131, 230n7, 232n1
Tobin, James, 67
Trigari, Antonella, 65, 70, 220n19, 222n36
Tsatsaronis, Kostas, 213n30

Uhlig, Harald, 173
Uribe, Martín, 215n19

Valles, Javier, 221n22
Venditti, Alain, 225n2, 227n14
Ventura, Jaume, 221n25
Volcker, Paul, 102, 183
Von Neumann John, 226n7
Von Wachter, Till, 98, 226n11, 227n18

INDEX OF SUBJECTS